As a prison chaplain, Louise Stowe-Johns spent many years talking to those who commit unspeakable crimes, yet it was 18-year-old Judy Neelley, who murdered two people under the threat of death from her batterer, who captured and held her attention.

In *Redemption of a Murderer*, Stowe-Johns delivers a fascinating and detailed picture of how Judy Neelley's abusive childhood and three teenage years living with Alvin Neelley led her to murder-as-survival and then, how the next sixteen years locked up on death row helped her reach salvation.

As a psychologist who studies battered women and children, it is not unusual for those who commit crimes, in order to survive, to have remorse unlike those who act out violently with anger. Whether it is redemption or healing from trauma, Stowe-Johns's analysis of this woman, still locked-up in our nation's unfortunate and unforgiving prison system, is compelling reading. I couldn't put it down, neither will you.

—Lenore Walker, Ed.D., Psychologist and Author, *The Battered Woman Syndrome*

It is educational and shocking to understand that receiving clemency on death row is not always a gift. This story awakens empathy for a murderer. Learning about the circumstances of a crime is enlightening. Judith Neelley's circumstances were beyond her control before prison and within prison. Witnessing her accepting to surrender her life on death row began to bring peace until clemency forced her to become a victim. *Redemption of a Murderer* shares the struggle of finding a meaning to life when your life is out of your control.

—Angela Grout, author *APRIL RAiN: The Murder of Jessica Briggs*, **and** *Dear Baby, Get Out!*

In this intimate and riveting true story, Stowe-Johns challenges media portrayals that sensationalize Neelley as a cold-blooded murderer who deserves the death penalty. Stowe-Johns exposes the physical and psychological abuse Neelley suffered at the hands of her co-conspirator husband, Alvin.

She examines the psychological complexity of domestic violence and a justice system that promotes inequity, impedes progress, and undermines humanity.

Through Stowe-Johns's forty-year relationship as prison chaplain and spiritual guide to convicted murderer Judy Neelley, the author examines factors that led an ordinary eighteen-year-old girl to commit horrifying acts of violence.

In the process of victim-offender mediation, Stowe-Johns shows the transformative healing that results when victims and family members of victims are brought together.

Redemption of a Murderer is a ground-breaking memoir as a testament to the healing and power of faith, forgiveness, reconciliation, and redemption."

—Christina Dunbar, Member, International Women's Writing Guild

Convicted murderer Judy Neelley didn't get a lot of lucky breaks. One that she did get was the enduring friendship and steadfast advocacy of author and self-professed pot stirrer Louise Stowe-Johns. At once a passionate outcry against a broken justice system and a compassionate account of Neelley's life inside that system, *Redemption of a Murderer* is leavened by Stowe-Johns's dry wit and humorous self-deprecation. I ingested this raw and compelling book in huge chunks, propelled by the story's inherent drama and the emerging portrait of Neelley in all her tender-hearted humanity.

—Autumn Stephens, author of the *Wild Women* series

I have known Judy Neelley and been her lawyer, off and on, since the 1980s, and I have had the pleasure of knowing Reverend Louise Stowe–Johns for almost as long. I've read all the previous attempts to tell Judy's story, and *Redemption of a Murderer* is the first to recognize Judy as more than a two-dimensional snapshot forever frozen in time during those terrible weeks more than forty years ago.

Instead of a caricature, Stowe-Johns presents Judy as a human being. In telling this story, Stowe-Johns does not dwell on the grisly details of Alvin and Judy's crimes, but without being exploitive, she honestly acknowledges their awfulness and the pain that they have caused. Stowe-Johns knows Judy better than almost anyone, and her well-researched portrayal of Judy's brief life outside of prison, her trial, and, more so, her four decades in prison, is both a cautionary tale and an important reminder that no one is beyond redemption.

Along the way, the book takes you on the author's own personal and spiritual journey as she came to earn Judy's trust, then began to prepare her for her execution. As an eyewitness, Stowe-Johns also reveals the untold backstory of Judy's clemency request and the Alabama Governor's shocking decision to grant it, miraculously sparing Judy's life and setting off a firestorm of anger and hatred that has not subsided.

Through these pages, we hear from Judy Neelley in her own words as she confronts her past and seeks spiritual healing and forgiveness through her faith. It is that part of Judy's story that needed to be told, and this book takes us along on the walk with Judy toward restorative justice.

—Barry Ragsdale, Attorney at Law

I left Tutwiler as the chaplain within a year of Judy's arrival and was limited in contact with her due to being a male chaplain in a female prison which posed some challenges and limitations. I believe Louise was a "God send" as chaplain at the right time for the women of Tutwiler and most certainly for Judy.

Louise challenges us as humans but most especially as Christians with the tension between redemption versus retribution and forgiveness versus punishment. She has done a masterful job of sorting through the formidable task of interpreting legal documents and the writings of those with multiple agendas who shared information about Judy.

Louise takes us on a journey to explore how sincerely we desire to not only give superficial affirmation to the truths of scripture but truly apply them. Perhaps we should seek comfort in Ezekiel 36:26 when he proclaims the power of God, "I will give you a new heart and put a new spirit in you; I will remove from you your heart of stone and give you a heart of flesh." Is it possible we are witnessing this work of God in Judy.

—Lennie Howard, Former Chaplain, Tutwiler Prison for Women, Elder, United Methodist Church (retired)

I was fortunate to meet Louise Stowe-Johns earlier this year at another local author's book event in northern Virginia. As we made small talk, she told me she was a writer, and I was immediately intrigued. I asked about her book, and she hedged my excitement by saying it wasn't for everyone. When she told me it was about a murderer on death row that she worked with for many years and her work in restorative justice, I was astounded. Getting to read her book, *Redemption of a Murderer: The Life of Judy Neelley* has been an honor. I was not familiar with the crimes of Judy Neelley or her life story so reading this book was eye opening. It's heartbreaking and necessary for anyone interested in the true crime genre, domestic violence, or restorative justice.

There is so much beyond the surface of the headlines we read about crimes, criminals, victims, and the justice system. Stowe-Johns does a remarkable job explaining how Judy became both victim and criminal at a young age, and what her life has entailed in the years since without minimizing the hurt and pain caused by her crimes. It is evident in the book that Stowe-Johns has spent countless hours researching, reading articles and trial transcripts, and interviewing those connected to the cases to write this book. It is well written, interesting, inspiring, and thought-provoking.

There is so much to glean from both Judy's and Louise's stories and how they intersect. I personally believe the work of restorative justice can do so much for our society, but it doesn't get the same attention as headline grabbing crimes and subsequent trials. This book shows just one example of a death-row criminal who participated in her own redemption over many long years on death row and in prison. It shows how restorative justice can help many others heal and find peace as well.

I highly recommend this book to anyone who is a reader of the true crime genre, anyone interested in criminal justice or restorative justice, and anyone interested in the effects of domestic violence, coercive control, and the intersection with criminal defense. It is truly a must read!

—Caitlin King, blogger and book reviewer

REDEMPTION

OF A

MURDERER

The Life of Judy Neelley

Louise Stowe-Johns

AIA PUBLISHING

Redemption of a Murderer: The Life of Judy Neelley
Louise Stowe-Johns
Copyright © 2023
Published by AIA Publishing, Australia
ABN: 32736122056
http://www.aiapublishing.com

ISBN: 978-1-922329-52-3

To all who have the courage to give and receive forgiveness
To all practitioners of Restorative Justice

Contents

Your words
of bullet casings and foreboding are
unnerving
disconcerting
rattling.

I witness the ache in your chest
and feel the invisible scars.

The despair in you
meets the audacity in me—
together
an illuminating blaze
fire hoses attempt
to douse.
They can
not.
You
and I
hold matches

Foreword

I met Louise Stowe-Johns in 1984 when she became chaplain at Tutwiler Prison. I was on death row. I didn't trust Chaplain Johns or anybody else.

Despite my cool reception, she came back. We had church together, prayed, and sang. Maybe I was testing her when I began to tell her about some things I had done. She didn't judge. She listened. As my trust in Chaplain Johns grew, I spoke about a desire for people to know my story as a warning. What I did was tragic beyond words. People didn't know what had been done to me. We agreed that she would take on the project. After she resigned as chaplain in 1990, she could begin writing. I had no idea what a monumental task it would be.

I had neither the courage nor the emotional strength to write about my past in the depth that would be required. As a trusted confidant, first as chaplain, then as a remarkable friend, Louise has done an amazing job with her painstaking determination and honesty.

Because our first conversations were in a death-row cell,

I didn't expect to live to see the story completed. But here we are, years later. I feel no small amount of guilt that I asked my friend to write my story, seeing what was required. Still, she persevered. Words are inadequate to express my gratitude.

Over the years, people have written much about me without my knowledge or cooperation. How accurate could that be? In contrast, Louise read the trial transcript. She interviewed people with knowledge of me and of domestic violence, both victims and professionals. She heard my stories from childhood to adulthood. She has never let me hide from the truth. I respect that she researched and cross checked. I would expect nothing less. In this book, she has been truthful, even when it's so painful.

For most of my life, I have carried indescribable guilt. Every time I was rejected, judged, or condemned, I've felt the hatred was deserved. I shouldn't have peace. I was not able to forgive myself and didn't deserve anyone's forgiveness, especially God's.

I've met a few people who were very supportive of me. Encouraging and forgiving. Unfortunately, the voices of condemnation far outweighed the kindness. I listened to the hatred and hated myself. For so long, I was unable to get beyond the shame and guilt.

One thing I've learned is how horribly destructive hatred can be. Hatred and unforgiveness eat us up inside. I know well the costs. It has only been in the last year or so that I've begun to forgive myself and accept God's forgiveness. We will not find peace until we figure out a way to leave the hate behind.

Slowly I became aware that to be redeemed by God, I had to express sorrow for what I did. I wanted to contact my victims' families to tell them how deeply sorry I am, even though I believed that I was the last person on earth from whom they would want to receive a letter. I wouldn't blame them. But I could offer details of the truth if that is what they needed. If confronting me would give them even a measure of peace, I was okay with that. So I expected the worst but hoped for the best.

I learned that in restorative justice, sometimes victims and offenders can meet. It may help victims heal, especially when the offender expresses sincere remorse. I wanted to give family members of victims a chance to meet me, question me, confront me, vent their rage. I wanted to show them that I'm not a monster. I wanted to ease their pain if at all possible.

While I was on death row, I tried to contact the victims' families. Through letters, I was able to correspond with relatives of victims. Their forgiveness was unexpected and humbling.

When I came up for parole, I heard that some were unaware of the details of the crimes. We tried to set up a face-to-face meeting. Even after multiple efforts by families of victims and me, I am disappointed that we were unable to arrange a time to talk. With all that happened to block it, I assume God was saying "no," or "not yet." I don't understand, but I accept. I can only pray that my victims and their families find a measure of peace.

Unforgiveness is a poison. Only when we forgive ourselves and others are we able to move forward. It is not about our earning it. It's about God's grace and mercy.

I also hope that victims of abuse will read this and realize that there is help and hope. You're not alone. Reach out. That will be hard and frightening. Many will not believe or understand. Nevertheless, reach out. You may save your life and the lives of others.

I want it known that I have never and will never receive one cent from anything ever written about me. I will never attempt to prosper financially from the horrible things I did. I ask only that people read this book with an open mind and heart—with a willingness to believe and name the horrors of abuse and the power of God's redemption.

Judith Ann Neelley

January 2023

Preface

Is it possible for one person to control the life of another to the extent that the one controlled goes against societal norms and even commits murder? Whatever your answer, Judy and Alvin Neelley—wife and husband—are a classic case study.

To unravel this question, you will need to go beneath headlines and prejudgments to see the potential for a life reclaimed and redeemed. I invite those who vilify victims of domestic abuse and sexual assault to hear their voices, to question clichés and society's quick judgments. I invite those who label lawbreakers as pure evil to refuse to dehumanize them. We are all a part of the human family. No one is beyond redemption.

I have spoken with inmates, female and male, who expressed genuine sorrow for their actions. They gained nothing substantive in telling me that. Lawyers make explicit to their clients that they are to have no contact with victims. How can a person change without facing the guilt? The question primed me to take note of a program to bring together victims and offenders of the same crime. I saw this as providential for victims who needed to hear an authentic "I am sorry" and offenders to hear of the pain they'd caused victims. I have mediated cases of violent crimes, including murders. I had the privilege of seeing the bravery of victims and family members of victims as they faced the offender and the offender's accepting responsibility and showing remorse. The interchange is painful, complex, and exhausting, but the healing is life altering when adversaries respect each other.

When someone harms another, "What did you do?" and "Why?" are logical questions to ask the offender. But "What happened?" may provide more fruitful revelations. A thousand little blows, psychological and physical, led Judy Neelley into depravity. She reached a point where she obeyed the commands of her husband. Actions have critical context. In my book, I have focused on what happened.

My responsibility as a spiritual guide is to decipher Judy's veracity. Despite my attempts to speak with Judy's husband, he chose not to speak with me. His death closed the possibility. I weighed letters between husband and wife, trial evidence, and testimony of witnesses against conversations Judy and I have had for over thirty-nine years. Memories are fallible; nevertheless, I have confidence that the arc of her story is trustworthy.

As appropriate, I have condensed and edited conversations in order to give coherence. Any errors or misunderstandings are mine. In most quotations, I haven't interrupted the flow by including "*sic*" for grammatical errors or misspelled words. When accounts differed, I have sifted, weighed, and researched the evidence. The healing power of truth and candor remains intact.

I have changed a few details and used pseudonyms to

respect the privacy of individuals. The book does not delve into the lives of the victims. Each newspaper article or story or inquiry—sympathetic or prying—can compound the heartache. I don't want to re-victimize family members. There has been too much harm already. Perhaps what I have written will bring insight into Judy's deep regret, character, and life, and enable an easing of pain from lives cut short.

Some may see my motive as a way to profit from the suffering of others. The South African poet Antjie Krog addresses the complex dilemma. "One has no right to appropriate a story paid for with a lifetime of pain and destruction."[1] Instead she gives witness to others' pain as a fellow voyager, not as a voyeur. Krog dives into the harrowing stories of apartheid and is nearly pulled under by the currents. It is in the spirit of a fellow voyager that I expose traumatizing events to sunlight's healing force.

I dreaded the emotional cost to Judy as she read the manuscript, seeing her life in the starkness of black letters forming words accusing and inescapable. Stories took on heavier freight in print. She forced herself through a recounting of crimes committed by her and against her. Tears dry, but the shame and harm remain.

Writing about Judy's life required a climate of trust and frequent interaction. Judy allowed both. She has relived scarring memories. She understands her candor exposes her to further denigration. It will come. Inside and outside the prison system. For years, Judy has been easy prey for verbal attacks, accusations, and lies. Although that has diminished, putting these words into print exposes her to renewed slander.[2] Judy's allowing her life to be literally an open book is courageous. People will question the radical change in her life and whether she merits forgiveness from God. Even so, Judy has taken another step toward healing, as she has sought to short-circuit lies that she is beyond redemption. Courage is not self-referential. It is action extended to others, seeking neither reward nor approval.

Significant events can't be sufficiently told by one person or one perspective. Our perception of an event is colored and amplified by what happened in the past. In Judy's story, victims of domestic violence can have divergent reactions. Those who escaped the beatings question why didn't Judy leave? Others who couldn't get away from the abuser understand the complexities of leaving: children, threats, no money, no transportation, and no secure place to go.

To deepen my understanding of the actions of Judy Neelley, I spoke with Dr. Kathleen Greider, Professor at Claremont School of Theology. I asked about the dynamics of domestic violence.[3]

Dr. Greider said that a person can suffer harm to the degree that they cannot be redeemed. "Some might say that the soul is resilient enough not to be killed by abuse, that it is resourceful enough. In some contexts, the soul can be killed. Waves and waves of deprivation, abusiveness, and humiliation: it would be remarkable if it didn't kill a person's soul."

Then she addressed Judy's life. "Many things held her: a diminishing of one's sense of value with excruciating slowness. It makes you wonder if you are making it up one day to the next. This guy loves me; I must be making it up. It doesn't surprise me that she stayed. I believe humans can be robbed of their sense of agency, and there are a variety of ways that happens. It is not surprising that she did what he told her to do. Theologically, there was soul-sickness in both."

In my work with Judy since 1984, I have focused on soul-sickness by helping heal the wounds. It is a sacred time of reconciliation with herself and others. Accompanying Judy has been a complex journey of transformation. She has reclaimed her soul by admitting guilt and expressing sorrow to those victimized by her crimes.

As you read, my hope is that you will meet a human being. Not an object to discard or demean.

To those who have suffered loss of loved ones through violence, I offer these words from Judaism: "May their memories be a blessing" and "May you know no further sorrow."

Introduction

As prison chaplain, I met a nineteen-year-old sentenced to death because she was found guilty of killing a teen. Judy faced certain death at an uncertain time. She was scared and in psychological distress as she confronted the pain of guilt. It was a necessary examination to assess her crimes committed in the skewed universe of numbing domestic terror.

The woman I came to know, in whose presence I have been for hundreds of hours, bears no resemblance to the Judy Neelley in books, media, and the minds of Alabamians and beyond. I don't recognize the teenage, lovesick letters to her husband as being from Judy's hand. My mind recoils from the cruelties Judy and Alvin committed against blameless victims.

I am troubled by the shadowy existence of Judy and Alvin's children during their parents' nomadic existence. The twins were mentioned in testimony, not as toddlers with distinct needs, but as inert objects in a motel room or in a car. Parenting was peripheral to survival. Judy's complicity was distressing. How could she have played every hand Alvin dealt as though it were her own?

Could she be redeemed before the state of Alabama put her to death?

Why bother?

Although my book centers on one woman, thousands of Judys are imprisoned with few opportunities to prove they have changed. Our criminal justice system advertises prison as a place for rehabilitation, yet little is done in a consistent manner that makes that possible. Many believe the United States is a Christian country. Is it Christlike to stoke righteous indignation and punishment without God's offer to embrace the prodigal?

I begin with an unflinching description of crimes committed by Judy and Alvin Neelley. Although they occurred over a brief span of time, they grew out of evil that had been festering for years. The purpose of telling is not for an alluring recitation of abuse and murders. It is the substructure on which Judy builds to communicate remorse to victims by bearing responsibility.

The following names listed in alphabetical order are pseudonyms:

Allison, Amanda, Brian Adams, Camilla, Cathy Rose Connolly, Corinne Adams, Deborah, Dee Jay, Eddie, Ginny Brandon, Gloria, Jack, Jordan Adams, Josie, Kay McRae, Keith, Kim, Laurie Campbell, Lily, Little Howie Adams, Marie, Melissa, Mike Deering, Mr. Edison, Paul, Reggie, Rita, Ryan Adams, Sabin, Sandy Adams, Sharon, Cindy Silva, Steve, Sylvia Bowman, Tina.

1.

Insatiable

September 1982

An unknowing darkening sky covered the town of Rome, Georgia. Children summoned inside, supper eaten, baths resisted. Behind closed doors and opened windows, families settled in.

Alvin Neelley drove into the neighborhood of trees, sidewalks, and porch lights. Judy, his teenage wife, sat in the passenger seat. He was casing the home of a teacher at the Rome Development Center for juveniles where sixteen-year-old Judy had her first stint as a juvenile offender. While at the center, Judy wrote letters to her husband describing empathetic staff. In response, Alvin peppered her with accusations and lies. The time had come for Alvin to punish those who had been voices of reason and compassion: the teacher and the assistant director.

Alvin was animated, Judy hypervigilant.

After finding the teacher's home, Alvin commanded in a quietly ominous tone, "Take the twenty-two and shoot out the window. Scare 'em good."

Judy's hand trembled as she gripped the gun. Alvin grabbed it and hissed, "Give me that. I know you; you'll miss on purpose."

He shot into the home four times, then sped off.

Sleep was fractured. Panic erupted in the home and among neighbors.

Alvin drove to a payphone and demanded, "Call the Rome P. D. Tell 'em you shot up that teacher's home for payback because of all the sexual abuse you went through at the center. Then hang up."

Judy was caught between her experience and Alvin's lies. His proximity reinforced a perverse universe. She complied with his incessant and menacing delusions.

"Now call that guy's house. Tell him tonight was only a beginning. He'll end up dead."

Mechanically, Judy dialed the number for Ken Dooley. She repeated Alvin's words, then ended the call.

Unhappy with his wife's tone, Alvin grabbed the phone and redialed. "That Youth Development Center of yours has been getting away with prostitution rings and using my wife. Tonight was just the beginning."[4] He hung up and smirked.

By the next evening, Alvin had located target number two: the address of the center's assistant director, Linda Adair. But he didn't tell Judy. He savored testing her.

One hand on the steering wheel and the other pummeling his wife, he demanded, "Which house is it? You went there. You're protecting her. If you don't find it in ten minutes, I'll kill you and throw you out on the road."

The terror in Judy's body made her heart throb.

Impatient to carry out his plan, Alvin drove to a gas station and then to an empty parking lot. Using a bottle, a motel wash cloth, and gasoline, Judy learned how to make Molotov cocktails.

At the assistant director's home, Alvin parked across the street and surveyed the premises. House lights were on. A yellow car was parked in the driveway.[5]

"Get out and throw it under the car."

Judy lit the cloth and threw the bottle. It fell short of its target, catching the grass on fire. Alvin gunned the car's motor and took off without Judy. Panicking, she yelled for him to stop. Alvin paused, giving Judy moments to jump in the car, while berating her for the lousy throw.

Neighbors alerted the Adairs that their front yard was ablaze. Police were summoned. Investigators got busy. Two people who worked at the same juvenile center terrorized. Menacing phone calls on both nights.

After Alvin heard reports of the crime on the police scanner, he laughed and schemed further. Those attacks were the beginning. Judy couldn't imagine what lay ahead. Thinking beyond the moment was a luxury. Surviving was minute-to-minute.

Two weeks later, Alvin revealed his plan. Judy was to pick up young girls for him to sate his quest for control through sexual violence. In two cars, they went to Riverbend Mall in Rome to search for a stray.

That same September night, a group of six girls and their chaperone went to the mall for an outing. They came from a group home for girls in foster care in Cedartown, Georgia. One of the teens was determined to go home to her family.

On a pretext, she left the group and went outside the mall. Spotting her alone, Alvin told Judy to pick her up. He stepped into his Granada and positioned himself so Judy could follow in the Dodge.

Judy pulled up beside the girl. "Need a ride?"

"…I came in a van with some friends, but I can't find them now."

"I can take you wherever you want to go."

The dark-haired thirteen-year-old hesitated, then got in the car.

Judy ignored the girl's request to take her home and fell in behind Alvin, the child in tow. They drove to Franklin, Georgia, and checked into a motel.

The next morning, in two cars, they headed for Cleveland, Tennessee, to retrieve their toddler twins, who'd been in the care of Alvin's parents. Alvin engineered their movements.

"The girl will ride with you. When we get to Cleveland, she gets in my car. I'll stay in town. You go on up to Momma's trailer and get the kids. Just tell 'em I was at work and couldn't come."

Alvin knew that police frequented the trailer on the lookout for Judy to question her about forged checks. If they caught her and took her in, Alvin would be long gone.

On the way to Cleveland, the girl ventured to speak, breaking the heavy silence. "He hurt me last night. I don't want to do it again."

Judy parroted Alvin's propaganda. "Oh, he doesn't want to hurt you. He likes you."

She got the twins, and they resumed their drifter life.

Back to Georgia. Alvin drove to a drugstore. He told Judy to buy a pack of diabetic syringes and drain cleaner. Not satisfied with the drain cleaner she bought, he ordered her to get another brand.[6] Alvin didn't offer an explanation; Judy didn't ask.

Three days of wandering. Low-budget motels and three states. Fast food. Rapes. The child's repeated requests to call her mother put off with false promises.

Judy never questioned what would happen to the child. Of course, Alvin would let her go. On September 28, the third morning, they drove to Little River Canyon, near Fort Payne, Alabama. A national treasure in the southern Appalachian Mountains with spectacular sights.

Alvin stopped at a lookout, seeing none of its beauty or hearing the music of Little River rushing between the cliffs. He focused on choreographing every act. "Handcuff her to the tree. Tell her you're going to give her a shot—that she'll go to sleep. When she wakes up, we'll be gone, and she'll be unhandcuffed."

Alvin had no intention of leaving a witness. He had a weapon he believed was as lethal as a bullet, syringes filled with drain cleaner. One shot would mimic a fatal heart attack—jailhouse jawing.

Crying quietly, the girl begged. "Let me go. I just want to go home. I won't tell anybody."

Judy knelt by the child. Alvin hollered from thirty or forty feet away, "Do it."

The first needle went into her neck.

"That hurts," she whimpered.

Judy reassured her. "Hang on; it won't hurt after a minute." Then she left the girl and stood by Alvin. They waited.

When he saw that the victim was alive, Alvin spoke icily,

"Shoot her again." He followed Judy to the car to monitor her filling a second syringe. The needle bent as she inserted it into the drain cleaner.

Alvin harangued her. "Dumb bitch. Just like your mother—don't know what you're doing. I shouldn't be surprised, Black lover, Black asshole. If you don't straighten up, I'm gonna kill you."

Judy filled another syringe and gave the girl a second injection.

Alvin was impatient. "Give her another."

Six burning shots and no death. Alvin was seething. He pummeled Judy in the head. "You can't do anything right. You are a sorry excuse for a human being. Bitch. Take her to the ledge; make her turn around. Shoot her in the back."

She pled with Judy again, even as she complied with Judy's directions. "Just let me go. I promise I won't tell."

Overriding the pleas was Alvin's hammering. "Hurry up. What's taking so long, bitch?"

Judy obeyed the man with a gun.

Cathy crumpled onto the edge of the canyon. Judy pushed her body into the ravine.

Alvin, the twins, and Judy left the canyon.[7]

The day and the victim were young.

They left the canyon and stopped for breakfast. Alvin was hungry.

At about 1:00 p.m., they drove to a payphone. Alvin drilled Judy. She was to call the "sorry and inept" police department in Rome.

A police lieutenant answered.[8]

"Are you looking for a Cathy Rose Connolly on the run from Harpst Home?"

"Cathy Rose who?"

17

Alvin listened and beamed his signature smile.

"Connolly. I can tell you where she's at. Go up to Little River Canyon in Alabama. Look off the side of the canyon where there's a powerline going across it, and look straight down in the canyon, and you'll find her where I left her."[9] She hung up.

Alvin tuned into the local radio station. He smirked when he heard the alert. "Call this station if you have a hot tip on the disappearance of Cathy Connolly."

Another payphone. A call to the radio station. Judy's programmed voice. "The Rome Police Department is hiding the fact that a girl named Cathy is dead. They and the Fort Payne police are hiding that. A social worker did it—killed her."

Another call. The Police Department of Fort Payne, Alabama. Same spiel.

Police now had several recordings of Judy's voice.[10] They followed her precise directions.

Cathy's body was respectfully freed from its first grave.

~

When Judy Adams ran away with Alvin, she was in love with a fantasy. When they said their wedding vows a year later, the fantasy had darkened. She had no vocabulary for the immorality into which she'd fallen. Judy loathed her role as procurer, the one to cajole the kidnapped victim into sex, then impotent witness. Alvin secured compliance from Judy over three years through beatings and threats of violence against her, the twins, and her family.

October 1982

After the abuse and execution of Cathy, and a similar killing in Georgia, Judy called on the last vestige of empowerment she had. The way to stop the killing meant turning herself in. Judy knew there was a warrant for writing bad checks. She didn't know there was a cross-country warrant for her arrest on suspicion of murder. Alvin's cheekiness in calling the police left auditory fingerprints.

Judy and Alvin's disjointed existence burst into the headlines of the Fort Payne, Alabama, and Birmingham newspapers. That was the onset of the public's absorption in the crimes.

March—April 1983

The capital murder trial for Judy in 1983 lasted fourteen days and attracted curious crowds and press coverage from at least three states. Her defense was that she was a victim of domestic violence and coerced into committing the crimes.

Found guilty by the jury, the Alabama judge in DeKalb County sentenced her to death. With only minutes to begin processing the judge's words, she was transported to death row at Julia Tutwiler Prison for Women on the outskirts of Wetumpka, Alabama, northeast of the state's capital, Montgomery.

2.

I Don't Want a Female Chaplain

April 1984

Before I heard the name Judy Neelley and before I resigned from my church job, came a crazy idea and a perplexing interview.

I was at a one-woman show about a civil rights agitator in Alabama, Julia Tutwiler, performed by Kathryn Tucker Windham.[11] "Miss Julia" had campaigned for prison reform in the late 1800s. Before the performance, friends told me that the prison chaplain at the women's prison was resigning and, logically, I ought to apply for the position.

Their proposition had synchronicity. They didn't know

20

that my job as a Christian educator at Church of the Ascension in Montgomery was ending. I had been ordained Deacon in the United Methodist Church the previous year; therefore, I was credentialed to become a chaplain.

The possibility of being a prison chaplain intrigued and intimidated me. Going on the intrigued part, I applied. I was an unlikely candidate, since I'd been in a prison exactly two times in my life. A year earlier, I ran, jumped, and laughed a lot with female inmates while leading interpretive dance.

Out of a leotard and professionally dressed, I sat in the warden's office to interview for the position. My application surprised me but not my family and friends. I hadn't gazed into the mirror and seen the words "prison chaplain" circling my head.

The tall, commanding warden said, "I don't want to hire a female chaplain."

Rather bad interviewing skills, I mused. Was I supposed to stand up and do parting pleasantries like, "It was nice to meet you?"

She continued, "We need more men on the staff in this prison." Then she spoke of a former male chaplain who'd hidden when a fight broke out in the prison.

If she was trying to dissuade me from applying, she was in full swing.[12]

Nevertheless, the warden listed duties of the chaplain. In addition to preaching, teaching, and counseling, I was to visit women in segregation. My stars, I thought, this is 1984. We can't still be segregating people! I was making plans for a march that might be coupled with protesting sex discrimination. But in one of the times in which my naïveté popped out to laugh at me, the warden explained that the chaplain would visit people who were in segregation for breaking prison rules, not for being a particular "color."

I was hired as chaplain for three institutions: Red Eagle Work Camp for men, Frank Lee Youth Center for young adult males, and Tutwiler Prison for Women.

The Meeting on Death Row

June 1984

A week after I was appointed chaplain, I mentioned to an officer at Tutwiler that I was going to visit death row to meet Anne Thomas and July Neelley. She cautioned me. "Don't read Judy's institutional file. It'll turn your stomach."

I believed I could be objective and see Judy as a person, not a fiend, while reading her psychological profile and learning about her crimes. The words horrified me. I realized the officer's words were a way of saying, "See the woman, not the crime."

I walked the long hall of drab walls and unforgiving concrete floor of the prison, searching for the corrections officer with keys to death row. When I found her, I made my request known, and she signaled she'd come when she could. She was in the middle of giving emphatic warnings to several inmates.

The June day was Alabama-hot. I retraced my steps to the unmarked door, with no hint as to the occupants behind it. Unremarkable. I leaned against the wall, feeling inadequate. I prayed for God's guidance, said hello to passing inmates and staff, and sweated.

The officer strode toward me. Quick pleasantries as she turned the key in the lock. From the barred doors at the front gate to the door before us, there were four secure barriers.

The metal door swung open, and we stepped into an area no larger than four by six feet. To my immediate left and straight ahead were floor to ceiling iron bars, food slots, and antiquated-looking locks, which separated the officer and me from inmates consigned to death cells. Along with a cupboard, the officer and I were pushing the limits of the tiny cubicle. Unnervingly close on the wall outside Judy's cell was a flimsy frame enclosing a slip of paper. It bore her name and date of the scheduled electrocution.

Two human beings sat on their beds in adjoining cells, warehoused until the state could have its way. Stainless steel toilet-sink combo. Single bed with mattress. A cupboard. Approximately six by eight feet.

Judy looked up warily.

"I'm Louise Johns, the new chaplain.[13] You're Judy?"

"Yes." Her voice was as flat as her expression.

The officer logged in the time and my name. My hand rested on the wall of bars for the shared shower. Anne Thomas was housed in a cell parallel to Judy's. To enter Anne's cell, one had to take a few steps through the shower area. Looking through two sets of bars, I pieced together Anne's face. She stretched her arm through the bars at a forty-five-degree angle to shake my hand.

I greeted Anne. She'd been on death row longer than Judy.

"How are you today?" she said in a welcoming tone.

I replied as I endeavored to make myself believe that the heat wouldn't suffocate me and claustrophobia wouldn't consume me.

Both Anne and Judy wore prison uniforms: a buttoned shift, pure white. The garment was engineered to fit all bodies and no bodies, erasing personal style. Black letters stenciled on the uniform could not be missed. ADOC: Alabama Department of Corrections.

Having finished her duties, the officer left, closing the door behind me, locking us in. I hadn't known that was protocol. Another bit of information for the novice chaplain.

I was confident the two women would be happy to see a friendly face and hear a kind tone in the midst of concrete and harsh rhetoric. My gracious presence would cast some mysterious spell on these outcasts.

I knew little of Anne's case. Judy's was the infamous one. I'd come with my best nonjudgmental self, and Judy's wary reaction wrecked my presumptions.

Anne and I conversed. Judy appeared uninterested in joining us. Unexpectedly, Anne spoke a brief prayer in tongues, which I couldn't interpret. Then she began singing "Victory in Jesus," and I joined in. The words came easily to Anne, less so with me. She was comfortable in expressing her faith. Judy was not. It was some time before I understood Judy's resistance came from her struggles with God's justice and a conviction that her sins could not be forgiven.

I was grateful when the officer's mandated thirty-minute check of death row liberated me. There was no spell. I walked out of the stultifying heat of the death-row unit, cooled by the reception I'd received from one of the women.

The day I met Judy, I knew sketchy details of about thirty days of her criminal life from reading the file. That left more than seven thousand days of living of which I knew nothing. In the unnumbered days left on earth for her, I didn't know if or how I could bridge the gap for either Anne or Judy.

Empathy on my part was inadequate. No life experience had the vaguest connection with what they endured. I could do skimpy pastoral visitations, spout comforting passages of scripture, and avoid psychological or spiritual entanglement in order to keep futile feelings from disturbing my sleep. Besides, there were hundreds of other inmates who needed spiritual guidance.

The number sentenced to death would grow. Some saw my job as straightforward. Get them ready to die.

3.

Marked

Judy's Early Life

Judy sat on the bed's thin mattress in a death-row cell. She leaned against the concrete wall, closing her eyes and breathing deeply. With the force of her mind, she transported herself away from the smell of the supper tray perched on the food slot and pushed out the prison walls.

The expanse of a sidewalk leading to the apartment in which her family lived opened before her. She saw her three-year-old self resisting the mother's effort to pull Judy up the stairs. She wanted to crawl. Images of her sister's tricycle escapade elicited a grin as she saw her tumbling down the stairs of their second-story apartment. *A real nut,* she thought.

She wiggled her toes, trying to take pressure off her legs as they rested on the metal edge of the bed. Her recollection moved to a duplex in Murfreesboro, Tennessee. Judy's brother was trying to shove her into a closet. She braced her leg against the door and felt her big toe get caught, ripping off the nail. The howl brought their father into the room.

He picked her up, sat her on the foot of the bed, and quickly examined the injury. "Stop crying! There's nothing wrong with your toe."

The pain hurt less than his reprimand. At five years old, she knew she needed comfort.

Judy saw her father picking up her brothers and showing them affection. Had he ever said he loved her? She could remember a few sweet moments: his arms encircled her as he taught her to tie shoelaces and steadied her when she was learning to ride a bike. She thought it was fun when she and Dottie caught minnows for their dad's fishing.

Wiggling minnows changed into images of their father's hunting vest with no sleeves and multiple pockets where he stored shotgun cartridges. She wrinkled her face in disgust when she saw the large pouch in the back, blood-soaked and brimming with dead squirrels, birds, or rabbits. She heard the voice of a small child. "Why do you have to shoot those funny little animals?"

The smell of the food on her untouched tray made her nauseous, taking her to a time when she was very sick. Her mother kept her out of school. When her father came into the bedroom, she pretended to be asleep. He called her name.

"He pinched me on my butt. It marked me. I was a little bitty thing." She didn't realize she'd spoken those words into the cell.

The door to death row opened noisily, breaking Judy's escape. She jerked her head as she pulled away from the wall. The officer took a tally of the women. Two. She noted it in the log, then departed. The door slammed. Judy heard the lock being secured.

She fell back, hitting the wall. The desperate sensation of being alone dulled the sharp pain caused by striking the hard surface. Of course, there was not one inch of her that deserved to be loved. She had to look no further than the father who called his daughter a fat rabbit and teased her about buck teeth.

Maybe she should have figured it out. She was not worth being loved or protected. When her daddy took a belt to her brother, would he come after her next? The hug her grandfather gave made her feel unsafe. Did no one notice how often that relative situated himself in his chair and called for one of the girls to come sit on his lap? Was no one paying attention when the girls were squirming in the lap, trying to free themselves? There was no protection—not by her father, her mother, her grandparents, or siblings. No child protective services intervened. Her sister wanted to speak out about being molested but didn't think anyone would believe her or would stop the abuse.

A male officer yelled at someone in the hall. It brought to mind hearing her father's argument with a gate attendant on a memorable and miserable family trip. He had helped construct Opryland in Nashville. Once opened, the work crews would get a free day to enjoy the music and rides. Jimbo and Dottie got new clothes. Dottie's outfit was red and blue. Judy wore hand-me-downs. That didn't matter to her. It was the trip that was to be anticipated—not what she wore.

Their daddy was more animated than usual as he drove. The children wrestled in the backseat.

Aunts, uncles, and cousins joined James and his brood at the ticket office. The children were fidgety with excitement. Proudly, the daddy presented his credentials to the man at the entrance. Whether the ticket taker hadn't been told about the agreement or a misunderstanding existed, the pronouncement was clear: they would get in like everyone else. They would pay. That was money the Adams family didn't have. But a promise was a promise! To exact justice, James chased and nearly caught the overweight attendant. The trip home was morose.

Her father's temper signaled danger. While in a bar, a stranger pulled a gun on James in a case of mistaken identity. James went home to get his shotgun. His wife begged him not to go back. Nevertheless, he left. When he returned for another shotgun, James's mother-in-law stepped in to keep the squabble from escalating. Judy thought all dads had a short fuse. Or was that all men?

After work and on the weekends, alcohol got between him, his wife, and five children. When he had a hangover, the children were forbidden to play or speak in the house. They might be exiled to the couch: sitting still, no talking, no whispering, no restless kicking the legs of the furniture.

The living-room wall, painted dark teal by their father, dimmed natural lighting, but neither the paint nor threats dimmed raucous children and innocent pets. He threw boots at the cat if it walked too heavily on the floor. Judy tiptoed and tried to quiet the other children with her obedience to house rules and anxiety about arousing anger.

They didn't have to tread softly around their mother. Sometimes they took care of her, being sure she didn't fall asleep with a lighted cigarette, and they got her up in the mornings. Although they might not be able to count on breakfast or supper, they could count on her saying, "I love you so great-hard," accompanied by a firm embrace.

Judy was the adult in the household. If the trailer was messy, she cleaned it up. Her brothers needed help to get ready for school. Mostly, she took pride in her grown-up behavior. Even with times of resentment, she found satisfaction in providing stability as she mitigated the chaos.

Despite the drinking, life got better. Their daddy started his own construction business. The family was stepping up, able to buy clothes they needed. Judy experienced times of tranquility. She relished sitting on their neighbor's fence, communing with the cows, singing to them. Unafraid.

Then came a car accident in 1973. James was in the back. On impact, his face slammed against the front seat. After multiple surgeries and long months of hospitalization, the family visited him. Judy was unprepared to see a stranger shuffling toward them in brown slippers with his arms spread wide. Her brothers and sister ran up and hugged the man in a plaid robe over blue pajamas. She saw the scarred and distorted face. Judy cowered behind her mother, who tugged at Judy to go hug the man with a "halo thing" on his head. To the fearful child, everything about him said, "Flee!" Then she was gripped with shame. Even when she knew it was her father, the sight of him repulsed her.

After James was released from the hospital, insurance money from the wreck paid for a motorcycle. On a Saturday night in March 1974, James got into an argument at a bar. In a rage, he tried to get himself and his motorcycle home. But a guardrail got in the way. He was killed instantly.[14]

"We're lucky," Judy told her friends and sister. If Dottie hadn't been in her best and only dress, and if there hadn't been so many relatives there, and if it hadn't been the day of their daddy's funeral, Dottie would have beat Judy up. Dottie thought Judy meant they were lucky that their daddy, James Adams, had died.

Nine-year-old Judy added, "We have so many people who

care about us."

That was a statement of wishful thinking.

Inside the Trailer

James Adams had tried to provide a better life for his family: he'd bought land, seven and three-quarters acres. After his death, his life insurance paid for a trailer to put on the property in Rutherford County, Tennessee.

The unkempt and weedy land had once been a river. The dirt was thin, the road unpaved. An old pond on its way to drying up didn't improve the land's appearance. But it was a place to call home. To Judy, it gave solace. They dreamed about horses, but that was as real as they would be. She memorized the land, could see it without opening her eyes. Grass and ground soothed her. The natural world fueled her spirit.

Walking into the woods was an escape from the discontinuity of a raucous household. On hearing the scuttling retreat of small animals, she wished she could tell them she came in peace. Judy noticed the woods had distinctive smells as the seasons changed and even at different times of the day. The heat and clamminess of a Tennessee summer didn't invade the complex woods.

She tried to imagine how different her family's life would be had the head of the family not died at thirty-four young years. Would he protect her from harm? Time aided in healing Judy's griefs of loss and betrayal. Nonetheless, her reality was unchanged.

The two years separating the girls fostered solidarity between Dottie and Judy. It also engendered wholesale fights and scary pranks. When Dottie put granddaddy long-leg spiders in Judy's hair, Dottie's defense was, "I pulled the legs off some of them for you."

Judy described herself as the "family snitch."

"I told Mom that Dottie had sneaked off from school one day to see her boyfriend. She hit me with her bony fist, and she could hit! I landed on the other side of the bed, hitting the floor. Now I had something else on her, 'I'm going to tell Mama!'" Gleefully, she admitted, "I wasn't always getting Dottie in trouble, just sometimes."

That story evoked another for Judy. "One summer when Kim and Rita were staying with us—they were Dottie and my best friends—they took some of Mama's beer to the back of the property to drink it. I solemnly promised I wouldn't tell. And I didn't. But when Mama came back, I pantomimed who had done it. I pointed to the refrigerator, and Mom guessed, then I acted like I was drinking something. They were grounded, and Dottie beat me up. She was a tough ol' girl." The skirmishes were uneven until Judy grew taller than Dottie.

"Ironically, all us kids were close. If one of us ever got in trouble, we knew there would be others there to defend us. We were so used to the fighting, I can't imagine not having done it; there was a lot of it." Judy gave me her critique. "Mama should've put her foot down; she wasn't strict, into discipline. We pretty much raised ourselves. We were kids, rarely drew blood—not from lack of trying, especially Bill. He picked up things to throw—puny little thing, skinny. Wonder he never caused major damage, knocking out several windows, never replaced. They were big ones; put plastic bags over them."

Judy took on a mothering role to Davey. He was the baby brother, five years younger than Judy. She gravitated toward the vacuum of parenting. "Davey was who I had to protect from Bill. We'd slug it out over how he treated Davey. That is sad!" She paused. "I feel so guilty about that."

After James Adams died, the toothpick scaffolding of their lives collapsed. The widow, Barbara Adams, had few resources to construct a sturdy framework that would support the family. She had little sense of self. She lost the wifely role of satisfying male expectations.

The family tried to live off social security. When those funds became inadequate, Barbara got a job making parts for heaters and air conditioners. She worked a few years, then was fired through a preventable setback. She'd been drinking with a teenager, the son of a policeman. They were both drunk, but she let him drive. After he wrecked the car, with minor injuries for both, she stayed out of work for two weeks without calling in.[15]

By the time she was a young teen, Judy cleaned, made beds, and washed the clothes. No one protested, and everyone accepted that role.[16] Cooking featured beans, potatoes, and cornbread. Jimbo left home and school. Dottie fell in love, got pregnant, then married when she was fifteen. Her husband was twenty-four. Between the pregnancy and the marriage, Judy's oldest brother and Dottie's boyfriend were in a car accident. The groom-to-be was paralyzed from the chest down. While he was on a respirator in the hospital, Dottie's mother signed for them to marry. The ceremony was conducted bedside. It was an odd scene with nurses smiling and wiping their eyes—the first and only wedding Judy has attended.

At home, the lives of the Adams family varied little from one day to the next. Davey and Bill could sink into the sofa, studying the television, or join their friends outside.[17] There were a few markers: a vague time when Bill went to Nashville to live with relatives, and when Davey briefly became a scout.

Judy, at fourteen, drove him to meetings.

Judy laughed as she told me how her mother fell through a chair. "We had a recliner that'd been my dad's. The seat was out of it. There was a pillow balanced on the springs. You had to sit on it just right. She plopped down; her feet went straight up. I could see her face through her kneecaps. She had a huge bruise. The big dummy! Once when she was in a bar, a guy put a wet ten-dollar bill on her arm and then pressed a lighted cigar against the bill. It didn't burn the bill. It burned her arm. She wouldn't yell. She had a bad scar on her arm from that. I'm like her—stubborn. Someone give me a dare, I'll do it if it harelips the devil, no matter how much it hurts me." Judy inhaled quickly as she told me. "That's stupid."

Barbara, or "Mama" to her children, had a heart big enough to divvy what they had. She didn't say no to a string of people needing a place to live for a while. Sharing was mandatory— food, beds, bathroom, privacy. Food was stretched. Since much of the cleaning and cooking fell to Judy, her resentment grew. She didn't fault her mother, at least not at the beginning, although life would be easier if the trailer wasn't a crash pad for all comers.

As far as Judy knew, those temporary boarders didn't offer their meager resources. In prison, Judy realized she was angry about how they'd used her mother. People came and went from the trailer. No one mopped or washed dishes after Judy cooked. "Everyone used Mama. She was such a sucker."

Barbara had new men in her life. They liked to wrestle with Judy, or maybe hold her, or get her to sit in their laps. Their hands wandered over her body. Repulsed by their behavior, she realized she'd have to protect herself. When drunken boarders wandered into Judy's room, she sat up and started yelling. They left. She didn't know if her mother was asleep, passed out, or didn't try to protect her daughter. It didn't make for a secure night's sleep or the sense that there would be anyone to safeguard her. That heightened vigilance robbed Judy of restorative rest. It would be years before Judy could lie down without fear of harm.

The trailer's luster was burnished off. Boys' roughhousing tore down doors. A sheet substituted for a door to Judy's room. The walls shared with her mother's bedroom were two pieces of paneling back-to-back, which exposed Judy to more than any young teen should've heard.

In a trailer of changing characters, there were pseudo secrets: what everyone knew, but didn't acknowledge and therefore never confronted. There was poverty and parental neglect. Her mom drank, and the door never closed to the trailer.

Keeping friends was complicated by unpredictable occupants and the smell of stray cats. It squashed one friendship when the girl Judy invited to her home was disgusted by the smell and spread the word at school. Embarrassed by the cruel banter, Judy stopped inviting. Her worn-out shoes and clothes made her easy prey for bullying in the elementary school.

School picture day, 1976. The twelve-year-old felt safer in jeans. Protocol was to wear a dress. That meant borrowing one. The next year, she showed up for the class picture in the same dress. She had nothing else to wear. It wasn't shorter; Judy was taller. The effect elicited painful teasing.

If anyone noticed in middle school that Judy was teetering, they looked away. She hoped for acceptance and joined 4-H Club and Future Homemakers of America. Nursing attracted her because of her instinct to nurture. She became a cheerleader and then faced ridicule at pep rallies and games; students made up derogatory cheers aimed at her.

The cute girls at school must be whispering about her as they looked her way, giggled, then regrouped to their huddle. She could tell others didn't feel like outsiders by how they played freely and touched other people, and it didn't seem to feel wrong or hurt. She longed for someone who valued her and heard her cries.

She intentionally chose friends she perceived to be as close to the edge as she felt. She judged herself as inferior by any measure. She couldn't hope to have the right clothes, or a steady diet, or a home phone. Being smart wasn't a key to popularity. Judy's brief tenure in high school was spent honing a calculated diffidence. One teacher, when returning tests, reported to the class the top three grades and the bottom three. Judy was in the top category but decided she would apply herself less. Fourth or lower was her aim.

Judy was comparable to other adolescents in the whiplash of body image. Her mom said Judy was pretty. It didn't make sense to her since her mother and Judy looked alike, yet her mother talked about how ugly she was. "How could I be pretty? Everyone called me beaver and nose. Those were the voices I listened to."

There seemed to be nothing on which Judy could build a sturdy identity.

Church and God weren't central in the Adams's home. The parents were paper members—on the inactive roll. Judy infrequently attended a Baptist Church, catching the church's van. She remembered being saved when she was twelve.[18] Had Judy talked with God more frequently, she might have questioned how God could abandon her when she needed protection. Those conversations were years in the making.

Splintering Toothpicks

Raised in the rural South, Judy understood the parameters of her life. She would marry while young, have children, and be obedient to her husband. Wedding vows sanctioned the authority of the husband over his wife's mind and body.

She saw her father become violent, and that was tolerated. He was not to be questioned. That must mean that's what husbands and fathers do. She was molested by her grandfather. She didn't like it, and no one stopped it, so it must be acceptable for men to molest women or girls. And since she didn't stop it, it was her fault. She was bad.

By the time Judy was fifteen, she'd been on two dates. One person with whom she had a date went to the same school as Judy. He was several years older. After the movie, there was no sitting in a parked car. She made him take her home immediately. The second date was a friend of her sister's husband. Gauging Judy by her mother's behavior, he made assumptions. She cleared that up promptly. A sixteen-year-old she had a crush on hung out at the house, sometimes sleeping there after he'd gotten high elsewhere. She thought they were close. The night he went into her mother's bedroom, the betrayal stung.

When Alvin Neelley and his friend drove up to the Adams's trailer, looking for Judy's mom, the young teen met a fun-loving guy who knew how to treat a lady. Around him, she felt special. It was June 1979.

Alvin began showing up regularly. He bantered with siblings and schmoozed with her mother. Unlike her father, he didn't drink. In contrast to the aggressive and inebriated men in the trailer, he was jovial, got along with everyone, and didn't molest her in a drunken haze. He was good-looking and good-natured, the complete package: a gentleman with marvelous manners, a kind heart, economic security, a ready laugh, and attentiveness to Judy. It filled her ache to be cherished.

Alvin was Judy's white knight, who'd come to his princess in burnished armor, offering all she'd been denied in her short life. She was dazzled by someone who would look past her notion of being ugly, the embarrassment from her pronounced front teeth, and rescue her from poverty. Judy's future seemed bright.

He listened as she told him that she did all the housework and the cooking. Overstatements, but to a young teen, that was how it felt. She'd taken naturally to mothering; now there was someone who would take care of her. Was he trying to be helpful when he said Judy's mom was using her to do all the "motherly" duties? Was he trying to shield her innocence when he suggested that Judy's mother used Judy as bait?

Judy drew Alvin's eyes because the nearly twenty-six-year-old man preferred young girls. Judy was mature in ways of taking responsibility for the home. But emotionally, she was younger than her years. She lacked the parental nurture and guidance that give a foundation for challenges and crises. Her mother was more like a sister than a parent.

Into that emptiness stepped Alvin. In destructive ways, they were perfect for each other. One craved affirmation. The other pursued dominance.

4.

Alvin & Family

The year 1953 was decisive in the marriage of Alvin Sr. and Jessie Neelley. Alvin was on trial in Alabama for murder. Pregnant and with three other children from a previous marriage, Jessie returned to Georgia, the state of her birth.

On Thanksgiving Eve 1952, five boys, mostly young teens, went to the Greenville, Alabama, Drive-In Theater. Two of the boys separated from the rest as they left the theater. They threw rocks at the Neelley home, hitting the tin roof. Alvin Sr. got his .22 rifle and went out to investigate. He testified on the stand that "he fired toward the earth without raising the gun to his shoulder and to the right of the spot where he saw some boys." Donald Henry, a ten-year-old, hid in the shrubbery.[19]

Defense argued that the bullet had ricocheted off the ground and hit the boy. Character witnesses for the defense testified to Neelley's moral character. Prosecution said that the forty-year-old mill worker had been lying in wait and intentionally shot the child. The jury deliberated about one and one-half hours before delivering a verdict: second-degree murder of Henry. They recommended a life sentence for Alvin Sr.[20]

The story passed down in the family was that the child's death was a tragic accident.

Five months after the trial, Alvin Jr. was born in Trion, Georgia, on July 15, 1953.

Almost thirty years later, the son was sentenced to life in a Georgia prison.

~

Six years after Alvin Sr. was paroled in Alabama, the state of Georgia took custody, then released him.[21] Those years away from his son and wife were pivotal. During pre-school, Alvin bonded with his mother. His father was a cipher. Alvin Howard Neelley Jr. was his father's one child, although the elder Neelley denied paternity. His mother doted on their son and made it clear to all her children and grandchildren that boys were superior to girls.

Somewhere along the way, the relationship between Alvin's parents became acrimonious. He retreated, and she attacked with accusations of infidelity. Alvin had no model for masculinity, and the solicitous mother may have felt suffocating for the son.

Young Alvin half-heartedly attended school. But he made friends with his jocular manner and sweet demeanor. His smile was ready and brightened his eyes and those around him. It didn't save him from being teased as he got older. Maybe to offset the hurt of bullying, as a juvenile Alvin started building a criminal record. He stole cars, then specialized in stealing from convenience stores where he was employed. It was an easy gig. Get hired. Steal. Leave town before he was discovered. New job. Steal. Leave town.

No father-son bonding was established between young Alvin and his father. To be named after his father was galling. Alvin Jr. also may have objected to the association with *Alvin and the Chipmunks*, popular in the late 1950s and 1960s. In the cartoons, Alvin was the smallest of the three chipmunks, easily distractible, a trickster, and adorable—attributes easy to see in the offspring of Alvin Sr.

In early 1982, Al badgered Judy about how she addressed him in her closing to a letter:

> *'Judith loves Alvin.' Why? I notice everything. I wasn't gonna say anything in a letter until I saw you in person, but you've gotten carried away with it. You know I hate Alvin. Barbara is the second [name I hate]. The best I can do is divorce you and get remarried fast and just plainly destroy you like you're trying to destroy me.*[22]

5.

Charisma

Judy sent me a meticulous inventory of her dwelling. It stretched from the "front door"—a set of bars, roughly twenty-three and one-half inches wide by seventy-two inches—through the "back door" to the far edge of the exercise area—approximately seventeen feet. The door to the securely fenced outdoor slab was solid steel with a one-foot-square Plexiglas window covered with wire mesh. Her bed was twenty-seven inches wide by six feet. The mattress was shorter than the frame by six inches and hard. The plastic was non-flammable with wool stuffing.

The bookshelf was four by four feet, twelve inches deep, covered by a white curtain. She had a thirteen-inch Sony television with, as Judy denounced it, one of the worst inventions for promoting laziness, a remote. The metal cabinet had one drawer and two shelves with a towel rack on either end. Her crafts sat under the bed along with shoes and plastic dishes. She had a pot for heating water for coffee and instant food, one dual cassette, including a CD player but no CDs. Earphones were to be used at all times.

She observed that if she were handling security, death row wouldn't have some of what was allowed, including a glass mirror, nail clippers, and electrical plugs. "God forbid we should fry ourselves before they do."

Moving to the exercise yard, accessed by both of the women on death row, she gave the dimensions of eleven by twenty-two. The overhead light used a recessed 200–watt bulb. It had to be frosted, otherwise it would cast too much of a shadow. It was turned on at 6:30 a.m. and turned off at about 10:00 p.m. In 1996, the time she provided me with this inventory, they had a few plants: tomato, cucumber, onion, and some flowers. Four plastic chairs surrounded the metal table.

On one of my regular visits with Judy in 1996, I suggested she tell me about meeting Alvin. A dry smile crossed Judy's face. We were in the death-row cell on the one place to sit: Judy's bed. I perched on the edge and could reach the door that led to the small exercise area, the wooden cabinet across from the bed, and the concrete wall flanking her bed. Judy could touch the toilet-sink combination and her cabinet. She leaned against the wall. We were inches apart.

Almost seventeen years earlier, an adolescent and naïve Judy laid eyes on the amiable Alvin Neelley.

"God, that was a long time ago. It was three days after my fifteenth birthday: June 10, 1979. He was driving a little yellow Gremlin. He and his friend Mike Deering were riding around trying to find my mom. Mike had talked with her on his CB and wanted to meet her. I was standing outside with my sister helping put her husband into the car: you remember—

43

he was paralyzed. We'd seen the car going back and forth on the gravel road. Finally, they pulled up and asked if we knew where Indian Princess lived."

Judy explained to me that after the death of her father, her mother got into CB radio, acquiring the handle "Indian Princess" chosen from her Cherokee heritage. She imagined that she had once been a princess for a tribe.

"Mike and Al didn't know her real name. I told them she lived here, so I turned around and yelled at one of my brothers to go get her. We stood there talking to Mike and Al. Eventually, they came inside, and I think Mike stayed the night, moved in; left his wife and four children."

Wistfully, Judy recalled the chemistry. "Al and I hit it off; he was funny, attentive. I wasn't used to getting attention; he was clean cut, very charismatic, likable, and adventurous. He took us riding around. My brothers and I piled into the car. It was fun and harmless.[23]

"My brothers loved him. Everybody loved him. He brought over bags of groceries and bought a hibachi for cooking hamburgers. He'd bring pork chops, steaks, food we never had money for, and take us picnicking at the river; anyone who would go. All the attention was big to us. Here he comes, flashing all this money, taking us places."

It would be months before Judy realized that, to fund the food feasts, Alvin was skimming off the day's receipts at a convenience store where he worked.

"We started going out to movies, but the only way I'd go was if my two younger brothers went with us. So he took all three of us. Eventually, we started going to movies alone. I thought he'd be a model husband and father.

"Al taught me to kiss. He was only the second guy I'd kissed! I kissed with my mouth closed, and he'd get frustrated.

I felt inadequate. 'You're so dumb; don't you know how to kiss?' It bothered me, little things here and there. I ignored them. He wanted me to go to his apartment. When I wasn't too eager, he'd ask me, 'Don't you want to be alone with me?' If we went to his apartment, he'd want to have sex, and I didn't want to. We'd started down a path; I couldn't retreat, back up.

"His kisses never started a fire. What was exciting was to know that an older man found me attractive, that he desired me. Plus, I was fifteen. At that age, you got hormones going on. I was trying to figure out what was going on in my body.

"He had an apartment in Murfreesboro. Soon I was going over to his place, cooking and cleaning. On his twenty-sixth birthday, July 15, just over a month after we'd met, he asked me to marry him. We were in the back seat of Mama's car; she was driving. I don't know where we were going. I was sitting up against the door; he was in the middle.

"'I want you to be my wife,' he said without much emotion.

"I was thrilled. I knew I wasn't ready to be married. I'd been proposed to before—teenager stuff. My response to his proposal was I went to hug; he went to kiss. It was awkward.

"Later, I told Mom I was going to the movies. We went by the theater to be able to say we honestly had gone. I told Mom the theater was too crowded, that we decided to go back to the apartment to watch TV. She trusted me. I'd always been a tomboy; I could take care of myself. If a guy put a hand on me, I'd slap him silly. She'd seen me handle myself. I didn't know it would happen that night; he'd been pressuring me.

"After he talked with Mama on the CB, we were sitting on his bed with a blue sheet. We talked for a few minutes. He started kissing me. He insisted I take off my shirt. I let him talk me into it. I was feeling a lot of pressure. It was over pretty quick. He was rough. Apparently, he didn't believe I was a virgin. He didn't care in the least about my feelings emotionally or physically. He satisfied his own needs and rolled off.

"I'll never forget that he looked down on the sheet to see if there was blood on it. I didn't know what he was doing at the time. The second time we had sex, he was particularly brutal. It hurt like hell. Definitely lacked the tenderness or warmth I'd expected. It was so cold, so disgusting. I wasn't comfortable with my own body. He didn't know how to excite a woman, a girl, to make it pleasurable."

Alvin hid many significant details of his life. He was married to Laurie, and they had three children. They met in Cleveland, Tennessee, when he was twenty-one and she was nineteen. Laurie and Alvin were both working at Alladdin Mills.[24] Their relationship moved quickly to living together and then marrying in 1975. Being married was not a deterrent to Alvin's philandering. His wife's pleas for him to be faithful were ineffective. He continued to move about, led by his sex drive or compulsion to subjugate women or both.[25] Despite Laurie's faithfulness, Alvin often accused her of sleeping with everybody in town.[26]

Isolation

Fall 1979

Alvin's charm captivated the teen who needed to be loved. It was easy for Alvin to slip into the picture and sow doubts, to convince Judy that her family didn't love her. With Alvin she was a princess. With Judy's family she was the maid and the madam who was to secure guests for her mother. It was time she stuck up for herself and left all that exploitation behind.

The stage was set for Judy's declaration of independence. Alvin dictated a letter that Judy wrote to her mother and siblings in which she cruelly denounced her mother.[27] With a mixture of emotions, Judy believed she'd dealt an irreconcilable blow. Her mother must hate the rebellious daughter. She didn't know that her mother searched for her. Even though Judy was certain she'd shut the door on her family, it remained wide open. That wasn't the narrative fostered by Alvin as he stoked Judy's isolation.

Judy's scrapes with the law began after Alvin glided into her life. Under Alvin's tutelage, Judy was an apt student. Forged checks in her hometown of Murfreesboro. Minor legal repercussions. It would get worse in every possible way.

Years later, Alvin's tactics became clear to Judy. In one of our sessions, she spoke in a tone of incredulity. "Al would tell me Mama was hitting on him. She had Mike; she wasn't doing that. 'All these women want me,' he'd say, 'better get me while you can. Your mom's wearing skin-tight shorts, tight in the crotch.' I was terrified of losing him. It was just another tool.

"He made me feel ashamed about my younger brothers. God, how do I explain? 'Why are you keeping up with your two baby brothers? You're older, too mature to hang out with them.' If I wanted to spend time with them, it showed I wasn't as grown as I pretended to be; that meant I wasn't worthy of him. He played on all the insecurities I had; damned good at it.

"We asked Mom to sign for us to get married; she'd signed for my sister when she was fifteen. She wouldn't sign for me; she wanted me to wait until I graduated. I'd just started the tenth grade. I was so in love. I got pregnant. It didn't take much for him to convince me to run away in October seventy-nine.

"We were driving home one night, and there was a car

directly in front of us. A man was driving; there was a woman passenger. The headlights were catching the silhouette of the man hitting the woman. I couldn't believe it. My daddy didn't hit my mom. I didn't know men hit women. She ought to hit him back. Al didn't say anything. Later, he told me he'd beaten up his first wife because she was sleeping around with Black men. I found one of her bras with blood; it never once occurred to me he'd hit me.

"He never laid a hand on me until Christmas seventy-nine. We were staying in Rome, in a cheap motel, nine dollars a night. We were running out of money. I got a job in a pizza place on the outskirts of Rome. It was a couple of miles from the motel." Judy spoke with pride. "It was only the second job I'd had. I was so excited. Al didn't like me being around all those men, said I was flirting. I never thought he'd be jealous. Everyone was so nice, like Paul, a tall, lanky guy who was a cook. After my first day, Al was to pick me up at five. I'd been waiting for him to come in to get me. By fifteen minutes after five, I went out looking for him. He was in the car waiting. I was telling him all about the day, all energized.

"We got back to the motel and were playing some board games." Her tone darkened. "I never knew he was getting angry; I knew he was quiet. He picked up the board from the game and hit me in the head. It hurt. I'd never been struck besides spanking. He slapped me when I started crying hysterically. He grabbed me by my long hair and started hitting me in my stomach with his fist. He was kicking me in the ribs and punching me in the head and face. It was crazy. He threw me across the bed, went around and started hitting me again with his fist and open hand. It was in my face, head, stomach.

"I was terrified, mostly trying to cover my head. I was begging him to stop. I was swearing to him I'd never do it again, even though I didn't know what in the hell I had done."

Judy's voice dropped. She matter-of-factly stated the pattern. For Alvin, violence and sex were twins. "I think after the first beating, I believe we had sex."

She knew she had herself to blame, although she couldn't figure out what she'd done wrong. It wouldn't happen again if she were more vigilant, more loving, more anything. But it did happen again, more frequently and more relentlessly.

"They say men who abuse women always apologize," she told me. "He never told me he was sorry. I apologized; mostly I never knew what set him off. The tension would lessen when the explosion was over, but he wasn't tender. There was never any of that. He would say, 'See what you made me do. It's your fault. If you wouldn't do such-and-such, I wouldn't get angry. I'm under a lot of stress.'"

Judy asked me what I could not answer.

"I don't understand. Why do it? It's not an explanation to say he was passing on what was passed to him. That would excuse it. I don't want to give him an excuse. I never went back to the pizza place. Al accused me of setting up a clandestine meeting with Paul. 'You wanted to sleep with him; if you hadn't made me mad talking about him, I wouldn't have hit you.' I started learning then how jealous and possessive he was."

A necessary silence lay between us. Then Judy spoke in resignation. "I had no idea the extremes it would go to.

"How could I be so stupid? There are fond remembrances. He took all of us down to Panama City one year. He took us to Lake Winnepasoaka near Roswell, Tennessee. People call it Lake Winnie. He used to be funny, had a sense of humor. It was a mask of who he really was; it was all a game. I'm unable to draw a full picture of him—too caught up in the painful past.

"He had jobs at convenience stores and wouldn't let me out of his sight. He made me go to work with him. While he was sitting on his butt, I was stocking shelves, mopping, and had to stack cases of drinks above my head in the cooler. He was beating me at regular intervals by then, often beating me in my stomach, trying to lose the baby. He accused me of having the child by a Black man." Judy despaired. "I had nobody to turn to."

Alvin told Judy that he was infertile. It was a lie not to take responsibility for their child and to accuse Judy of committing the "unforgiveable" sin of lying with a Black man. Although a phantom, he appeared to be real in Alvin's mind.

Her shame and guilt grew. Abuse became a daily reality. It was hated, and it was predictable. In a lopsided existence, even the violence had a warped stability.

After Judy got pregnant, she described him as "jealous, hateful, frightening" and sexually voracious. "I could never satisfy him. Sometimes he wouldn't wait until he got off work. He just had to have it then, right in the store where we were working, anywhere he wanted to. He made me lie down on the concrete floor, and he did what he wanted until he was satisfied, and then he'd go back in the store and make me clean up the rest of the store …" She began to sob. "I felt like a piece of meat."[28]

After a moment, she continued. "I'd been very sick the entire time I was pregnant. Oh my God I was sick; I lost a lot of weight. Skeletal. I was fifteen; my body wasn't ready. By then we were in Albany, Georgia, and already involved in criminal activity. It never occurred to me I could miscarry. I didn't know it could happen.

"One day, I couldn't stand up right, the pain was so strong. It lasted several days. I was throwing up. In terrible shape. Al finally decided to take me to the hospital on February 13. They kept me. The following morning, I miscarried. I named her Barbara, after my mom. I hated that it was Valentine's Day. They wouldn't let Al in the room with me. He came to see me the next day. When I woke up in recovery after the D&C, he fussed because we didn't have a car. He had to walk to the hospital; he didn't have any money. He blamed me for that."

Judy's recollections were hard to hear and harder to fathom.

"Then he got me back to the motel. Oh my God, the things he did to me. He took either a mop or broom handle and kept shoving it up in me. He beat me with his fist. He wasn't big on using his open hands. He'd pick up whatever was handy, usually guns, his hand revolver. He said I lost the baby on purpose so I couldn't prove it was a Black man's: over and over. He was calling me everything but a cedar bush! 'Bitch, slut, whore, Black lover.' He hates Blacks.

"When the beatings started, I used to think this won't happen again. I know what makes him angry; I won't make him angry again. We'd stolen money in Kennasaw from a convenience store; he held that over my head, telling me he'd turn me over to the law. A lot of verbal battering. If I mentioned going home to visit, he'd say that if I ever ran away, he'd hunt my family down and kill them one by one, and when I showed up, he'd kill me. I believed him because he'd put a bullet in the back of his first wife. He never let me out of his sight more than ten minutes. He'd time me. I had to account for every minute and every penny.

"We were married July sixteenth, 1980. Justice of the Peace in Ringgold, Georgia. It was the day after his twenty-seventh birthday. It was legal for me because I was pregnant. That happened immediately after losing my daughter in the miscarriage."

Once Alvin established domination behind locked doors, it was easy for him to move into public spheres. Even when she was in youth-detention facilities, he hammered her with propaganda. The child who said when she was young that she feared her own shadow was easily cowed and reduced to becoming Alvin's alter ego.

~

Something shifted in Alvin. Prior to his 1981 incarceration, his violence was limited to Judy and, before that, Laurie. By the summer of 1982, Alvin's predation was circling outward in scope and intensity. As his lust for control grew, he was losing control. Judy's compliance was cemented. The goal became survival, even at the expense of victims.

They fled his parents' home. It was a narrow escape from an arrest after Judy passed a bad check. They went to Murfreesboro, in motels and in the home of Judy's mother.[29] Alvin bought a Confederate flag and hung it over the kitchen door, memorializing it with a picture.

Alvin & Judy 1982

Alvin's left arm, wound around Judy's neck, was like a boa constrictor. Judy's hand clasped the wrist of that arm as a sign of affection or restraint. Alvin's dark mustache gave definition to his good ol' boy grin. Then that detail: Alvin's possession of a handgun in his right hand, pressed against Judy's chest.

Asymmetrical: smiles, gun.

I asked about this during a telephone call with Judy. "Was anyone concerned that he had a gun in the house and it was pointed at you?"

"No. It wasn't loaded. At least I think it wasn't loaded."

I restrained my urge to express skepticism. "Who else was there?"

"My younger brothers and sister. He took a bunch of

pictures."

Later, he announced he was leaving. After an hour he reappeared and insisted Judy get in the van. She resisted.

"He took out his gun and pointed it at me and told me if I didn't get in the van, he was going to kill me where I was standing. When I hesitated, he told me I better not try to run because I knew what he had done to Laurie, and he wouldn't hesitate to do it to me."[30]

Judy acquiesced.

A few hours after driving into the country, Alvin insisted that she'd been talking on the phone. When her answers didn't please him, he stuck the gun to her temple and cocked it. "[He] told me he was going to shoot me if I didn't tell him. I was crying. I told him I was sorry; I didn't want to make him mad." Then Al "put the gun to the back of my head and told me I had to the count of ten and he was going to shoot me if I hadn't told him … When he got to ten, he fired the gun up the back of my head, I guess about an inch from my head. He told me he'd make sure the next one didn't miss."[31]

On the run when they had two cars, Alvin led. Judy was to follow, never letting another car between them. During her testimony, Judy explained. "He wanted to watch me in his rearview mirror to make sure I was not looking at other men in other cars or flirting with anybody." He said, "that he was going to blind me, and I wouldn't ever be able to look at anybody else again."[32]

Judy's siblings were unaware of the extent of Alvin's abuse. When he said they were all going to Florida, they were excited. Alvin was not interested in a suntan. He told Judy that she was to procure her sister for him. Judy's protests were ineffectual. One afternoon while her brothers played on the beach, Alvin and Judy's sister had sex. Her grief was two-fold: the abuse of her sister and the flaunting of his infidelity.

After Florida, Alvin reverted to one of his earlier obsessions. The juvenile facilities in Georgia. Alvin laid out the scheme. Judy was to lure workers from the Macon center and "he was going to kill them, especially the Black security guards."[33]

Alvin wanted a rifle. Since he was a felon, he didn't risk purchasing it himself. While they were in Tennessee, Alvin, Judy, and her mother went to a big box store. He picked out what he wanted, told Judy to buy it, and left the store. Judy purchased it in her mother's name, using her mother's license, because Judy wasn't twenty-one. At that time, Tennessee didn't put pictures on the license, so the ruse was successful. The purchase was finalized with a bad check. Later, Alvin bought guns in his mother's name.[34]

By mid-September 1982, Alvin's combustible personality was nearing ignition. His appetite for revenge intensified. The external constraints of the prison had masked the heat building within him. Underneath a glacial blanket was a lake of lava, with hints of escaping steam and stench. The warnings were there, but no one monitored Alvin's seismic activity. His rage smoldered; outbursts of rapes and beatings became his norm.

Calling the Cops

October 1982

Judy and I sat in the confines of her cell as she unraveled events leading to her arrest.

"He'd been beating me with his gun. I had on a V-neck top. There was blood all over me. Al was taking me to my mom, saying he was leaving me. We got stopped by the cops. Al gave them his brother's driver's license. He used other IDs to avoid arrest, including his son's name and social security number, and the name of the man from a stolen income tax check.

"I thought about jumping out and turning myself over to them. But I was too scared. That night, Al left me with Mom. She saw the shirt with the blood and was upset. I said I couldn't explain, but I needed for her to do me a favor: call the police. I gave her the license plate number of Alvin's car. I asked her please to do that for me. She didn't want to, but did it anyway."

Judy lay bare Alvin's frame of mind. He had turned people into objects, normalizing violence. Things have no feeling and are designed for the owner's usage. "He was going through human beings like you go to McDonald's: order what you want and throw it away when finished. It was for his own satisfaction. When finished"—she spoke as if she couldn't believe the import of her words—"he'd throw them away."

Despite the call to the police by Judy's mother, Alvin was quicker than they were in finding his wife. "Al returned, demanding that I go with him. When I wouldn't get in the car, he started shooting. My two brothers were there. I knew he'd shoot them if I didn't leave, so I got in the car. We went uptown to Murfreesboro, passed by a million cops. They never found us because they were looking for a girl.

"We picked up his next random victim and took her back to a motel. She was sitting alone at a shopping center. I pulled up and asked her if she wanted to go for a ride, go get drugs. We'd been on the prowl all day and hadn't found anyone; it was late. Alvin was getting frustrated and desperate. She was in her late twenties, a hooker. He had his thing with her in the hotel. I was outside. We stayed in the motel that night. She was handcuffed to the bed. Early the next morning, there was a knock on the back door of the motel. I went to answer it. There was an old, old cop with an arrest warrant for forging checks. Al said he would come down later and get me out. Cops were everywhere.

"Al took the hooker and dropped her off uptown. Then he went to his mom's; the twins were there. He tried calling the cops to get me out. It didn't work.

"One of the times I called the cops in Cleveland, trying to get them to pick me up for bad checks, they never did. If they had"—Judy stopped abruptly—"If they had …"

Her words hung around us.

Judy described Alvin's going to the jail to try to get her out. "Mom went into the station with a bag of clothes. Al was in the car. By then, they'd found a warrant for the bad checks he'd been writing. When they went out to arrest him, he tried to get away, running. Bastard! They hauled his butt to jail," Judy said with satisfaction.

"On the fifteenth, cops converged on Murfreesboro. They questioned us for hours and hours and hours. I think it was the next day they signed extradition papers and took me to

Fort Payne. That's when they charged me with Cathy's murder. They took Alvin to Georgia. It was the last time I saw him."

After three years of losing control of her life, barely escaping death at the hands of her husband, Judy had drawn on her dormant morality when she begged her mother to call the police. She saved at least four lives: two children nearing their second birthday, Judy's unborn child, and herself. The "old cop" could not know the import of that day's duty.

6.

The Transcript

State of Alabama v. Judith Ann Neelley, defendant

Spring 2001

The 2,600 pages of court proceedings and testimony of Judy's trial is about one and one-half feet high.[35]

I was delighted when, in 2001, the law office of Barry Ragsdale sent the 1983 trial transcript. Ragsdale had been appointed to represent Judy in the appeals process. I was not prepared for the effect those pages would have on me.

I read late into the evening. Then the testimony leaked into nightmares. Judy and I were in a house. I had a sense of foreboding because I knew Alvin was also there. When Judy and I left the house, I told her that she shouldn't go back, that Alvin was evil. I thought, *if she doesn't go back, the appalling events won't happen.* But even in that murky dream world, I knew it was too late. I was unable to prevent anything. I slept intermittently and awoke with a start, certain I'd heard someone in my bedroom. That restless and frightening night taught me I should read earlier in the day.

As I studied the transcript, I noted the consistency between Judy's court testimony and her revelations to me over the years. I noted Alvin's presence in the courtroom while physically miles away. He didn't have to be there to be there. Police who interrogated Alvin testified to a kind and sweet soul. To them, Judy was in control.

March 1983

Judy's feelings were stuffed in a paper bag, then in a locked suitcase. Alvin had the key. After she was arrested and took responsibility for every crime she and Alvin had committed, her lawyer tried to find the key to the sealed emotions. Sometimes his efforts were too overt and too demonstrative. She found that confusing.

If she constrained her feelings, she could speak about the acts of violence. They were abstract. However, every day she was outside the reach of Alvin's fist and cruel accusations, a tiny dent was made in her psyche. The more she felt, the more she hurt. Maybe it was better for her to remain in a state of numbness.

As she sat in the jail cell in Fort Payne, Alabama, waiting for the trial, she was glad to be away from the fear induced by Alvin. Yet she loved him, and he loved her. She was loose in a hollow place and feared the jumble of contradictions. Like waking from a nap that has lasted too long, she felt sick and disoriented, unnerved by what she was facing. It seemed she either was entirely responsible for every criminal act committed or guilty of nothing by virtue of Alvin's domination. Balance was impossible.

The trial for capital murder began on Wednesday, March 9, in the DeKalb County courthouse.

A court official administered the oath for jurors and they took their seats. Judy's court-appointed lawyer, the Honorable Robert B. French Jr. gave his opening statement, laying out what he planned to prove. He planted the disparity between two people: the fifteen-year-old Judy and the adult Alvin—the naïve child and the practiced con.

The first witness for the defense was a major coup: Laurie, number one wife of Alvin.

She thought she'd escaped the control of Alvin Neelley. She'd tried to put their marriage far into the past, had remarried, and was living a quiet and lawful life. Then Judy's lawyer found her. In an act of selflessness and bravery, she traveled to Alabama prepared to take the stand. French was elated.

The county's district attorney, the Honorable Richard Igou, was not delighted. He objected because of irrelevancy to Judy's case. He knew of "no case, no evidence ever allowed by disconnected third parties to give this kind of testimony." French retorted that Alvin's treatment of women was an unbroken line of abuse. The back and forth, before the Honorable Randall L. Cole, Circuit Court Judge for the Ninth Judicial Circuit, was out of the jury's hearing. In his typical manner, Judge Cole listened intently. Then he ruled that testimony by Laurie would be allowed as to what Alvin did, but not what he said—a crucial legal distinction.[36]

French's questions to Laurie elicited descriptions of

multiple beatings.

"He was just imagining this stuff that was going on, but it was real to him, and these things wasn't happening. He would just get into a rage and just start hitting me, and I hadn't even done anything." In the midst of the beating, he told her that if she admitted she was going out with other men, he'd quit. Desperate to be freed from his abuse, she'd "come clean." "Well, I would just admit it just to get him to stop, and then he would put—get me in the car and would go on these wild chases hunting these guys that was in his mind."[37]

One of the duties demanded of both wives was personal care that required helping dress him and kneeling to put on Alvin's shoes and tie them.[38] During one pregnancy, Laurie was on her knees when he kicked her in the stomach. Another time he was beating her, and she crawled under the bed. She screamed, hoping that someone who lived downstairs would call the police. It worked, and officers showed up at their apartment. Alvin gave her two orders: get out from under the bed and get rid of the policemen. They asked to be let in to "settle this." Obeying Alvin's orders, she told them there was nothing going on. They asked about the bruises, and she told them that she had fallen or run up against something.[39]

In a similar scenario, Laurie recounted another instance of being beaten and crawling under the bed. Alvin countered by bouncing on the bed with the heft of his two hundred pounds.

Laurie couldn't stop the tears as she spoke. "And I was pregnant at that time, and I was already hurting from being beat, and I told him to stop, and—but he wouldn't stop it. And the springs would hit me in the stomach, and it just was painful."[40]

Igou objected numerous times to Laurie's telling what Alvin said. The court sustained those objections since it constituted hearsay.

When they were commuting to work, Laurie often drove. If Alvin was in one of his "spells," he beat her, sometimes with his fist and sometimes with items he found in the car, like an ice scraper and screwdrivers. He kept a gun under the seat and used that as a weapon to pistol-whip Laurie.[41]

French asked if she could tell when he was in a "mad spell." She said she could hear it in the inflection of his voice, but also, "His eyes—it was something about his eyes when he got mad that scared me. He just had a gleam in them."[42]

A furniture scam while he and Laurie were living in Cleveland, Tennessee, delighted Alvin. When he "got into some trouble," he decided it was time to move. Running low on funds, Alvin sold the furniture to an auction company, but he owed money to the furniture store. The store wasn't amused.

Laurie testified that, "When the furniture store found out that he'd sold the furniture that wasn't even paid for, they got after him, and so we just picked it up and took off to Albany, Georgia."[43]

After a brief time in Albany, they moved again, landing in Laurie's Georgia hometown. The beatings stopped while living with her family. He exhibited his best behavior, "laughing and cutting up" with her mother. The affable son-in-law made Laurie's reports of abuse untrustworthy. She needed someone in her family to believe her and send Alvin packing. No one did.[44]

Three or four months later, they moved into a trailer in Tunnel Hill, and the beatings picked up where he had left off.[45] It was one of many relocations: Alabama, Georgia, Tennessee, too many to count over the five years of their living together. Alvin's jobs in multiple convenience stores were his piggy bank.

Laurie described Alvin's inflicting corporal punishment on

the children. "Well, he would try to whip them for no reason at all, for something little that wouldn't amount to anything, but I would always jump in … [H]e would hit me instead of the kids. He was hardest on Little Howie."

French asked about Alvin's response when she tried to protect the children.

"He would hit me in the face, and he would tell me to sit down and shut up, that I didn't have no business in this matter."[46]

To prepare Laurie for prosecution cross-examination, French asked about thoughts of escaping. Why didn't she leave? "Didn't he ever sleep so that you could protect yourself?"

"[H]e never did sleep hard, you know. He was a light sleeper … [H]e heard about everything that I was doing, and he would always sleep with a gun up under his pillow, and he was always afraid of somebody coming after him."

"Did you ever attempt to do him any bodily harm while he was asleep to get away from him and save yourself?"

Laurie replied that she didn't; she was too frightened.[47]

She found a fleeting period of protection when she was able to leave Alvin by going to her mother's home. He took the children to his mother, then about a week later, demanded that Laurie return. She couldn't resist his schemes to get her back. Alvin told her that she'd never see the children again if she left him. Back she went, along with her thirteen-year-old sister, Tina. That was Alvin's idea.[48] He had plans.

Laurie told the court that Alvin "produced some little white pills that he wanted me to take and told me that they were caffeine pills, and they would make me feel funny, you know, happy. And so, I went ahead and took 'em, and then during the night I started feeling drowsy. I was just half out and half in, and me and him was in bed, and the next thing

I knew my sister was in the bed, and he was trying to make out with her. I was lying there telling him to leave her alone, and I couldn't do much because these pills had me so droggy. (crying.) And I was just floating off and on, and finally I heard my sister. She kept saying—telling him not to touch her, and she kept hollering for me, and I couldn't do nothing for her." Recalling her inability to protect her sister, Laurie's tears continued.

"And finally, I guess he just gave up, and Tina, she went to the other bedroom ... and the next morning my sister woke me up, and she was screaming, and he had went and put a sheet up over the window; he was trying to rape her, and she was hollering my name, and I got to the door, and he was over her, and I told him that he better leave her alone, that I would kill him. And so he went on into the kitchen, and he got mad at me for stopping it, and he started beating me ... and I just told him to let me and Tina go and to stay away from me. So he let me go to the phone.

"I went and called my mother to come after my sister, and I told her not to tell anybody, because I was ashamed of myself because I couldn't help my sister. And she said she wouldn't tell anybody, and she didn't tell anybody up until recently, and she told my daddy, and he was mad about it ..."[49]

Igou objected to "quadruple hearsay." His objection was sustained.

Laurie escaped another time until Alvin called with news that he'd gotten picked up for stealing where he was working. He bullied her by saying he would tell the police about her involvement, which was sufficient to convince Laurie to go back to him.[50] Once out on bail, they skipped town. Back to his mother's trailer.

Early one morning, another jealous berating and beating

by Alvin broke out. Laurie was in bed, and although she was naked, she ran out of the trailer. Following her outside, a naked Alvin grabbed a mop handle and began hitting her. She saw people looking out the window from a nearby trailer and begged with her eyes for someone to come out and just say, "Leave her alone." But they just watched.[51]

Alvin's racism was displayed after stealing from an Alabama convenience store in which he was working. Inside their apartment, he called the police to report that he'd seen two Black men trying to break into the store. Alvin was delighted to hear on his scanner that the police checked out his tip.[52]

Another brief separation occurred when Alvin kept Laurie's driver's license, and she needed it to cash her payroll check. After a series of telephone interactions with Alvin, Laurie, her brother, and her sister went to the convenience store in Dalton to meet Alvin. As they were getting out of the car, she saw Alvin pulling up behind.

"[H]e told me that I wasn't going to get away with doing him this way, and the next thing I knew I heard a loud noise, and I didn't even know I was shot until I got in the store, and he shot me in the back right down below—well, really in the behind end, and when I got in the store, I felt something running down my pants leg, and that's when I seen the blood, and I passed out … My brother, he tried to chase Al down in the car, but he couldn't catch him."

Laurie recounted a call from Alvin while she was in the hospital. She cried as she recited his menacing words.

Igou objected: again, she was reporting hearsay.

French shifted. "Were you concerned for your life again while lying in the hospital?"

"I was concerned for my life ever since I met him."[53]

Alvin's threats frequently were accompanied with his .22

Ruger. Once, Laurie was able to dissuade further harm when she pled with him about her salvation. "I told him if he killed me that—I wasn't a Christian enough, but I still believed in God. I told him if he killed me that Jesus would be mad at him ..."[54]

Again, Laurie fled to her mother's home, but Alvin pulled her back into his orbit. The grip Alvin had on his wife was slipping, but it was enough to coerce her to go riding. Rather than stopping for the soft drink he promised, Alvin kept driving through Georgia towns and on to Alabama. Laurie's pleas to take her home were met with accusations that she had a date. Unable to convince Alvin, she became quiet.

"When I wouldn't talk to him, he took his gun that he had, and he hit me right here in my forehead, and that just started bleeding, and when he done it, there was a car that was going beside of us, and I was screaming and trying to get this person to maybe pull Al over and let me out of the car, but he told me that if I didn't be quiet, that if that car would stop him and cause him any trouble, that he would just finish me off."[55] The driver of the other car didn't stop.

On the stand, Laurie's composure withered, precipitating French's focusing on the developing relationship of Alvin with Judy.

Laurie felt relief when Alvin brought Judy into the store where Laurie was employed. Alvin hoped she'd be jealous. She hoped this was her replacement. Laurie described subsequent times she saw Judy. "Well, he would come in the store, and he left her in the car one night, but he was parked in front of the glass window where she could see, and he would ... try to rub my hair or put his hands on my breasts or try to kiss me ... and I told him that I didn't want any trouble, that I didn't know the girl, and I just wanted him to leave me alone."[56]

Time for Igou's cross-examination.

He addressed her by her married name and gave reassuring words. Mrs. Campbell, "I'm not going to be harsh with you, but there are a number of questions that I do have to ask you. Are you prepared for us to go ahead with that?"[57]

Laurie said she was ready.

Igou asked about births and marriages to put Laurie at ease. As most lawyers do on cross, Igou gradually increased the pressure. She stated that her mother didn't believe the stories of her being beaten. Igou met her admission by asking how the jurors were supposed to believe her if her own mother did not.

Through tears, Laurie replied. "He would put an act on in front of my family. He would be nice to them, but behind their backs he was mean."[58]

Igou circled back to the robberies, reminding her she stated she'd taken money from the cash drawer. "You knew that what you were doing was wrong, didn't you?"

"Right, but I didn't have no other choice."

"You knew what you were doing was wrong."

"Right; I knew it."

"You didn't have the choice of not doing it?"

"Right. (crying) … I knew if I didn't do it that I would be beat."

"The fact is, Mrs. Campbell, you chose to go ahead and do it knowing it was wrong, didn't you?"

"Right. (crying) … I was forced to do it."[59]

Laurie had never been questioned by the police about cash she'd stolen. By admitting her guilt in court, she opened herself to prosecution. Igou seized the opportunity to imply that she could be arrested. French took exception, describing his allusion as "threatening comments to the witness."[60]

Igou pivoted. He strived to convince the jury that Laurie

freely chose to be with Alvin and pounded on her going against her morality.

Laurie reiterated that she had no choice about participating in the robberies and no choice in going back to him when he told her to come.[61]

"I went back to him just to see my kids. He took my kids away from me. (crying)"

"How did he do that?"

"His mother threatened me and told me if I didn't sign the adoption papers, she would turn me in for all this … She brought abandonment charges against me the night that I left the trailer, but I didn't leave sight of that trailer until Al got back to that trailer."[62]

To discredit Laurie, Igou reinforced that she left the children while they were asleep, in spite of Alvin's having made threats against them.

"Only one," she interjected.

"Was that one child there?"

"Little Howie, yes. I thought about taking them down the street with me, but was hard carrying three kids."[63]

"I didn't ask you what you thought about. I ask you what you did … How long did you leave the children with him?"

"What you mean, at the trailer?"

"Wherever it was you left them. It's hard for me to keep up." Igou shifted. "It seems to me the pattern throughout the things you told Mr. French that you are always wanting somebody else to help you. You wanted the people who were looking through the window outside to help you."

"Right."

"You wanted the people in the car next to you to help you."

"Right."

"You never tried to help yourself."

"I tried to. (crying.)"

"But you would continually go back to him."

"It's not that I would go back to him. It's that he would come after me. (crying.)"[64]

The prosecutor used Laurie's blurring answers to where and when particular incidents occurred as fodder for painting her as an unreliable witness. Who was living where with whom? Where were the children? How many times did she go home to her mother? Were they in homes or trailers, at the trailer of Alvin's parents? Frequent moves compounded the incoherent timeline.[65]

Maybe Laurie was to be pitied. Believed? Probably not.

Conventional wisdom is that lawyers don't ask witnesses a question for which the attorney doesn't know the answer. An exchange between Laurie and Igou might have gone further than he planned.

"Did Alvin ever force you to kill anybody, Mrs. Campbell?"

"If I had stayed with him longer, I probably would have. (crying.)"

"I'll wait just a minute so you can answer my question. My question, Mrs. Campbell, was this: did he?"

"There was one time he asked me to get this guy off in Dalton by his self and asked me—and that was the night that we come back from Georgia, the last night he beat me, and I promised him I would if he would take me back to Tennessee."

"My question is this, Mrs. Campbell: this is my question: Did he ever force you to shoot anybody?"

Igou peppered her with questions about what Alvin forced her to do and whether she'd been with Judy and Alvin when they kidnapped and killed their victims.[66]

"Were you subpoenaed, Mrs. Campbell, to come here today?"

"No, sir."

"You didn't get a subpoena, did you?"

"No."

"You don't like Alvin very much, do you?"

"Huh?"[67]

Igou's cross ended.

In French's redirect, he wanted to clarify a key point. Despite Igou's objections, which Judge Cole overruled, French asked Laurie why she'd come if she wasn't subpoenaed?

"Because I want people to know what he did, what he can do to you, and what kind of … influence he can have on you."

French, addressing a weeping witness, asked, "Mrs. Campbell … Can you, in your wildest imagination, think of anything Alvin Neelley would have told you to do that you would not have done?"

"No."

In Igou's recross he was blunt. "Would you have shot a thirteen-year-old girl in the back if he told you to do so?"

"Yes," she responded, tears flowing.

"Would you have injected her with Drano and Liquid Plumber into her body if he told you to do so?"

"Yes, because I knew what the consequences would be … I would be beat."

"So, you would have killed a little girl instead of suffering a beating yourself?"[68]

Losing what composure Laurie had left, she begged him to stop the questions. Igou instructed her to tell them when he could continue his questions.

When she stated that she was ready, Igou pushed back. "No, ma'am, I don't think you are. Let's wait until you are really ready."

Judge Cole instructed Igou to continue.

71

"Mrs. Campbell, would you have shot a thirteen-year-old girl in the back because you would be afraid if you didn't he would have given you another one of those beatings? You would have injected a thirteen-year-old girl's body with Drano and Liquid Plumber because you would be afraid if you didn't he would give you another one of those eight hundred beatings?"

With sudden clarity, Laurie spoke, "That's a different story when your mind's being overpowered."

Igou repeated his question.

"Yes," she affirmed through tears.

Inferring Laurie's freedom to choose, he delivered one more lob. "You would have, just like you stole the money because you wanted to?"

Laurie answer was unchanged. "Yes."[69]

The court adjourned its seventh day. Laurie was on the stand about five hours.

The transcript of Laurie's answers showed the patterns Alvin established: he prepped his wives on how to rob; they took the money and gave it to Alvin.[70] Wives disliked cooperating with stealing but were demoralized by calculated cruelty. The wives were frequently accused of infidelity. Threats to harm children and family members were cudgels. Parallels between Alvin's grooming of Wife Number One and Wife Number Two consisted of threats, beatings, rapes. Repeat. Two marriages. One M. O.: Alvin's method of operation.

If Judy had fathomed the aberrant life into which she'd fallen, how would she get help? The concept of domestic violence was unknown to her. As long as she was under Alvin's domination, Judy's help was occluded. She needed knowledge that there was a place to go. Knowledge would not, however, give her a telephone and a way to get to shelter. Those were physical barriers. She also needed to have the children or at least know they were safeguarded from harm. When Alvin and Judy were with his parents, they showed by their lack of involvement that they would not help her. Mrs. Neelley protected her son, cooking his breakfast, feeding him first, and even cutting up his pancakes. Judy was the seductress. Alvin was the model of the good son.

Imbalances from sexism and age differences between a teen and adult put the husband in charge. Their vagabond subsistence kept her in geographical disorientation and Alvin's orbit. Judy was beyond hatching any escape attempt.

Judy's testimony described how she felt his eyes on her. "If I was looking out a window, he would've sworn I was making signals at some man or looking at some man or talking to some man." Amid the accusations, Judy tried to reassure and calm him. "I begged with him. I pleaded. I told him I loved only him; I didn't want anybody but him. I talked to him constantly about it, and the more I talked to him, the madder he would get about it, and he would accuse me more, say I was protecting somebody.[71]

"He would tell me about the FBI that he knew and how he could get away with a lot of stuff illegal and not have to worry about it because of the connections he had … I believed him … He told me if I ever left him that he would always know where I was. He would come for me … and if he couldn't find me, he would, ah, get each member of my family until he did find me, until I came back … He said he would kill each one, one by one, until I came back."[72]

Laurie's baring of life with Alvin exposed the cracks in the foundation of his alternate reality. Judy had bought into his lies about Laurie. When Judy's efforts to placate fell short, Alvin would say that Laurie did everything to please him. Judy said she tried to "out-do her … trying to top that."[73]

A house with a fissured foundation requires an expert to diagnose the problem. Laurie was Judy's expert. Laurie's words began to awaken Judy. There was a sickening familiarity in Alvin's treatment of his first wife. Her witness to life with Alvin mirrored Judy's life. When the prosecution questioned Laurie's stories, Judy knew the answers.

Laurie's testimony was the courage Judy needed to begin to give a full accounting. I imagined a melodramatic courtroom showdown in which Judy erupted from her stupor and shouted as Laurie spoke, "Listen to her. She's telling the truth! Believe her. Believe me! We are not monsters."

But Judy's legs would've been wobbly and her voice constricted. Unlike lightning that illuminates for miles, the brief and revealing moments were perceived only by Judy, their clarity transitory, fading into a dark pit of confusion. Was she guilty or innocent? The impact of what she'd done was devastating. Judy had to grasp the coercive control Alvin had over her, while taking appropriate responsibility.

A photograph of Judy at the defense table during her trial showed a lowered head. The viewer couldn't know that her defense attorney told her to keep her head down, hands clasped in her lap, and never, never show any reaction to any testimony, court proceedings, or noise from the audience. No expression could provide universally positive interpretation. Smiling: a sure sign of cold-heartedness. Fry her! No smile: same thing. If she cried, she'd be denigrated as emotionally unstable or faking remorse to win the sympathy of the court and courtroom.

Interlude: Moral Complexity

Three spectators of the Fort Payne trial talked during a recess.

"Why did she stay? She had ample opportunity to get away."

"I get that she was abused, but that's no excuse for what she did. She wasn't locked in a room where she couldn't get out. If Alvin was such an awful man, why didn't she kill him?"

"I just don't believe in this battered-woman syndrome or whatever they are calling it. And don't give me the excuse of a dysfunctional home life. My father was mentally ill, and my mother was an alcoholic. I was abused. I didn't murder anyone. She had choices."

"People are abused because they are co-dependent, masochistic, or enjoy being a victim." The assertions continued. "The minute any SOB puts his hands on me will be the last time!"

One of the three women was reticent to discuss the case. When she finally spoke, her words were measured and her tone quiet. "The trial is dredging up memories." When she paused, the others were unsure how to respond. The quiet emboldened her. "If you had seen me years ago, you would've thought I had everything. I was a rising star in the company. I had expensive clothes and was the picture of success." She hesitated. "That was not what I saw in the mirror.

"At company happy hours, my husband was by my side, or rather I was by his side, his arm around my waist, keeping me close. My coworkers nicknamed him 'Eye Candy.' He was gorgeous!"

"You're single now, right?"

"Yes, and happily."

"So what happened?"

Her censoring evaporated. "I shot him."

"Oh, my God!"

"You're kidding—right?"

"No. It's true. I loved him—or the person I thought he was."

"It must have been self-defense."

"Yes." She exhaled. "That's not how the D.A. saw it. He labeled me a cold-bloodied murderer, and worse than that. Some believed me. Most didn't. Behind locked doors, drawn curtains, behind the public face, was not the man I married." She looked at her hands as she shook her head. "I didn't pull the trigger. Yes, my prints were on the gun. I told the police everything. The woman who killed that man was the person he'd hammered me into. My guilt and regret are enormous because I am not a killer. But in that instant, I was trying to annihilate the evil that had stolen me."

Although the scene is imaginary, the conversation of the three women is realistic in its depictions of beliefs and misconceptions about domestic violence.

The judge gaveled the trial back into session.

Keep Judy on the Stand

Judy's lawyer, Bob French, had a strategy: keep Judy on the stand to "humanize" her and prove Alvin's hold on his client. On the ninth day of the trial, March 16, he began reading letters from Alvin to Judy.

French read, paused, and asked questions for clarification, to make his point, or to lead the witness. District Attorney Igou objected, saying that French was testifying for Judy. When Bob read the first letter into testimony from June 1981, he asked Judy what a phrase meant.

Igou was on his feet. "Judge, we object to this. Let her take these words that were written, and let her make up something of her own volition to try to give the jury a different meaning to it?"

French: "Bear with me a little bit, may it please the court."

Igou was unmoved. "Let the evidence speak for itself."

French was ready. "The evidence will scream in a few minutes."

Judge Cole overruled.[74]

Alvin's letters were long and rambling, vacillating between professions of love and expressions of anger. He spoke pejoratively about Judy and women generally. She was easily replaced. The June 22, 1981, letter stated that Judy was "fixing to have a baby by someone else. Mom was even told." Alvin alleged that he received a letter sent from the Youth Development Campus in Macon, Georgia, where she'd been sent. Judy wasn't pregnant.[75]

A letter dated June 29, 1981, Exhibit number 42, elicited Igou's objection. French countered that Judy's interpretations of the letters were crucial to show she was subject to Alvin's intentions. French told the court that the letter would "connect it right to the death of these people where he says they're going to do it. He's going to get out and start killing people." Again, Cole allowed the reading.[76] Igou's objections went from minor misreadings by French to Igou's protesting that French's readings were "theatrical."[77]

When Alvin wrote on August 10, 1981, he gave his

virulent assessment of women. He believed Judy was "messing around." He averred that she'd planned for him to get locked up so she could be free.

> *When you get used and suckered you could come*
> *back to me. Wrong. I'm this way about it, and so*
> *are most men. Women that easy and that screwed*
> *up were only good for using for a while, and all*
> *you have to do is tell them what they want to hear,*
> *then dump their dumb ass and laugh, like I used*
> *to do when I went with a married woman. I said*
> *just what she wanted to hear to get what I wanted,*
> *when I got all I wanted, she got dumped, because*
> *just like I know, and everyone else know, if she*
> *screwed one man around she would another one.*
> *So, all she got was used, suckered, and dumped, and*
> *if her husband found out, she didn't only get used,*
> *suckered, and dumped, she got screwed up and lost*
> *her family and everything and usually a man that*
> *really loved her.*[78]

Alvin's letter dated December 4, 1981, after he was transferred to another prison, began amiably:

> *To my beautiful wife. Hi, Sunshine.*
> *Well, I'm finally out of Dirty County ... The*
> *officers here are okay. Things are neater than peanut*
> *butter, I guess you could say.*[79]

Pages later his mood becomes ominous.

> *Make sure you smile like you used to when I took*

pictures of you. The last ones made me fighting mad when I saw that look on your face. If you can't smile, don't get in any of them. I don't know if we can ever get back together, but I'm gonna have to have a talk with you.[80]

Closing the letter, he stated:

Don't write me a letter like your first after you got home. It was dumb. The twins could have wrote one better. Another like it, and we're gonna fight.

One month later, he berated Judy. He'd instructed her to number her letters so he could be sure he got all of them. He was missing letters seven through eleven. Then he commanded her to send information.

I need it for my parole sheet. You not that dumb ... I said get it here, and I meant it. I hope you do leave when you turn eighteen years old ... You still could do time and be locked back up. Catch my drift? If you want to leave, fine, but don't try to keep me locked up ... I was offered a job today when I get out ... It pays well, and its going to last just a few hours. The man who offered it to me can just hand out thirty or forty thousand dollars when he wants. So, it should be good.[81]

Alvin's letters to Judy while he was in prison revealed a man who felt misused and betrayed. He vowed revenge when he got out, and gave frequent harangues against a spectrum of people. [82] But in his eyes, Judy was responsible for the catalog of hurts he endured.

Her letters began romantically and sometimes passionately, but rather than sounding like love for Alvin, they subtly expressed fears of losing him, and the penalties she would pay if she went against his demands. Judy's writings were the juvenile's mix of bravado and insecurity.

From jail on December 27, 1980, Alvin wrote Judy an eight-page letter:

> *I got your letter today. The one you wrote last I guess. It was like some of your pass one's, that makes me mad.*
>
> *Some of your letters say one thing, and some say another. Love, it looks like your lieing to me, and that hurts me as much as not being with our kids.*
>
> *By some of your letters it looks your wanting me to call everything off betweet us, but my love for you can't be stoped that easy. The way your hurting me, I wish I really could sometimes's. your killing me by the way you do thing's, and by doing what other people say, and by not doing what I ask, and tell you.*
>
> *Judy I know enough on you to put you in prison for along time, but I've took the hurt and said nothing. I'm not saying I'm going to tell, I'm just saying you've hurt me, and I love you so much. I have feeling too, you know. All you ever do is tell me how hard it is on you, and how I better write you nice letters.*
>
> *I could get out of my cell at night for visits with people like Teresa, and Beth if I wanted, but I've been true to you. What have you done for me?*

I love you, that's a big joke ain't it. Well that's how you make it look … Over where you were locked up. I saw some of their reports. and I like some of the thing's I read … I won't ever tell how I seen copies of their report's. some of them they wouldn't let me see now. They said, it would hurt me to bad.

They also all said they didn't believe you would be a very good mother, or wife. They all said one way or another, that you was easy. that like to have killed me … I love You, but look where you put me. just look around and you'll know why I get up set some time's.

I don't really look for you tomorrow. You'll find some reason not to come. You say you love me, but you never really show me. Please think about me some time, I don't want to be forgotten.

Love Al

Alvin's parents were caring for two children from his marriage to Laurie. By late 1980, the twins of Alvin and Judy also stayed with his parents in Tennessee if either Alvin or Judy was locked up.[83]

Judy described one exception. "Before they sent me to juvenile detention, I left the twins with my mom. She kept them for a few days. When Alvin got locked up, he sent his mom to Murfreesboro to get the twins. She didn't know I didn't want Mrs. Neelley to have them, so Mom gave them to her.

"I was mad at Mom for doing that; although she was very, very poor, she was a good woman. She had a heart of gold, never talked badly about people. She would have taken care of

my kids with love; there was no love in the Neelley household."
Judy exhaled. "But she didn't know all that. We never discussed
it; I didn't want to hurt her. I hadn't asked specifically for her
to keep them, can't blame her."

Each time Judy was released and Alvin was in prison, she
went to live with Alvin's parents. The twins and Judy were
where Alvin wanted them: under the watchful eye of his
mother, Mrs. Neelley.

Alvin told Judy to save his letters. I found a few from Judy
to Alvin. In a meticulous narrative, Judy's six-page letter on
August 13, 1981, captured the tension in the Neelley home.
She addressed it to "My Darling, Loving Husband."[84]

*Hi Babe. How are you feeling? I hope you are doing
good. I want to set something straight with you
right now, okay? I have not been out running the
streets! I have only taken the kids down to the store
and back. I have always had them with me, except
for once.*

*And before you start jumping to conclusions,
let me explain why I went alone then. I had taken
both Lily and Mikey down to the store and I bought
them some candy with the money Mom gave me,
for them. I bought Mom an Examiner.*

*We walked back to the trailer and I gave Mom
the paper. She said she didn't want that kind, that
she wanted a "Star." She told me to go back and
exchange it.*

*It had started raining while we were arguing
about the paper. So I finally had to take it back.
But since it was raining, Mom said Lily and Mikey
couldn't go because they would catch cold.*

Sweetheart, I haven't been fooling around on you. I never have and I never will. I am your wife and I love you with all of my heart. You are my one and only love.

Well, I noticed that you seem to admire this little Julia. Saying that she is a "beautiful sixteen-year-old" and that she "has more smarts than most 30-year-old women." Well, let me tell you something, she might be trying to get you by what ever means she can. But she will Damn Well Have to Kill Me to do it. And I will sure as hell not give the little bitch the upper hand. I'll kill her before she ever gets you from me. Damn it, I Love You! And I will prove it to you! Just wait!

Alvin's parents got into an argument.

[Mrs. Neelley] told him that he was a lazy SOB and wouldn't even go to get the twins some juice.

He started saying he would take me. Mom kept fussing with him and I was getting pissed. So me and Lily walked on out the door.

In Judy's P.S., she excused Alvin's flirting because he was "irresistible."

Write soon. I love you. Your loving wife, Judy

Miles apart, Judy clung to a fairy-tale version of Alvin. Each reunion reestablished fear—not love.

Smoldering Volcano

Before their incarcerations in 1981, Judy and Alvin were vagabonds, low-level criminals. A letter in November 1981 telegraphed Alvin's eroding psyche.

They're gonna try to hold me until I cool off, but my time will be over before I cool off. I'm gonna kick a-blank-blank-blank when I do get out here in Albany, Rome, Macon, and some other places, even Cleveland. Let's not forget good old Dalton. Smile … I will see that everyone that has made me mad while I've been locked up, I will make sure the rest of their lives will be unhappy and destroyed. I try not to get mad, but everytime I see [my lawyer] or anyone that has had anything to do with us or our case I get mad enough to kill. I'm really gonna laugh when I get the ones who don't even know that I know about them. Smile.[85]

He boasted that he "jumped two deputies" from the sheriff's office and would settle scores when he gets out.

> *I'm gonna go ahead and finish with Laurie and a few others in this state, fast. Enough about my fun.*
> *I'll just drop out of sight. Then people will start dropping. Smile. I may smile, but on the inside I want to destroy, and if I can I will when I get out … I won't be a fool next time and let them set me up again. I've let things go so long and get so bad the past four years, they have forgotten just how mean and nasty and cold I can be. I'm white and I'm right. I'm not a honky.[86]*

Alvin bragged about being a drug user:

> *I used to be one of the biggest drug users in the state.*
> *That's no big deal.*

But Judy said he didn't do drugs and rarely drank.

> *Keep your nose clean. I don't want to hear the wrong*
> *things about you again, or there's two things I can*
> *do, love you or destroy you. It's up to [you] which.*[87]

In his letter from January 11, 1982, he scolded her for not sending all the photos she took:

> *If I have to, I'll blind your frickin' ass, or if I can't*
> *get there, I'll have someone else do it. You really*
> *realize you put yourself in danger when you make*
> *me mad.*[88]

The January 13, 1982, letter maligned Judy's mother:

> *What's she gonna do when everyone has had her*
> *twice or more and no one wants to keep her for*
> *good 'cause they know she's been had by everyone,*
> *and they just use her when they're between women.*
> *I guess she's better than nothing when you're horney*
> *…*
> *   Is the kids being sweet and nice like me, or like*
> *you, mean and nasty?*

Alvin moved to payback against unnamed men:

I'll see them all dead or worse when I get out, and their wives will be screwed, and by Blacks, and not just a few. They'll watch too. It's really funny. You're gonna be right along with them if you don't get your act together now ... If you're waiting for me to cool off, this is it. I'm past mad.[89]

I know at least one or two families in every town in Georgia, big or small. There's a Black girl I could write. I won't say how many in all. I've even had [offers] from Cedartown and Rockmart ... At least there's no place in this state now I can't do what I want. Smile.[90]

When you come to see me . . . bring this letter with you. When you answer this letter, take and write down every part just like I have, word for word, and then answer it. Then go on to the next part and answer it, and bring your letters with you.

Not only, in his claims, is he omniscient about all Judy's movements, but also he knew the mind of God.

Answer me honestly, Babe, do you really think for a second God will ever let you have a good and happy life with someone else after how you've treated me? You can lie to others and yourself, but you can't lie to him ... It says in the Bible what you do to others always comes back to you worser.[91]

His biblical reference was convoluted. The Bible says that what you reap you sow, a natural consequence, not a "worser" consequence. Jesus and others in scripture urged people to repay evil with good.

Alvin was getting antsy for sex. If he were to be transferred to another facility, he could go out on the town on Sundays:

They have frickin' houses there ... At Walker, if you're out with the right detail boss, he'll let you take an hour or so to mess around if you come back and not tell.[92]

Then it was on to warning her about the mind games the staff play on teens in the youth centers. His description of the techniques was an eerie template of his behavior:

They usually work first at turning you against the people you trust. They're good at it, too ... They get you to the point where you do things you actually hate ... It usually takes someone who gets out of the YDC. a long time to get back to their real self, and when some do, and they see how they've been used, they want to die. I want to kill every time I think of it. You really had a job done on you. You don't even know it, but you will.[93]

Alvin's letter on February 5, 1982, began:

To my beautiful wife. How's our kids and yourself doing?

He had a caveat for her next visit:

If you weigh only one-hundred-sixty now you're too light for me, so don't try to get near me until you do something about it, fast. I'm not joking. I'll leave the visiting room if you try to get near me.[94]

Nine days later, Alvin taunted Judy about leaving him, the consequences, and his accusations about her running off with a "punk." Despite no evidence that Judy was being unfaithful, Alvin was plotting.

> *Thinking I can't find you, 'cause I can. Smile. When y'all do, y'all are going to be like little crying kids. What's the punk gonna do when he has to face me? I'm not a dumb little girl who falls for things … I'm gonna prove to you that I can find you, and I do know where everybody's family live. When I start y'all are gonna be crying and begging me to stop, but I'm gonna be as fair as y'all have been. Smile … Some of you won't live through.*[95]

The January 25, 1982, message was unequivocal:

> *What can I say but I love ya and you're one super lady, the only I've ever loved and the only one I have actually cherished with all my heart and love. That's why I would destroy you before I would let anyone else have you and why I could destroy anyone near you.*[96]

Letters from Alvin read by French consumed nearly one hundred pages of the trial transcript, including interaction with Judy and objections by Igou.

As Judy listened to the letters during the morning session, she registered little emotion. That changed in the afternoon of the ninth day, March 16. French's Q&A moved into Judy's description of Alvin's behavior following his release. His subdued manner changed by that evening.

"He got real mad at me because he said that my body had been ruined since he had been away from me by all the people that I had been with, and he started ... beating me, using his fist hitting me, and he just—he got pretty violent and was ... kicking me and punching me and pulling my hair."

Alvin's parents were in the trailer; Judy stated they didn't interfere.[97]

French knew the answer when he asked, "At the time of that beating, Judy, did you notice anything strange as far as he was concerned?"

"He had—when he was hitting me, I saw that he had an erection."[98]

French questioned further about the beatings. "Judy, would you tell the jury what you took from this man when he began to use foreign objects in your private parts and things like that?"[99]

"He would use more objects beating me, such as a gun and sticks and a leather strap or belt and a piece of hard plastic, and sexual intercourse was always involved with the beatings."

"Judy, when did he break your tooth?"

"Around the first of April." She explained that Alvin hit her in the mouth with the barrel of the gun.[100]

"When he broke your tooth, did he stop hitting you?"

"No; he kept on. He was laughing."

French retrieved Exhibit number thirty-three, a ball bat. "Are you familiar with that bat?"

"Yes, sir ... He used it to hit me ... in the arms and legs and in the head, and sometimes he was able to get me in the sides with it."

"What else did he use this bat for, Judy?"

She sobbed as she described the bat's use. "A few months later … he told me that since I had slept with Blacks that he was going to show me how big my hole was, and he tried to put it up in me. And it wouldn't go, and he cut me with it, and I was bleeding real bad, and he got mad when it wouldn't go in, and he started hitting me with it … He hurt me real bad."

"Judy, after the severe beating he gave you on the third day that he was back and the tenor of the beatings picked up, what did your relationship become?"

"It was—He was always very demanding. I never made a move without him there. He wouldn't let me out of his sight. I was terrified of him."

"Did you ever question anything he told you to do?"

"No, sir. If I did, I got beat again."

"Do you have any more scars?"

"Yes, sir … I have some scars on my hands where he hit me and left some scars, and I have a place on my wrist where I had six stitches where he hit me with a hacksaw."[101]

Girls can be "Soaped"

During the trial, Judy talked about Alvin's instructions to ensnare Ginny Brandon, one of the staff at the Rome Youth Center. Judy was to tell her that she had left Alvin. Judy needed assistance in finding a job and a place to stay. They set up a meeting for the following day.

Alvin's scheme was to tie Brandon in a chair. She was to reveal where she took girls to rendezvous with the men in the alleged prostitution ring and to list the names of everyone involved in the ring. Alvin would coerce her with his gun.

Judy was to kill her after he got all the information. "[W]e were gonna have all our stuff in the car and just leave without anybody knowing it." Then she added, "The motel room was in my name."

Late in the day, a call came to their room informing Judy that Ginny had been called out of town and wouldn't be able to help her. As Judy had no proof of the call, Alvin accused her of tipping off Ginny. The penalty was beating Judy with a baseball bat.[102]

She lay on the floor with him swinging with both hands. "He would just hit me hard enough to bust my head and bruise up my arms and my hands real bad."

At trial, French was determined to make the most of the scene. His questioning elicited tragic-comic relief. "He didn't draw back like this and hit down on you, did he?"

Before Judy could respond, Igou objected. "Judge, we object to Mr. French trying to—I don't know what he's trying to do. We object to his demonstrations."

French countered, "That's no objection then if you don't know what I'm trying to do. We object to him interrupting my examination, Your Honor."

The tone I imagine in the judge's ruling was that of an exasperated parent. "Gentlemen, I sustain the objection."[103]

Trial lawyers must perform. French enjoyed the courtroom drama. He was passionate, hard-driving, cocky, competitive, and a risk-taker. He needed every part of his persona to argue "not guilty" in Judy Neelley's case. The crux of his argument was that Judy lost agency of her life. Alvin owned her like a loaded gun. She was in his hands.

The last prosecution expert was the psychiatrist who examined Judy prior to the trial. Dr. Alexander A. Salillas, M.D., worked for the Alabama Department of Mental Health in Tuscaloosa, Alabama, Taylor Hardin Medical Facility. Judy was there for nearly a month during January and February 1983. She was committed shortly after giving birth to her third child. The hormonal changes after childbirth produced a challenging range of physical and emotional adjustments. Judy was also dealing with losing her child. He'd been put in the care of her grandmother in another state. She had no time for bonding.

Salillas was one of three psychiatrists who constituted the Lunacy Commission to determine whether Judy was "competent to face charges." He assessed her to be a normal woman of high IQ with a dependent personality disorder. In that scenario, one "subrogates his or her interests to that of the person that is important to her."[104]

Police records, social history, and sessions with Judy were sufficient for Salillas and the other commissioners to determine that there was no indication of a mental disorder or deficit "that might diminish her criminal responsibility."[105]

Igou's questioning of Salillas was to establish that Judy knowingly, and with an understanding of right from wrong, injected drain cleaner into Cathy's body and then shot and killed her. He wanted to prove she wasn't crazy and must be found guilty for her crimes.

Salillas subscribed to Choice Theory, developed and made popular by William Glasser, an American psychiatrist. Salillas contended that, although Alvin was a sexual sadist and did abuse Judy, it was her choice to kill. She remained her own agent even when she was fearful of her life.

Bob French's cross of Salillas was to plant in the minds of jurors the horrors endured by Judy. The prosecution expert and the defense attorney agreed on one critical factor: Alvin was sadistic. Salillas offered that "from a totally charming—

ah—prince, he had turned now to something like a monster or an ogre."

French pounced. "We haven't even started with him. He's just beginning to show himself."[106]

French had to destroy the theory of free choice, or at least, cast reasonable doubt. To get there, he used hypothetical questions to dispute the expert's claim that whatever the hypothetical wife did, she was making those choices, not acting in the stead of a husband.

The defense rolled out coercive persuasion and led Salillas to agree on the fundamentals. The battered-woman syndrome was in its infancy legally. In a culture that found no issue with the man being in charge in all aspects of life and with nearly unlimited license in the treatment of a wife, even a wife who was beaten and raped held little expectation she would get justice. Salillas agreed with the basics of coercive persuasion listed by French: isolating an individual, controlling "channels of information and communication," assigning repetitive tasks, manipulating guilt and ratcheting up anxiety, and degradation of the victim.

The psychiatrist asked the lawyer, "Where are you reading all those from?"

French told him it was from an article written for attorneys on coercive persuasion.[107]

Salillas agreed with the assertions that we are shaped by our culture. But the psychiatrist steadfastly maintained his belief that the debilitated brainwashed prisoner "is not as incapacitated as to be unable to make decisions."[108]

After French presented a series of hypotheticals that paralleled Judy's life, Salillas contended that such a person was vulnerable to external pressures, but not conditioned.[109]

The psychiatrist's demeanor was unflappable, and he was

not swayed in his bedrock conviction. He took as a given fact that girls are routinely deflowered, that they can be "soaped," that is, seduced by lavish attention.[110]

Salillas acknowledged that the girl was entangled by the ogre but insisted that available resources, such as shelters and police, would make escaping a simple act. "There's the police, or maybe the beatings that you mentioned were not that bad at all. Maybe there were times when he was tender. So, in the end, maybe she stayed because she wanted to, not for any other reasons." Later, he opined that the beatings were "no big deal."[111]

French was incredulous, rehearsing the details of her situation: domestic violence, distance from home, cut off from family, psychological warfare. "A fifteen-year-old pregnant girl should have got up out of that motel room, after he beat the tar out of her, and gone to the police?"

The expert calmly replied that he couldn't tell "anybody anything … Maybe there was a beating once, twice, or twenty times, but the end result was she decided to stay. There are many ways she could have stopped that if she wanted to." Then Salillas expressed skepticism. "I cannot see how she can stand it, frankly. The severity of the beatings … somebody would have to love punishment to take that without wanting to break free." Perhaps, he added, it filled a need she had.[112]

District Attorney Igou didn't let French have free rein while interrogating the psychiatrist. Igou's objections were often sustained. It wasn't quite an objection when Igou said, "Judge, I would ask Mr. French if he's asking the jury the question or the witness. He keeps prancing in front of the jury and making an argument to the jury."[113]

Briefly, Salillas weakened his position when he stated that the wife's criminal acts were committed because she was "following his orders." He posited that she obeyed without question and probably "without feeling." He went further when he stated, "There wasn't enough sense in her to judge that this is something she had not done before, and the gravity of the act itself has not failed to put an impact on her at all."[114]

The doctor's core dogma was that no matter how severe the violence and threat of violence, a person has the requisite ability to make a morally appropriate decision and to act on it.

Salillas comported himself well. The prosecution was pleased.

Later, French characterized his cross-examination of Salillas, as "lawyer in desperation."[115]

Inside the Lion's Den

For my life is spent with sorrow,
and my years with sighing;
my strength fails because of my misery,
and my bones waste away.
I am the scorn of all my adversaries,
a horror to my neighbors,
an object of dread to my acquaintances …
For I hear the whispering of many—
terror all around!—
as they scheme together against me,
as they plot to take my life.
Psalm 31:10–11,13

The trial of Judy neared its end. Prosecution examined about twenty-eight witnesses including law enforcement, a victim, potential victims, and social workers. Defense called two wives, one former and one present.

The jury began its deliberations late afternoon on Monday, March 21. They resumed the next morning. In less than four hours, they elected a forewoman and found Judy guilty of a capital offense. The penalty phase came after the judge gave his charge. One hour later, the jury returned with its advisory sentence. Many in the courtroom were astonished or angry. Not death, but life without the possibility of parole (LWOP). Ten jurors voted for LWOP. Two voted for death.

It was a victory of sorts. At least Judy would not die by electrocution. She would spend the rest of her life in prison, reliving all the sordid events in her life. That cheered some, because they liked the thought that she would have more days to suffer.

Unless.

In Alabama, the judge could override the jury's recommendation.

One month later, Judge Cole convened court for his sentence hearing.

French's opening statement lasted nearly two hours. It was quintessential Bob. He sought common ground with the court. In defending Judy, he had concluded that she was not filled with evil. When Judge Cole asked Bob French to take the case, his thinking was she should go "to the chair."[116] He admitted that earlier in his career in handling divorce cases, he got tired of hearing women whining about claims of abuse by their husbands. If it was so terrible, she ought to leave. "She took him for better or worse. He's just a little worse than she took him for." Bob came to understand that women in our society are routinely blamed and violated. He gave voice to Judy by reading from several of her letters. He decried the injustice of killing someone who had helplessly become obedient to another's control.[117]

Richard Igou's opening statement was brief. The state supported "the sentence of death as altogether appropriate and even a proper and necessary sentence for this case."[118]

Bob summoned Judy to the stand and spoke to her in a strange juxtaposition of logic. The words "death penalty," spoken in the same sentence as telling Judy that nobody wished her ill, stretched the imagination.

"I want you to realize what's at stake, the death penalty for you, and I want you to realize that you can be comfortable here because there's really nobody that hates you or wishes you any wrong … I have known Judge Cole for many, many, many years, and he's a compassionate man, and you have nothing to fear from him. I want you to tell Judge Cole just exactly who is Judy Neelley."

Often, French called Judy a child during the trial. His directive had the ring of an adult talking down to a child.

She replied in kind. "Judy Neelley is a caring person, gentle. Ah—I don't hurt anybody. I don't do anything wrong. I like to help people. Ah—I'm very quiet." Her words strained the convictions of many who listened. "I'm very confused about some things, very scared. Ah—ah—I'm very worried about myself and about my children, very lonely."

In response to further leading by Bob, she acknowledged that she had no thoughts or feelings of her own while with Alvin. Knowing the penalty if she didn't do exactly as he told her—verbal and physical abuse—she built her life around pleasing him. At Tutwiler Prison, she could at least laugh when she wanted and cry when she felt the tears.

After Judy left the witness chair, French presented his closing argument. He began with his learning curve, researching for the trial: coercive persuasion, brainwashing, learned helplessness.[119] He called her a "girl" to signal the misadventures of childhood and the possibility of rehabilitation. He addressed Judge Cole, pleading for mercy:

"I know that you are dedicated to duty enough that if you feel it's your duty, you'll do it. That's why you've got me so scared. I know it. I just ask you, in all your humanness, to not allow this just to be an automatic hearing … which results in the destruction of an eighteen-year-old girl. I just ask you to consider that her life has never started …

"There's nothing we can do for the victim. We can only create more. She was incapable of independent thought … she had no premeditation or intent, and the only thing we can do is make it worse."

He hadn't been opposed to the death penalty before Judy's trial. Changed by the case, he could no longer "extinguish a human life form under any circumstance."[120] French laid on Judge Cole the potential for colluding with Alvin:

"I ask you not to let Alvin Neelley kill three women and get away with it. Whether he gets away with it or not, the result is the same. He has totally killed two, and one's very life hangs in the balance. I know the responsibility of the position [of judge]. And it's for that reason that I have the fear that this girl that's been placed in my charge will be destroyed, and I just have to beg you not to do that … [S]he has a good heart, she's a good person, and she needs to live."[121]

Igou gave his closing argument. "We've heard Mr. French state, very eloquently, as he's apt to do, his feelings in this case and feelings about himself, but I would submit to the court that it doesn't matter how Bob feels about it. It doesn't matter how I feel about it." Igou stated that he had seen no remorse expressed by Judy and that was "highly significant."

With the same courtesy and equanimity Judge Cole showed during the trial, he expressed thanks to the defense team:

"First, Mr. French and Mr. Bussman … I want to express to you gentlemen the appreciation of the court for your representation of this defendant in this case.[122] When I appointed you gentlemen to represent her, I expected that you would give her a good defense, that you would represent her well, and indeed, you have … The dedication and the zeal with which you have represented this defendant certainly is commendable, and I speak to you as officer of the court in saying that I am grateful to you for the representation that you have provided this defendant."[123]

Cole stated the requirement that he had. By balancing the mitigating and aggravating circumstances of the crimes, he came to his decision.

He detailed the mitigating elements. Her youth was in her favor. Yet having "adopted the lifestyle of an adult," the age factor was lessened. The second factor was that she was "substantially influenced by her husband." Nevertheless, the degree of influence didn't rise to being brainwashed or under the hegemony of her husband. Third, the defendant herself "voluntarily set in motion a series of events which led to her arrest and the arrest of her husband by telling her mother … to notify the police that she was in the area and could be arrested."[124]

Judge Cole continued as he listed the aggravating circumstances: murder was committed after a kidnapping. It was "especially heinous, atrocious, and cruel." A child was abused and sexually violated. Even though Judy's participation in that couldn't be proved, she was an accomplice. All of those actions were "to a degree beyond which is common to most capital offenses."[125]

In rapid succession, Cole delivered his verdict and appointed legal counsel for appeal:

"Mrs. Neelley, the court hereby fixes your punishment at death. Your conviction and this sentence are subject to automatic review by a Court of Criminal Appeals. Mr. French and Mr. Bussman, the court will appoint you to represent her in that appeal."[126]

"[F]ixes your punishment at death." Judy's head went down as she slumped in the chair. It was April 18. Judge Cole set the date of execution for May 25. Judy had thirty-seven days to live. Protocol took over her life. Handcuffed, deputies escorted her from the courtroom with French by her side. Taken to the jail cell by a deputy, she was to change into her jeans and shirt. In a sheriff's car, the destination was an alternative universe.

The first person to address her at Tutwiler Prison was Shirlie Lobmiller. In an inscrutable tone, she delivered her message. "I am the assistant warden. You will be staying with me for a while."

Mutual dislike was instantaneous.

When Judy entered the prison, she wore handcuffs in front of her. That changed. New restraints pulled her arms and hands behind her back. Judy said, "They put leg irons on me, just to take me down the hall. That was a shock, a big shock, 'cause I'd never had shackles. At Fort Payne, they cuffed me. They took my picture at the front gate. My hair was long and falling in my face. I couldn't get it off my face because my hands were cuffed behind me, and they're wanting to do a mug shot and no one is moving my hair for me. I heard later officers resented me because I supposedly flipped my hair like models." She grew indignant. "Excuse me, what do you expect me to do!"

Three short blasts of the prison's buzzer signaled lockdown of all inmates. Death row inmate on the move.

"When I got to death row, the officers told me to take off my clothes. They put me in the shower and turned on the water to wet my hair and my body. Then they turned off the water and gave me a little medicine cup with this pale blue liquid—Cuprex—to kill lice and nits. I had to put it on the hairy parts of my body and stand there ten minutes, while the officers watched me. It was so humiliating."

Her uniform had no buttons. Since they could be swallowed, they were a hazard for the newest resident of death row. Short-sleeved dresses for all the women revealed a woman's past from dark needle tracks to scars of self-harm. No hiding of one's body in prison.

A letter and a number awaited Judy: Z-429. That identified her as an end-of-the-line person. There are two Z-levels: 1 and 2. Once her behavior posed no threat, she would be classified as Z-2, allowing her to wear a dress with buttons.

The first night, she didn't cry herself to sleep. For a scratch in time, death presented itself as a loving friend.

Judy isolated into sullen depression. She trusted no one. The environment was an enigma. Kindness raised her suspicions. If she felt hate, it was familiar. She had to get up by five in the morning, but what was the point? She tried to wrap herself in the numbness she perfected while with Alvin.

Years later, a reporter asked Judy what it was like coming to Tutwiler. She didn't hesitate. "Terrifying! When I was sentenced, they gave a date. No one tells you that is a technicality, that there is a suspension because of the automatic appeal. On the day I was to be executed in May, I kept thinking they would come and take me."[127]

In Judge Cole's statement of sentencing, he directed the defense to begin the appeal. But what convicted person processes anything between hearing a sentence of death and an execution date a month later?

Without proof—only Judy's word that Alvin was present and complicit in the murder of Cathy—Alvin wasn't charged with a crime in Alabama. He was, however, charged with murder in Georgia. No parallel transcript of Alvin on trial exists, because his cases were settled out of the courtroom. He was sent to prison with two life sentences plus ten years for killing Kay MacRae, Judy's second murder victim.

An interview Alvin gave in 1984 is fascinating for what it reveals about him. He savored ascribing an impulse for control as a central motivating factor for Judy.[128] He told the reporter that his wife did the killing for the feeling of power it gave her. "I've met hardened criminals in jail that I fear less than her." Neelley portrayed Judy as "a clever, manipulative woman who held the threat of jail over his head and enjoyed killing and torturing her victims." Her motive for murder, according to Alvin, was to keep the victims "from telling anyone about her involvement in a prostitution and pornography ring, and because she liked feeling powerful."

Neelley fabricated a story that there were police officers in Rome running a prostitution ring. His rationale for participating in the killings was that he feared Judy would turn him in for jumping parole on a grand larceny charge. She didn't kill him because then she could pin blame on Alvin for whatever she did. He pled guilty to the MacRae murder in Georgia because "I didn't have proper legal representation and a few people had things to hide." He was never charged with domestic violence.

Appeal Number One

June 21 & July 1, 1983

Two months after the death sentence was pronounced, the appeal process began. The judge and the lawyers were back in court. Same courtroom. Same prosecutors. Same defense team. Same defendant, now offender. Judy had been temporarily moved from death row to a jail in Fort Payne. June 21 was the day to examine and cross-examine witnesses. French had twenty-three amendments to the motion for a new trial.[129]

Bob was thoroughly prepared. He called a reporter as a witness. The reporter covered the trial for the *Birmingham Post Herald* and heard comments that could have affected the jury's deliberations. The witness testified that he heard one spectator say, "I'll gladly pay the electric bill to barbecue her ass." Another witness, a businessman from North Carolina, heard a comment that drew the attention of several jurors. "The chair's too good for her. They ought to use Drano."[130]

Amendment four was for illegal search and seizure of evidence from Barbara Adams's home, Judy's mother. Soon after Judy's arrest, law enforcement showed up at Barbara's house. She knew at least one of the men. They said they didn't have a search warrant, but they could get one. She told the court, "I let them search my house because they had badges and guns and they said they wanted to search."

French had been frustrated in efforts to build the defense. "We had difficulty in marshaling the facts because of our initial interviews with [Judy]." When Judy was arrested, she admitted, as if reading a script, to everything. Alvin was guilty of nothing.

After a parade of witnesses, Judge Cole adjourned court at French's request because his expert in domestic violence was not available until July. Her testimony might change Judy's future. The battered-woman concept hit French broadside. He argued that the court needed to consider the depth of the evil exploitation Judy had undergone, even though such abuse was not available as a defense in Alabama.[131]

On the first day of July, Judge Cole gaveled the appeal back into session. Dr. Margaret Nichols, a clinical psychologist in Atlanta specializing in domestic violence, was the star witness. She was sworn in. Nichols noted that, although women have been abused for centuries, the medical profession in the last twenty years had formulated the behavioral characteristics that are typical of battered women. French led her into questions about Judy, whom she had assessed.

The psychologist opined that Alvin's influence had diminished but continued to be present in Judy. Trusting someone other than Alvin required dissecting the tactics.

"I believe she was trying very hard to be as honest as she possibly could. It was obvious from both her choice of words and from her body language, how she sat. She shook. A large part of the time she was crying as I was talking to her, and ... it was very, very difficult for her and she was trying to choose other ways of giving the information [leaving] out some of the most painful details, and it was with a lot of prodding from me that she was able to talk about these things."[132]

Dr. Nichols said Judy's situation was "the most severe extent [of a battered woman] that I have seen." Alvin's repeated accusations of her infidelity and efforts for revenge are acute obsessions with battering men. Ultimately, unable to gauge when abuse would occur, Judy gave up, numbing herself. Feeling is not allowed.[133]

"The most extreme beating … was the turning point for her," referring to the beating after Alvin was released from prison in March 1982. "From that point on [Judy] never knew when she was going to live and when she was going to die." The violence of that extended episode coupled with the "humiliation and the degradation" put Judy totally under Alvin's dictates.[134]

French asked for a causal explanation of Alvin's behavior. Although she never met him, Nichols gave her clinical assessment of batterers. "First of all, that there is a feeling that by being able to make another person look and feel subhuman, that the individual who was doing the humiliating and the degradation then feels like more of a man. He feels bigger. He feels stronger. There were also aspects clearly in this case of a great deal of sexual excitement and arousal on the part of Alvin when he was beating or degrading Judy … It's called sadism.

"Alvin successfully stopped thought processes, leaving Judy to rely totally on his worldview and skewed morality."[135]

In Igou's cross-examination, he tried to discredit Nichols's credentials and expertise. He had several openings. She'd never worked on a case in which a child was tortured and killed by an abused person.[136] Dr. Nichols parried that psychological degradation and its effects, coupled with physical violence, surpass any other battering of which she knew.

Igou pushed her on whether Judy was a sociopath and whether she knew what she was doing was wrong. Nichols responded. "I think that she was so completely emersed [*sic*] in Alvin Neelley's mind and ideas and under his influence that I don't think that she thought about whether or not it was right or wrong." Considering the morality of an action one must have some self-determination. By Nichols' analysis, Judy did not.[137]

Repeatedly, Nichols underscored the impact of "psychic abuses [that] go right into a person's sense of themselves [and] are much more profound, long-lasting, and debilitating than any broken bones."

Judy's teenage brain could not extricate itself from the deadliness of her relationship with Alvin. Unconsciously, she was enabling him. No checks and balances aided in recognizing the unintended and unwitting complicity. She was in a confined space as her sight dimmed. No door or window was opened. Her capacity to see collapsed into darkness so profound that nothing penetrated except the sound of Alvin's demands.

In prison, Judy began to reassess her life. If she stayed in the chasm of lies and depravity, that was where she would die. She was near death when rescued by being arrested. It's shocking to put death row as better conditions than being married to Alvin. There is no plausible logic to state that death row was a way to save her life. One can posit that it saved others' lives because Alvin was insatiable.

If the justice system had its way, the end would be death by electrocution. If Judy had her way, she would face death having made amends. Time was short, and she had no idea if those expressions of profound sorrow would make any difference to those whom she had harmed.

The court ruled on the June/July 1983 appeal. Death sentence upheld.

Z-Row Goes to Church

On death row, the world contracts to a small cell and limited contact with humans or nature. For Tutwiler, that meant access to the small exercise area during hours of sunlight. Through the window in the back door or in the exercise area, an inmate can focus beyond three fences. The third, topped with concertina razor wire, surrounds the prison. Across the four-lane highway is a forest of trees that put on a magnificent spectacle of seasonal colors and an occasional dusting of snow. That view surpasses most death rows.

By 1989, the number of women on death row had grown to four. I wanted the women to be allowed to spend time in the chapel. I understood it would be the exception, but I'd gained enough trust from the administration to venture the request. I was elated when the warden granted permission. The women were often engaged in crafts, and since it was December, I gathered supplies so they could make decorations for their cells. I made dough with which they could create small figures for a crèche.

The entire prison is on lockdown to move a death-row inmate. Dorms are secured. Anyone who tries to leave where she is will get a disciplinary. To open a death-row cell, there must be two officers. The inmate is shackled and handcuffed. As she shuffles down the wide hallway, she walks in front of dorms. Most inmates never see death-row inhabitants. In that rare opportunity, they stare, make comments, or yell out their names, most in friendly greetings.

The change in scenery and creating decorations made every

awkward and embarrassing step from their cells to a brief time outside and then into the environment of the chapel worth the discomfort. Looking across the highway through one fence line to view the stark scene of winter's austerity boosted their spirits.

Three of the women said yes to the invitation.

We had snacks as they chatted and crafted items to beautify their cells. I led a service with communion. Each of the women expressed appreciation. Judy wrote:

> *Chaplain Johns, I wanted to let you know how much the day meant to me. The communion was especially beautiful. I've never done it that way. For me it was more of a sharing experience.*
>
> *The entire day was like that. Out in the chapel we were able to walk around freely, no bars or fences in sight. Each of us were aware of the outside restrictions. But for a short while we were just a group of friends—sisters—sharing the day. Making crafts, talking, laughing, and sharing a lot of love.*
>
> *It meant a lot to me. More than I can express. Thank you for giving that to us. May God richly bless you. With love, Judy*

Her assessment of the snacks: "delicious."

Finessing and Challenging the System

I resigned from the chaplaincy after six years to establish a regional program in victim-offender mediation and to design a spiritual program called Epiphany for youth offenders.[138]

Three years later, in 1993, Tutwiler's warden, Shirlie Lobmiller, called and asked me if I would be a spiritual counselor for Judy. By then I was pastor of a congregation and continuing the two programs I'd started. I met with Judy and said I was honored to assist her, but I couldn't promise frequent sessions. The honesty and willingness with which she was determined to dissect how she'd landed on death row inspired me. Soon it became bi-weekly sessions.

Looking back on the access I had and the number of requests I made, from bringing in art supplies to changing the dates of visiting Judy, I'm amazed at the latitude I was given. The visits weren't conducted through glass and a telephone. I could always go into her cell; then we were locked in. Officers made mandated checks, but conversations were confidential. Occasionally, I comforted Judy by embracing her. If we heard the sound of the key in the death-row door, we were quick to end the hug. My act of caring could easily be interpreted by an officer to stoke rumors that Judy and I had a homosexual relationship. I walked out of the prison. Judy remained.

I was allowed to take in a laptop so I could do a rough transcript of our sessions. Lawyers use laptops, and that was part of my pitch. Routine security clearance focuses first on the person: pockets pulled out, no tissues, no cellphone, no billfold or purse. For women, a bra search: stretched forward or popped to be sure nothing was hiding in the cups. With one's back to the officer and arms outstretched, hands slide down the sides and then on the inside of legs. Laptops are opened and cases scrutinized.

On one steamy Sunday afternoon, I also had a few sheets of typed notes to give to Judy from the last visit. The prison rule was that when you went beyond the gate separating the front lobby and inmates, you were not to "take anything in or anything out." I sought approval for every item or scrap of paper that traveled either way. I valued my clearance too much to risk breaking a rule, even if sometimes it was onerous to comply.

Heat was building in the death-row units; the air in the cells was dead.

Judy had written me the previous week that she thought her cellmate, Marie, wanted to be able to see the laptop. "I know our time is short, but can she play a few games on Sunday?"

With Judy's request in mind, I went to the door of Marie's cell. She invited me in, which gave us a few minutes to talk after exchanging a hug. She showed me her months-long project: a cross-stitch portrait of a woman in a black-and-white blouse. The pointillist effect of the stripes—with touches of purple and blue in the black, orange and yellow on the white—was stunning.

"Marie, want to come play some games?" Judy called.

Her reply came in the form of her appearance in Judy's cell. Suddenly, the officer, who'd been engaged in logging my movement, took notice. He saw all three of us spread on Judy's bed around the computer.

"What do you have there?" the officer asked.

My attention pivoted to the officer. There should be

no problem at this point. I had permission to bring in the computer. The case had been inspected, but I envisioned his reporting that all I was doing with the computer was playing games, not helping Judy therapeutically.

I explained quickly that they were trying out a few games, and soon Judy and I would settle into the work at hand. Marie and Judy were oblivious to our conversation. Hearts and Solitaire went on uninterrupted. Satisfied with my explanation of the laptop's use and the warden's blessing, the officer changed to a subject dear to his heart. He broached a conversation about a verse in the Bible.

The officer was known for his Bible study. A question to him about a passage could produce a long and detailed commentary. It was tolerated by some inmates, appreciated by others, and potentially misused if one inmate had been instructed to engage him in conversation, to "catch the heat," while another inmate was busy breaking Tutwiler's rules. Even with being an occasional pawn, the officer helped inmates and was well regarded because of how he interacted with everyone.

He left the unit. Marie went back to her cell.

I handed Judy the edited transcript from the previous week's visit during which we had talked about her falling in love with Alvin and falling into the snare of abuse.

"Don't send it in through the mail; if you think I need to see it, bring it with you. You know what I mean," Judy said.

I knew. The policy of opening mail rankled inmates. Legal correspondence may not be opened. The volume of mail prevents wholesale reading by the mail clerk or anyone else. Opening mail is necessary for contraband: money, drugs— anything not approved by the department, even a stick of gum. Judy's mistrust about how people portrayed her kicked in. She'd seen one book and article too many on what she'd supposedly done or said and knew people's morbid interest kept her name in more chatter than other inmates on death row in Alabama. She couldn't bear the thought of her most tormenting memories being paraded about again should they be sent in the mail.

Judy began our time telling of an incident when another inmate betrayed the trust she was trying to cultivate within herself.

"One day I was outside and talking with Clair. She was in disciplinary segregation."

They could visit because the chain-link fence of the patio for death-row inmates butts up against the larger exercise area for segregation.

"We talked about regular ordinary things," Judy told me. "Then, like an idiot, I mentioned when Al had done something to me with a plant. Every time I see that kind of plant, it brings back the trauma."

I hadn't heard about Alvin's cruelty with a plant, but my attention needed to be on the interaction.

"Clair's response? She told me I'm just plain crazy." Judy's tone was melancholic. "It was important to me, hadn't told anyone else. Every time I put myself out there, get kicked. Maybe I choose the wrong person to talk with." She sighed. "Sometimes I think I overreact to their reaction." She began crying, her toes tracing cracks on the concrete. "I don't trust my own reaction, not about emotions, anyway."

"That sounds wounding," I said. "Would it help to use a different lens with which to see people?"

"A different lens? I'm too old, too set in my ways." She paused, speaking about herself obliquely. "You've been holding onto reality with one rope. It's a disgusting situation, but this is all you know; you're dangling over this unknown and you

112

want to mess with my rope?"

I asked, "What is your rope? Anger?"

"Maybe. I've always held onto the rope. I don't know what's below, what will happen if I let go. Even though uncomfortable, this is my reality. I have no clue what's beyond. It's very frightening." Judy's tone expressed her despair. "Every time I trust somebody, I get kicked in the teeth. It does make me angry.

"I don't fear being alone. I do have a fear of not being loved, not having someone to love. Someone who cares enough that when I need to talk, the person can be trusted. I liked solitude growing up. Sometimes I'd go off and walk, sing songs, talk to God, mostly just 'be.' I keep giving people a chance to prove they love me. I'm insane."

I asked, "What do you think you ought to do?"

"Quit trusting." She looked at me with a hint of impudence. "I've got a headache. You realize this is going to make me analyze other situations and relationships. I jump in too fast. Like with my lawyer, Bob French. I wouldn't have gotten close to him if he hadn't manipulated or encouraged. He'll tell you. He set out to transfer my dependence from Al to him." Judy looked down at her hands, as if those thoughts were too weighty.

"Al had run out of money, and since he wasn't working in a convenience store where we could steal receipts, he drove us to a mall in Rome, Georgia. We were in our car, and he was telling me to take the gun and hold up some shopper. I was just sixteen and scared to death. He said if I wasn't going to do it, he'd find Wicked Wanda, and she'd do anything he told her to do. I have no idea who he was talking about."

"Wicked Wanda probably existed only in his mind," I speculated.

"I don't know." Judy seemed to be remembering the day like seeing a film. "There was a woman walking to her car not far from where we were parked. Al picked her out for me to rob. I knew if I didn't do what he said, he'd beat me, so I got out of the car, pointed the gun at her and took her purse. She just had a few dollars and checks. I told her not to do anything for two minutes. The funny thing is that she had a package with a label from a jewelry store. I didn't take that. Al didn't tell me to take anything but her purse.

"I got caught when I tried to write checks on the lady's bank account. I was eight months pregnant." She smiled. "It wasn't hard to identify me."

Judy hadn't comprehended that she'd slipped over a line into criminality. Holding a gun on someone upped the severity of criminal charges. It was Halloween, 1980.

"I remember being in the courtroom with a lawyer, prosecutor, judge. No one else was there. They discussed my case, and the judge said he could sentence me for ten, but only gave me two years, considering age and first arrest. It scared the living daylights out of me. I was in an emotional state. Part was relief that I'd be away from the beatings Al gave me. I had an absolute terror of being around him. Yet I didn't know what to do on my own; he was my puppeteer. I was desperate to keep in touch, wanted to see him. Still thought I was in love.

"When I got locked up, I had a big bruise on my arm. I lied and said I'd hit my arm on the car door. What really happened was Al hit me with his gun. I'm sure I had a busted lip—always had a busted lip. This was early—abuse not yet at the extreme to which it got. It was already pretty bad."

Being arrested became a curious blessing for her.

"I was sent to the Youth Development Center in Rome on November ten. I was experiencing pain in my back and asked for Tylenol. One of the employees figured out that I'd gone into labor. When I got to the hospital, they told me I was having twins. I had no idea since I hadn't been to a doctor. It was lunchtime on November twelve when I had the twins."

The youth center had a maximum of one hundred twenty girls between the ages of nine and seventeen who were housed in cottages. The schedule was strict. One daily routine for Judy was writing Alvin.

While in the youth facilities, Judy couldn't internalize the staff's assessment of the trauma in her life. Alvin fed her outrageous lies; the staff was brainwashing her. Yet her experience with the staff's kindness didn't comport with that, creating a confusing muddle in her mind.

Linda Adair, a tall, blonde woman, was the assistant director of the Rome Center. Judy spoke of the kindness Adair showed. "After I had the twins, she took me to the doctor. Took me and a few other girls to her house; took me to Weight Watchers. I spent a lot of time in her office, just talking. She was a classy lady. Mostly we talked about Al and the kids, what I planned to do. I remember telling her and the house parent I'd been abused, not the full extent. They urged me to get out. The chaplain at the Regional Youth Detention Center in Macon said I didn't need to go back. I needed to get the kids and leave. We wrote for a while after I got to Tutwiler."

The report of abuse warranted scrutiny of correspondence between Alvin and Judy. Linda read their letters and stopped the correspondence because his influence was damaging. Alvin filed a grievance, and Linda's intervention was overruled. The strongest influence on her thinking was Alvin's constant presence in letters and in her mind. No one cracked the armor Alvin had fashioned.

The two-week break Judy got for Christmas in 1980

came with a stipulation. Judy was not to visit Alvin, who was incarcerated in Georgia for stealing money from a service station. Judy went to Cleveland, Tennessee, to be with in-laws and the children. It wasn't the happy holiday she envisioned.

"Growing up, we always had a live tree, Christmas decorations. At the Neelleys, there was no tree, no decorations. It was sad. There were four kids: twins and stepchildren, four and six. We didn't wrap anything. Mrs. Neelley got two shoeboxes, put them at the front of the TV. In the deeper part of the shoe boxes, there was something for the step-kids. The twins got something in the lids. It was skimpy." Judy repeated, "Nothing wrapped," as if no words could explain that egregious omission.

"They weren't dirt poor like we were growing up. They didn't have money to waste but had some resources. I'm ashamed to say I was so caught up in getting a box for Al, I wasn't concentrating on making much of Christmas for the children. After Christmas, I went back to Rome.

"When I was locked up, Alvin was always accusing me of sleeping with the guards. He said there was a prostitution ring; employees would take girls out to a hotel. They would pimp for the ring. There was none! I would've known of that. One of the excuses for beating me was always, 'I'm under a lot of pressure; I am wanted by the law.' I believed if I did the right thing, he wouldn't be angry. I had this perfect marriage pictured in my head."

Juvenile authorities released Judy nine months into a two-year sentence. That was good news for Alvin. He directed her to go to Albany, Georgia, and confess to the robbery for which he was in prison. The police bought her confession and arrested her. After an investigation determined Judy could not have committed the crime alone, she was put on probation for six months.

Alvin was released. His freedom was brief. Back to prison on a ten-year sentence. Since Alvin couldn't successfully connive through Judy, he hatched another plan. It wasn't original. He worked out a deal with the cops to testify against a man who'd been charged with killing one police officer and shooting another. The man was put in the same cell as Alvin. Soon he concocted a story that the man had admitted to the crimes. The falsified statement landed a ninety-nine-year sentence for the purported cop killer. The man's sister contacted Judy for help. She wanted to do something to exonerate the man, but she had no hard proof and feared Alvin's backlash.

Volcano's Lava

March 1982

In our sessions, small talk was minimal. Time was limited, and Judy had a hunger to voice her story as completely as she could, with no judgment from the hearer. She uncoiled graphic details.

"When Al got out March 22, 1982, he was angrier than when he went in. He'd been in seventeen months on a ten-year sentence, which indicated to me he had some pull by turning state's evidence. He talked all the time about his connections—KGB, ABI, GBI, FBI. When he threw out KBG, he didn't like that I corrected him. He always pretended he was more than he was, that he'd written some songs, been a professional wrestler, ego things. His brothers thought I was stupid, crazy. I used to confirm it."

We repeated the tropes. Often people blame the one who is beaten. The victim causes the partner's outbursts and violence. The victim takes on the guilt. She will admit to what she hasn't done to try to curtail the abuse.

"For a couple of days, he was constantly harassing me. 'Admit what you did.' The more I told him I hadn't slept with anyone, the more he beat me. He changed his tactic. On the third day, he was saying if I'd just admit it, we could put it behind us, and he'd never bring it up again. I knew he was lying. He'd been on me constantly for those three days. I'd had little sleep. He talked, talked, plus I had to get up at four thirty, waiting on him hand and foot. Waiting on kids. Maybe getting two hours of sleep a night. The torture. I'd reached a point I couldn't stand it anymore. I'll tell him what he wants to hear. Just leave me alone."

Judy may have been teetering on an episode of PTSD as she stated, in the present tense, "I'll tell him what he wants to hear. Just leave me alone." The moment passed, and even though she surveyed the beatings from a more secure distance, the recollection held her.

"I didn't think it could get worse by telling him what he wanted to hear. Finally, I lied and told him I did it with the security guards at the Center in Macon. I chose them mostly because he kept harping on them, particularly a Black security guard.

"At first, he was quiet. He didn't start beating the hell out of me; he started drifting off to sleep. Some twenty minutes later, he started hitting me in the head with his fist, mostly in the side of the head. He had a twenty-five automatic. He put it on safety and was hitting me in the forehead, the side. There was a lot of blood. I'd try to wipe it away so I could see what he was doing next. When I cried out, he would hit me

118

in the mouth and tell me not to make any noise. Because if his mother came in—they were in the next room—he'd kill me. If I grunted, he'd hit harder.

"He straddled my chest, then pinned my arms down with his knees. I couldn't block him. He just started indiscriminately in my face, broke my nose. He would choke me and tried to smother me with a pillow. Just as I was losing consciousness, he would let go and start again on my face and head. When I got my arms freed, I'd block him the best I could. He'd hit me in my ribs. When I lowered my arms to protect my stomach or ribs, he would hit me in the head."

Judy broke down, stuttering as she tried to continue. "This was the night that he made me go into the half-bath next to the bedroom, take the stick off the plunger and bring it to him. He made me lay back down on the bed."

I knew what came next. I wanted to hear no more. Was her vivid retelling therapeutic or toxic? I studied her body. Was her recounting like vomiting, the vile feeling as it grows in one's throat and the relief when the poison is expelled? I prayed for God's guidance and presence.

"I can still feel it, all over my body, the plunger handle, everything. I understand that was a long time ago. I know it is not really happening now, but I feel the emotions of it." Struggling to breathe, she stuttered. "When he was using the plunger, he said I had already been ruined for letting that Black screw me. The terror, the confusion. I can't convey how it felt to be trapped in the bedroom. I couldn't scream. I couldn't run, fight. I was completely at his mercy.

"That night, he bit a plug out of me. He was standing in the corner of the bedroom. I was down on my knees. He would have me begging. He took my right hand, bit into the wrist. He kept biting and biting. You could see the teeth marks

119

six months later. He made me open my mouth and urinated in my mouth. Made me swallow it. Beating was interspersed with having sex.

"He beat me all night. He went to sleep about three or three thirty. I had to get up at four thirty to cook breakfast. Don't remember if I slept."

Judy's tears as she spoke caused her nose to run. When she blew her nose, I jumped, betraying the tension in my body. We laughed at my startle reflex. The lightened mood didn't last as the night's physical combat morphed into psychological combat.

"Alvin instructed me to tell his mother that he'd heard someone out around our cars during the night. He went out to check and had a stick. I was supposed to've sneaked up from behind, and he swung around and hit me before he knew what he was doing. My eyes were swollen shut except for a tiny slit out of my right eye. My face was one huge bruise, distorted beyond belief, severely disfigured. I didn't recognize myself.

"When I told Mrs. Neelley what I was to tell her, she didn't say anything that I recall. She went on preparing breakfast. Mr. Neelley said not one word. It was a school day, so I had to get Lily, Al's daughter, up and dressed. She was almost seven. When she saw me, she started crying. I squatted down. The closer I got to her, the more she would scoot back trying to get away. I wanted to take her in my arms and comfort her, but she was so scared I couldn't touch her. 'Lily, I'm okay; it was an accident. It is still me inside. I just look different.' It was an odd thing to say. Lily kept crying. Al wouldn't let me out of the house for several days until the swelling in my face went down."

Judy was narrating the story sixteen years after it happened. Wounds on her body were healed, but not the embedded scars. I wanted to cry. For Lily. For Judy. Even for Alvin and his parents.

As if to diminish Alvin's cruelty, Judy observed, "When you're feeling numb, it doesn't hurt so much."

The session paled in comparison to the terror of that night; even so, the reliving was punishing. I prayed for the spirit of God to comfort her. Later, I considered the sacred trust she had in me. She believed I would hold her words gently and respect her by listening without judging.

To break the sway of those memories, Judy turned to their jobs in twenty-four-hour convenience stores. "I helped him in his second shift, and then I worked the third—sixteen straight hours. We lost one job at a Zippy Mart in Dawson, Georgia, because I fell asleep. Al would sleep during the third shift. I was exhausted beyond words. No one ever came in at three a.m. Once I went to the back to lie down a few minutes. I didn't mean to sleep. The next thing I heard was the bell. The cops came flying in. When they saw the two of us, they thought we'd been robbed and shot. I got into a lot of trouble from that. It was so embarrassing. I got us fired. Al said I was lazy and knew better than to sleep."

Judy mirrored what she'd been taught: she was the one who got them fired. She was lazy. She shouldn't have been sleeping.

"One store we worked in, there was a lot of money coming in on Friday nights. About seven thirty, the place was deserted. I knew something was going to happen. Word had gotten around. A guy came in asking for cigarettes. As soon as the register was opened, he opened his jacket, and I saw his gun. He told me, 'Don't say anything. Just give me money.'

"Alvin was in the store, and all I said was, 'Al.' He caught my tone and turned around. I thought he would stop it. I kept putting money into a bag. No peep out of Al. The guy snatched the bag out of my hand and tore out. Al yelled, 'Call the cops!' When it was all over, I was shaking. Al was mad at the guy. How dare that guy rob the store! Cops got there fast. Al said there was a second guy with a shotgun. He didn't do anything to stop the man because he said he was afraid the guy would shoot me. Bullshit. I picked out the guy from a line-up at the station. He had a gap in his front teeth. They had him smile, and I said, 'That's the guy!' We had to go back to the store and lock up.

"We never went to court on it. We got fired not long after. For a while, Al had been the assistant manager."

Judy told me about schemes they used to steal money from the convenience stores. She said the stealing disturbed her, since she'd been taught that it was wrong to steal, while simultaneously she experienced excitement.

"There was always the fear of getting caught, but then it was like getting one over on the system. Al hated cops. That got transferred to me."

7.

Fact Checking

In conversations, letters, phone calls, journal entries, and visits, Judy's stories uncoiled. When she jumped at a loud sound in the hall, she apologetically explained her fears about what would happen next, about never wanting to have her back to others. Alvin's eerily muted anger could surface in the most mundane situation. She fantasized that if she knew what was coming, she could repel it more adroitly or escape the beatings.

I couldn't help Judy if I blindly accepted every aspect of life with Alvin. I've checked myself for years on my perceptions of Judy. One way to test a story's truthfulness is whether it changes markedly in retelling. Judy's testimony at trial, our many conversations in the prison cell, and letters are consistent without embellishment for effect.

Another avenue was to speak with Alvin. I sent a letter to

him while he was in prison in Georgia to ask if I could visit. I told him I knew Judy. He wrote back that his lawyer advised him not to accept my request. I believed meeting him seemed more fair than long distance analysis and filtered accounts. In 2005, the door of opportunity shut when Alvin died in prison after surgery.

~

In the spring of 2001, I was a chaplain in residence at the United Methodist Seminary, Claremont School of Theology in California. To asssess my work with Judy I interviewed two professors of pastoral care, the Rev. Dr. William (Bill) M. Clements and the Rev. Dr. Kathleen Greider.

I asked Bill Clements what my antennae should be with Judy. I knew I had to entertain psychological diagnoses long enough to tilt me toward them or away from them.

"Be sure she doesn't have an antisocial personality disorder herself. Antisocial people can be extraordinarily believable. If she were antisocial in prison, she would be flouting the rules, not taking responsibility for any of her actions."

I replied that she reclaimed her voice in prison, speaking up for herself and others, but she wasn't a rule breaker.

Bill seemed satisfied with my characterization as he built a psychological profile.

The conversation turned to Judy and Alvin's children. "Does she have contact with them?" he asked.

I told him of the relationships that had been reestablished with the twins. But the younger brother was adopted. When I'd talked with the adoptive mother a few years prior to this conversation, she thought the fifteen-year-old didn't know the identity of his biological parents. I explained to Bill that Judy had sent him handmade presents for years and simply signed them "Judy." His adoptive mother asked that Judy stop all contact with him. She knew his curiosity would be more and more aroused by the gifts and notes. Judy stopped. It nearly devastated her, but she respected the request.

"That tells me she's not antisocial," Bill said. "An antisocial personality would've sent the gifts anyway and said, 'It's your problem, not mine.' Antisocial people cry crocodile tears when they get caught. They aren't sorry for what they've done, just the circumstance they're in."

All right, I thought, she was off the hook with the antisocial personality disorder, but I wanted to understand if there was a psychiatric illness that had contributed to her buying into Alvin's gentlemanly manners and his lavish gifts of food.

Clements spoke about personality disorders. "Often, relationships are stormy; they get very angry and very frightened. There's nothing in moderation. They're instantly in love and out of love. It's like the fine-tuning dial is missing. It's all hate or all love. They flip from one to another really quickly."

Bill had read excerpts from the trial transcript and didn't hesitate to assess Alvin. "He is paranoid, sadistic. To have a strict diagnosis of an antisocial personality disorder, you have to know about them as a young adult. Alvin's behavior is consistent with antisocial personality disorder."

Reflecting on the ways personalities interact, I mentioned the possibility of Judy's having a personality disorder. "What would the interaction be like between two people in a marriage with personality disorders … even though they would be differently defined?"

"Some with a personality disorder are sensitive to rejection. They'll attempt to do most anything to avoid rejection, might believe the unbelievable. They'd feed on each other. She would be much more susceptible to his directions and have trouble saying 'no' and making it stick … A fear of rejection or physical abuse would be greater than her fear of going back to juvenile detention, so she'd do what he wanted even though it might be illegal. We don't see any history of independent, antisocial action on her part prior to her knowing Alvin. It could be true that all her criminal activity was in conjunction with him. A question would be, when she wasn't with him, was she arrested for stuff when he was in prison?"

I shook my head. "No. There was no unlawful activity."

"You should look at posttraumatic stress disorder with what Judy has been exposed to. In PTSD, you begin to try and avoid things that trigger the flashbacks. It's not healthy to do that when you're no longer in the traumatizing situation, to be afraid unnecessarily. It happens normally when your life is threatened, like the kind of stuff Alvin was doing to the thirteen-year-old. If she'd survived, she probably would've suffered from posttraumatic stress disorder. In a pool of one hundred people experiencing the same event, about thirty would have PTSD."

I related an episode Judy told me. She and another inmate were playing around. Unexpectedly, it evolved to Judy's being hit on her forehead several times with a wet washcloth. She had no outward injury, but she regressed to a time when Alvin had abused her. It was frightening.

I wanted Bill's take on why people had a hard time believing Judy and labeling Alvin a "lovesick slob" incapable of doing anything other than what she told him to do.

"They haven't seen the welts on her arms; they haven't seen the vaginal tears. They see a guy who is superficially charming."

I asked about violence against pregnant women by their partners. "Judy had one miscarriage. The beatings began before

126

she became pregnant. When she was at risk for miscarriage, Alvin made no attempts to seek medical help. During pregnancy, there was a marked increase in the intensity of the physical battering. Is there a relationship between pregnancy and abuse?"

"It's not proven, but there is speculation that the man might be sexually frustrated, so without coping skills, he reverts to violence."

Bill referenced Alabama where he'd lived. "In Alabama, we'd be likely to say if a woman killed her abuser, 'Yeah, she did it, but he deserved it!' She'd likely only get a short amount of time."

I wasn't sure there would be many people who would find in favor of the woman.

Next, I met with Kathleen Greider, also a professor at the seminary. I intentionally covered similar territory to get another read. As with Bill, I gave her transcript excerpts and an overview of Judy's life. She read the material attentively, her forehead furrowed.

"I understand sociologically how Judy could be beguiled by Alvin," I said. "But I have trouble connecting the dots psychologically. It's not the simplistic question of why she stayed, but what were the hooks that kept them enmeshed?"

"What does Judy say about why she stayed?"

Judy and I'd talked about that. "Love and fear."

Kathleen's quick read produced volumes of insight. "In cases like this where there has been a lifetime of hardship, emotional deprivation, loss, and neglect, there is a power that has got her trapped. In situations not so dramatically wounding, people stay. In this case, the trouble starts before the father's dying in a motorcycle accident when he'd been driving while drunk. It's self-destructive as well as putting others at risk.

"It's not a stable home environment. How does a kid get started in life? She had a sibling she took care of which gave her agency. She is intelligent. Did anyone notice her? Did she get support in school because of her abilities? Did someone say, 'You're smart enough to go to college?'"

I asked how she defined "agency."

"That's the experience of being effective on one's own behalf or on behalf of others that produces self-confidence and personal value. There can be a disconnect between innate abilities and external forces in a teen's life."

"She wanted to graduate from high school," I said. "I think she got satisfaction out of school, but she felt like an outsider. She didn't have nice clothes. She didn't see herself as attractive. That colored her academic successes."

"The question is, what did she have inside her and around her when she was fifteen?" Kathleen said. "She would've had some sense of where she was heading. Having a man like Alvin would be about what she could hope for: someone who would treat her with courtesy and respect."

Kathleen continued. "I'm thinking of a metaphor of a suction cup on a window. It's hard to pull it off after the vacuum is established. She had a vacuum in her, and she was stuck there when Alvin came along. The vacuum was tornado stuff inside Judy—an emotional energy that pulls one person to another in some situation of crisis. Then this guy comes along, and he looks pretty darn good. An inner hunger gets awakened. He shows respect, and it's hard to underestimate the potential pull of that.

"In this description from the transcript, it sounds like Alvin would have an antisocial personality disorder or sociopathic personality—infamously charming, initially quite responsive, generous, and complimentary. He's gentlemanly and courtly."

I concurred. "He cast a spell of graciousness."

Kathleen described the gradual process. "One of the dynamics used by perpetrators of abuse, sometimes consciously, mostly unconsciously, is a gradual sucking in. I'm going to get you to run away, common rule breaking, romantic. There's a little bit more every time. In that process, there's an increasing fear quotient. The changes aren't dramatic. One may say, 'What am I doing?' But if you combine that with a campaign of fear, of threat, 'I will turn you in: I have more and more on you.' If you're seduced into a behavior that's shaming, it's a potent mix.

"As a person of good intelligence who has been taking care of the house and her brother, her behavior violates who she thought she was. The message she got from her environment says she should've been able to say no; she should've been able to convert him to be a good man. If she'd been a good woman, she would've been able to clean him up. It's enlightenment thinking of will and rationality: you ought to be able to do these things."

Kathleen's assessments continued. "Sexuality is such a huge thing here in terms of her childhood and her relationship with Alvin and the abuse. For those who haven't been violated sexually, it's hard to imagine what it's like in that intimate part of one's life. You can be abused in the workplace, but if you have a loving, safe bedroom, if you have someone to hold you with love, you have some safety. Imagine having all the other forces, and you come home, and the bed isn't safe. How soul-killing that is! You're not worth anything."

I threw in one more charge leveled against Judy. "I've heard that not only is the abusive person controlling, but the one who stays is controlling as well."

"We're all controlling to some degree," Kathleen responded.

"We get controlling actually or in a feeling way when we feel our survival or being is at risk. I start from the premise that is theological, and as a pastor and clinician. We should be protective and in a positive sense, controlling, if we have an image of ourselves in God. We should be treated with honor and respectfulness. In some relationships, I need someone to set a limit on me, and if you don't, it enrages me. I can't seem to set it on myself. It can produce rage."

The level of violence escalated rapidly after Alvin was released in 1982. I tested that with Kathleen. "I've often thought that rage must've been building inside Alvin while he was in prison. But considering what you've just said, it could be the opposite. In either case, whether there's pent-up rage or sleeping violence, it's scary to think of Alvin back on the streets. Some people do well in prison with the limits that are set but lose it when they get back on the streets."

"It may be either," Kathleen said. "Perhaps in that environment where there are set limits, it helps him manage himself. It gives him self-respect. He's able to have a joking relationship with the guards. He feels good about himself. When he gets out, it's a social affront; the containment isn't there to keep him from committing another crime."

She continued, "I don't believe we're ever completely powerless, although we may feel powerless. That's most tested in the presence of someone who wants to kill us. That's where resurrection comes in. The power isn't in our physical lives."

The conversations with Kathleen and Bill deepened my knowledge and motivated me to learn more.

The Media

Craig Rivera was persuasive, and it didn't hurt that he was good-looking. Judy was smitten by him when he interviewed her at Tutwiler on behalf of his brother, Geraldo Rivera, who was working on a television special, *Murder: Live from Death Row*, that aired April 1988.[139] Craig told her that if she appeared on the show, she could speak about the dangers of being in battering situations. It might help the public grasp the hold batterers have on their victims. The three hours Craig spent with Judy as she described abuse by her husband were quashed. Judy wanted to inform, but Geraldo wanted to sensationalize. Judy was presented as a hardened murderer.

In the program's opening, Geraldo Rivera stated that the viewer would meet some "horrible people." Those included Charles Manson, Richard Speck, Judith Neelley, and others. He interviewed family members of victims to "comfort the victim" alongside "confront[ing] the criminal."

During the live interview, Judy and her lawyer, Bob French, sat in the warden's office at Tutwiler. The frenetic pace, as Geraldo quickly switched from one person to another, heightened the program's drama with minimal depth. Judy felt ambushed by the questions and quick cuts to another story. Had I not known Judy, I would've concurred with the portrayal that she was an evil human being, and the sooner she was executed, the safer Alabama would be.

A decided disadvantage, for all who were interviewed remotely, was no monitor of the show. The people being interviewed could hear the assertions, masquerading as questions, but never saw Geraldo. His disembodied voice baited Judy. "Do you see how easy it is for normal people to totally disbelieve your defense?"

She stated that she understood that but insisted tersely, "because it's the truth."[140]

The word "normal" conveyed his dichotomy of normal and "horrible people."

Rivera skimmed over cases and didn't deal with complexities. It was unfair to viewers and guests on the show to give the illusion of solid journalism. The content was packaged to titillate, not to give in-depth reporting.

Judy was seething and wanted French to intervene; he didn't. In an interview after the show, he said that "the show merchandised revenge, hatred, and anger." And Geraldo's "interviews with grieving family members of murder victims bordered on cruel exploitation."

The cover of the November 14, 1988, *Newsweek* bore the headline "Trash TV." The picture of Rivera's face shows the broken nose he got on one of his shows. Daytime television in the 1980s pandered to human's basest behavior. Rivera was adept at sensationalizing stories and baiting guests.

A year later, I became angry when I arrived at the Tutwiler prison chapel and found it bustling with people. Interviews were being conducted with inmates. Geraldo Rivera had been approved to tape two television shows at Tutwiler on the upcoming Friday. A family member of an inmate would be brought to the prison for a "surprise" reunion. I was angry because I had no knowledge of the takeover of the chapel and feared that inmates would be used. I was protective of chapel use. I wanted it to be a place where the women could come to grow spiritually and escape the craziness of the halls and dorms. Ingenuously, I believed that all events scheduled in the chapel had to be approved by me.

It's hard to ignore the flash of fame. Some public relations value can occur in airing a program from a prison. But televising emotional reunions does little to increase people's understanding of the human cost of mass incarceration. I wrote a strong letter of disapproval to the public information officer for the Department of Corrections:

> *I wish to go on record as being opposed to G. Rivera's doing any show which deals with inmates in Alabama. I have seen enough of his handiwork to know that he distorts, inflames, sensationalizes, misleads, stereotypes, and manipulates. He uses people for his own ends.*

I admitted it was possible that Rivera would do a credible piece of reporting. But even if he did, I questioned the rationale of the DOC to allow a man of his reputation to use inmates for ratings. What benefit was it to host sensationalist "journalism"?

I was unpersuasive. Geraldo was coming. Believing I should be present for events that affected the entire institution, I attended. We sat on bleachers put up temporarily on the scrappy south yard. Later, I saw the shows aired on television. Rivera did better than I'd anticipated. A low bar, I will admit. There were a few reunions of children with their inmate mothers. That was a positive outcome.

Free-World Spectators

The women on death row were not usually asked who could come into the outer cell of their units. The door would be unlocked, and they would be feet away from any person approved by the warden. They were to be grateful and gracious hosts. Judy felt used by heavy-handed evangelists who appeared to be more interested in getting points for conversions (to give them chits with God) than meeting a person—not a stereotyped and desolate death-row inmate. Judy found it exasperating when they presumed that they alone were bringing Jesus into the prison.

One prison ministry, Worldwide Evangelists for Jesus, riled her.[141] They got access to the death-row units with their books and video cameras. Judy didn't give consent for them to make videos of her and was incensed when she found out the videos were being used without permission in promotional literature. On the back cover of a book, distributed to prisoners around the world, was a quote attributed to Judy and another death-row inmate. Those quotes appeared to endorse the book. Neither had approved.

Judy contacted her appeals attorney, Barry Ragsdale. He wrote the president of Worldwide Evangelists for Jesus. Barry was clear. The letter demanded "that you and your organization immediately cease and desist from using Ms. Neelley's name and/or photograph and cease attributing allegedly quoted material from Ms. Neelley." Failure to comply would be met with legal measures.[142] They complied, as far as anyone could know.

I was annoyed with the ministry for using several of the death-row inmates, but I interpreted it as more of an error in judgment than intended exploitation or misrepresentation.

Summer 1997

I returned home to the parsonage in Union Springs, Alabama, feeling wrung out after a day of traveling many miles and tending to challenging spiritual concerns. En route, I summoned my martyr complex.

When I opened the back door of the parsonage, my husband called to me from the living room, "Louise, come here, I want you to meet someone."

A dark, quiet corner was what I wanted. My husband, Dick, bless his heart (said in the South as a prelude to a not-so-subtle critique) never met a conversation he couldn't start. I didn't have the stamina to enter an exchange with anyone.

Yelling from the kitchen that I was not available seemed a poor option, so I made an appearance, and Dick introduced me to a reporter from Birmingham, Alabama. Tom Gordon was doing a story on the effect of welfare reform and decided to come to a small town to "check it out." He sought out Dick on the recommendation of someone from the Department of Human Resources because word had gotten around that Dick had brought folks together to explore starting a community food pantry. Gordon thought it was worth pursuing.

Presuming he was a nice guy if he cared about welfare reform and food pantries, I started working my Birmingham connections. I asked Tom if he knew Brooke, my daughter Michele's college roommate, who worked at the same newspaper. Yes, indeed, since she handled the switchboard at *The Birmingham News*. Dick, again, bless his heart, for some unknown reason had been telling Tom about my work with Judy. Tom came to a small town in southeast Alabama to poke around for stories needing to be told, and as synchronicity would have it, he was the reporter from the newspaper that had covered Judy Neelley's trial and subsequent appeals. I was talking to an eyewitness! My fatigue vanished.

I had three goals as I listened: one was not to reveal anything of confidential nature about Judy; two, to get as much information from him as I could; three, to gauge his assessment of Judy. I told Tom that Judy had written letters of apology to employees of the juvenile system in Georgia. I wanted him to know that Judy had been straight with me about her crimes, and that she was earnest in her desire to make amends.

A month later, I received at least thirty-nine of the articles he or other staff had written about the trial and its aftermath. They were a treasure trove of investigative reporting of research, analysis, and interviews.

One article covered a police interrogation of Alvin. It yielded fabrications, not facts. Rather than confessing to what he'd done, Alvin spun a story that he and his wife were "recruiters and enforcers for a prostitution ring." Alvin told the police that he had information about at least ten unsolved murders spread across multiple towns and cities in two states. The headline, "'Prostitute recruiter' suspect in deaths of 10 women" fueled the fires of public indignation and fear.[143]

Alvin's statements about a prostitution ring were investigated and discredited. A police chief commented that, "It appears he's a sensationalist." Another officer wondered if Alvin were "trying to work a deal."[144] Did he like the attention his stories garnered? Even after it had been proved that the Neelleys had nothing to do with a prostitution ring or the deaths of unknown others, the story lodged in people's imaginations. His tales revealed his belief that he was smarter than the authorities.

Journalist Tom Gordon traveled to Tennessee to talk with Barbara, Judy's mother. His article begins, "[Judy] was quiet, the best-behaved of five children." The headline recast Judy. "Husband 'changed' accused murderess." The charges against Judy dazed her mother. She described Judy as being shy, uninterested in boys, good at helping with household chores, and an apt student. "After she met Al, she changed." Her mother had not approved of Judy's contact with him, but she "didn't try to interfere." About three months after they met, Barbara came home to an absent daughter and a note saying she'd be all right and her mother would hear from her. The next communication was from the Department of Youth Services. Judy was in the Macon Youth Development Center.

After Judy's first stint in juvenile facilities, she and Alvin visited Barbara. Her mother was astonished. "She'd changed completely ... She wouldn't say nothing to nobody because her husband was so jealous he would accuse her of going out with anybody she ever spoke to ... She was afraid of him, deathly afraid of him ... He'd have her crying just about every other day."[145]

Gordon's reporting was consistent, researched, and objective. It's a credit to him and *The Birmingham News* that he was assigned to the case. He stayed with it through appeals and commutation. He retired in 2010 from the newspaper, passing the reporting to a plethora of news outlets for Judy's legal issues.

I found no coverage of Judy's crime in a Montgomery, Alabama, newspaper until late 1984. Even then it was an Associated Press report. By the time her case was argued in the state supreme court in 1986, it was being reported. That may explain why I was unaware of the notorious killer in a prison about twenty miles northeast of my home in Montgomery until I became chaplain.

8.

Pulling in the Pain

Confront the dark parts of yourself,
and work to banish them with illumination and forgiveness.
Your willingness to wrestle with your demons
will cause your angels to sing.[146]

Nineteen ninety-four was a year of tragedy for Judy. In May, Judy's friend died of suicide and Judy attempted suicide. Three months later, her fifty-year-old mother died of ovarian cancer. On a visit in late August, neither of us was prepared for a session when the recollection of an assault disrupted Judy's psyche.

We were sitting outside in the enclosed exercise area for death row. "One time in Macon, we had a little league baseball bat." Memories embedded the seemingly mundane statement. The sun and words were bearing down on us. Judy tried to continue. "He took the small end and tried to shove it up in me. It wouldn't go. He said I was gaped open from sleeping with Blacks; that was one of his ways to prove it. I bled for a long time from that."

She faltered.

We'd built a safe space to which all her life could be brought and honored. I had to take responsibility for entering a place of emotional danger. I gently suggested she continue if that was what she needed. She stopped; tears came without restraint. Later, I wrote, "If you don't feel that I'm helping you, you should say that. I don't want to put you through anything that will harm you." I wouldn't walk away out of my reticence or repulsion, but I couldn't further injure her.

Nearing the thirteenth anniversaries of the deaths of Cathy and the young Georgia woman, Kay, Judy began shutting down. She'd lived through twelve years on death row. Her spirit was a nothingness, a buffer but not a shield. Judy felt a cold emptiness. She mourned in "deep sorrow for the horrible things done to a precious, innocent thirteen-year-old girl. I'll never forget. Never." Her thoughts about the second victim, Kay, were equally acute.

Because of the experience of despair, Judy moved deeper into spiritual and psychological inventories of her life. That became apparent as she slept. Astonishing dreams emerged out of fears and aspirations. When she wrote me about one dream, the mother's wisdom astounded me.

Her nightmare in September 1995 took place in a jail. Alvin appeared. Without intervention by bystanders, the two began to fight. It was brutal. He didn't expect her to put up a defense. She felt she was avenging his crimes against her and other innocent people.

"I'd thought I would enjoy hurting him as he'd hurt me so many times. Instead, I was disgusted and broken-hearted." The fighting escalated to broken bones and blood. Finally, Judy said she couldn't bear it anymore. "I dropped to my knees, crying hysterically. I wouldn't fight anymore." She crawled away and called for her mother.

"Mama pulled me up into her arms, holding me as I sobbed. I asked her why hurting Al didn't make me feel better, but instead made it worse. I asked her how to make the pain end … She softly told me to pull the pain and memories to myself instead of trying to push them away." As Judy began waking up, she fought against losing her mother's unexpected wisdom. But she slipped away.

That dream reinforced Judy's weighing the interconnectedness of expressing remorse to persons she'd harmed, forgiving those who'd hurt her, and envisioning God's forgiveness. Each action was integral to the other.

Extending Forgiveness

Happy are those whose transgression is forgiven,
whose sin is covered.
Happy are those to whom the Lord
imputes no iniquity,
and in whose spirit there is no deceit.
Psalm 32:1–2[147]

1997–1998

If a year has been difficult, New Year's Eve can be a portal to designing a better future. Newness provokes aspirations.

Judy wasn't considering aspirations or resolutions. She was praying as the new year began. She wrote in her journal:

> For the first time I asked for blessings for Alvin Neelley. Normally I ask for blessings for family, friends, children, authorities, etc. but when it comes to Al, I'll usually just pray that he will tell the truth. I've no idea what moved me to pray for good things for him. I must be losing my mind. I haven't told anyone about my praying. I guess I feel that this is some sort of growth for me. I actually prayed for the man I despise.

Judy was moving toward a goal she hadn't imagined. The weeds of hatred impeding her path had to be unearthed.

One and one-half years later, the weeding continued. Judy vented in a letter to Alvin. Her intention was to say that she'd forgiven him. The first letter was the kind one writes to exorcise venom, but definitely not the letter one should send:

> Al, there is much I want to say to you. I know that none of it will make a difference to you. It will change nothing about you. But I am not doing this for you. I'm doing it for me.
>
> For many years I have wasted an enormous amount of energy hating you. I have despised you with every fiber of my being. Despite knowing that

my rage and hatred didn't affect you in the least, but was eating me up inside, still I raged.

I'm sure you're well aware [that] more than likely I will be executed before this year's out. As I write that I wonder how it makes you feel. But I already know the answer. You have no emotions, so you do not feel for others. The only thing you will feel is pride that you have literally gotten away with murder.

But really you have not. It only seems that way. You've never been convicted in the justice system for the murder of Cathy Rose Connolly, and you never will be. But you and I both know what happened. More importantly God knows what happened. You may escape punishment on this earth, but you cannot escape from God. You will answer for your sins just like the rest of us … I'll leave true justice to God.

The letter wasn't mailed. She quit writing before she was able to express forgiveness. About one month later, she tried again:

Al, I am writing for one reason. I want you to know that I forgive you. For all of the horrible things you did, I forgive you.

I do not do this lightly. For a very long time I have despised you. The rage and hatred I've felt for you has controlled me and eaten away at my soul. No amount of intellectual reasoning would lessen my feelings.

The memories of all that you did remain vivid.

143

The bitterness I've felt for the justice system has been a big problem for me ...

It's not my problem now. I told the truth, as you well know. I cannot make anyone believe me. But I will not try anymore.

You and I know what happened, Al. But more importantly, God knows what happened. For your sake I sincerely hope that you have confessed to God and sought His forgiveness.

I will not forget the things you've done to me and others. I wish I could. But for the first time in my life I can recall those nightmarish memories without feeling the rage burning within. I've given it to God and set myself free ...

By now you're, no doubt, thinking I've lost my mind. The irony is that I have never been more sane. But it matters not whether you believe me.

There's one other thing I want to say to you, Al. I want to thank you for my children. Despite the horrors of their lives they have grown to be wonderful, intelligent, sensitive young adults. I am very proud of them.

I wish you well, Al. I do pray for you. I hope you have found the help that you need. And I pray that you find peace in your soul. As long as there is breath in me, I'll keep you in my prayers ...

God heal and guide you.

Sincerely, Judy

I received a jubilant letter from Judy after she wrote to Alvin.

I'm free! (Smiley face.) Free.

The smiley face had crinkle marks at both ends of the mouth.

Still in Tutwiler unfortunately. But free where it counts. Inside.

I feel so lighthearted! As you know, I started a letter to Al some weeks ago. Never finished it. Now I know why, there was still a bit of bitterness in me.

Last night I talked to God. Aloud I spoke the words that I forgive Al, and I prayed for him. I cried some.

She understood that there would be times when she'd question the sense of freedom in forgiving Alvin. But she believed that God intended healing in her life. On that, she would build her future.

Years later, I recognized spiritual work I needed to do. I also had to forgive Alvin. How could I counsel the need to let go of anger or the desire for retribution, if I was holding onto it? Letting go or holding on set an example for Judy.

I will admit, that since I learned Alvin Neelley Jr. hated the name of Alvin, I've taken restrained pleasure in always referring to him as Alvin—a gray area related to forgiveness. However, if I were speaking with him, it would be Al.

Neither Judy's nor my forgiveness affects God's judgment on Alvin. It does change us—for the better.

Alvin didn't respond to Judy's letter.

9.

The Tentacles of Relationships

She hadn't seen her twins, April and Jeremy, since they were two. Her youngest child was a shadow. The twins lived into their teens with Alvin's mother, Jessie Neelley, who intercepted Judy's letters to the children. Judy made gifts and sent them. She didn't know if anything was given to them.

The third child also received handmade gifts, but the adoptive parents judiciously guarded him from knowing the source. He learned later about his birth parents.

Judy told me that Mrs. Neelley was unwilling or unable to bring the children to visit at the prison. Judy was certain unwillingness was the reason, and that angered her. Some people offered to drive to Mrs. Neelley's home and bring the children to see Judy, but Jessie would have none of it. I commiserated with Judy over the separation. Then I decided to act.

With enough hubris to believe I could change the grandmother's mind, I wrote to her. I expressed sympathy regarding the challenges of child rearing. After a few preambles, I beseeched her—also known as begging—to allow the children to visit. Then I hit the judgment button. She reportedly read her Bible and attended church. It was time she started reading those passages that mentioned standing before Jesus. I said that keeping her grandchildren from their mother would be one serious error against her. Someday, she would have to answer for that. The letter swayed between empathy for the strains of parenting and dishing out blame: Why is it that the children can visit their incarcerated father, but not their mother?

I waited for her reply. I waited some more. I never heard a word. I admitted that I was not as persuasive as I thought I was. Judy advised me to let it go. She noted that the grandmother was capable of reprisals against her or, worse, the children. Let it be.

By the time the twins had become teens, Jessie had had enough. The state would have to take over. That was a good-news/bad-news time for the twins and Judy. At least with Mrs. Neelley, Judy knew where the children were. She could send letters and gifts and pray that someday they would see them. Going into foster care put contact into jeopardy, along with anxiety over the quality of the placement.

Almost ten years later, April had a sharp recall of the day's events as she described it to me in a telephone call.

"We were taken into foster care in the seventh grade. Granny said she was too old, couldn't take care of us. I did the cooking and a lot of cleaning. I didn't want to leave my friends." Her voice rose, and she spoke with emphasis. "The worst part was they came to school and got us! I was angry and embarrassed. I asked them why they picked us up at school. They said they were afraid we would run away from home." Her incredulity increased. "If we were going to run away, we'd already have done it. Then they evaluated us, a funny day to evaluate! They were checking our attitudes. I was angry and didn't want to talk to anyone. They reported I was sulky and needed to come out of my shell. One year later, they wrote what a remarkable change had taken place in me. I told them they ought to know why I was upset. When they were taking us from Granny's, my aunt was there. She lives in another state. She was financially able. She had a big house. She was crying, but she could have taken us. I thought, 'Screw you!' It breaks you or makes you stronger."

August 1995

The improbable occurred. Foster parents, Keith and Gloria, brought the twins to the prison. They were almost fifteen. Thirteen years of separation rendered them strangers.

A hot month in Alabama, and Judy's emotional state fluctuated widely. No guarantee existed that they would make a connection to someone whose life was in the hands of the legal system. Why should they attempt to bridge the years? They'd already had the heartbreak of losing their mother once. Why open themselves to loss again?

Hundreds of letters, cards, and handmade gifts couldn't solidify a parental bond. Judy mourned and berated herself that she hadn't been with her children to help with homework, sibling squabbles, falling in and out of friendships, clean clothes for school, or comforting a crying child. She missed giggling and bedtime rituals. At the core of her angst was one complex question: Can they forgive her?

Everyone endeavored to be in the present. Issues, questions, and misgivings can't be settled in a few hours. An observer, unaware of the back stories, would see awkward interactions and expressions of love. But that observer couldn't know the turmoil in each.

After the twins and the foster parents left, Judy worried if they'd see each other again.

When April Neelley was twenty-eight, the *Times–Journal,* a Fort Payne, Alabama, newspaper, interviewed her. A reporter from the town in which Judy's trial had taken place captured the dislocation April and her brother experienced.

Until their early teens, the twins had lived with Alvin's mother and for a short time with grandparents. The grandfather died when the twins were pre-school age.[148] There were secrets in the house. Items from the lives of their father and mother hidden in a tall box, taller than the children—clothing and news clippings. The twins' older half-sister read the clippings. From that box came more confusion than a child can process.

School was a tough place to negotiate and an academic refuge. From April's perspective, her older half-sister got the heaviest brunt of the cruelty of fellow students, although she and her brother weren't spared. But teachers were protective of the siblings.

At home, she often heard from Mrs. Neelley that women were whores. April remembered her grandfather more fondly than her grandmother. In foster care, she was allowed to "be a kid again," what she'd missed as a child.

In 1998, April Neelley was chosen as the Foster Child of the Year in Tennessee. The House Joint Resolution listed her accomplishments. The junior in high school was an honor student, excelled in public speaking, was drum captain in the school band, a class representative, and on the Tennessee Youth Advisory Council. A photograph shows April outside the Tennessee capital with a large, framed certificate presented by the governor. Her hair fell slightly below her shoulders with a turn on the ends. She was poised and photogenic.

Before they reached eighteen, the twins had lived in multiple settings: in motels on the road with their parents, with Alvin's parents, and in four foster homes.

Long Trips

August 1997

Before dawn Judy's family started the drive to visit her in Alabama. In the car, sat Judy's sister, Dottie, her husband, and their children, and Judy's oldest brother, Jimbo. Judy hadn't seen him since 1982.

During the meeting, Dottie studied Judy, while Dottie's daughter appeared disengaged, or maybe tired from lack of sleep. Jimbo struggled with claustrophobia in the windowless room. Dottie's husband, Dean, remained quiet.

Judy practiced conveying what the family must comprehend. Her voice belied the anxiety she experienced when she told them she was running out of appeals and might be executed in the next year.

She warned them that "Reporters may contact you and

say, 'I'd like you to tell me what Judy is *really* like.' Or, and this one got me with Geraldo, 'If you share your story, you can help other battered women.'" Judy laughed nervously.

"I want somebody to know the truth, so when all of this is over, Chaplain Johns is going to write about it. You can trust her. I tell her everything. We trust each other; that is no small thing. Talk to her if you want to. What district attorneys and judges, what no one understands, is the harm this does to families."

I sat beside Judy, and when she could no longer contain her tears, I took her hand. Then Jimbo stood. I expected him to leave the room, overcome by the news and maybe the feeling of walls closing in. To my amazement, he walked to Judy and put his arm around her. She clung to him.

Judy tried to regain her composure. Addressing Jimbo, she said, "You haven't seen me in fifteen years, and I lay this on you!" With her execution looming, she reiterated, "I don't want you in the state of Alabama when this happens."

Dean asked quietly, "Who will be there for you, Judy?"

As repellant as the thought was, I knew I'd be there. But that wasn't a satisfactory answer; I'm not family.

Maybe the family was beginning to think about the probability of Judy's last months. During her incarceration, family visits were infrequent. A trip from Tennessee to Alabama is costly, and entering a prison is rarely a happy thought. When it means confronting a prisoner's impending execution, some are unable to handle that reality. Although death-row inmates are approved one special visit every six months, the officials allowed Judy to have more, showing kindness. Time was running out.[149]

November 1997

The second visit with Judy's children. The day before Thanksgiving.

I arrived at the prison early for Judy's visit with April, Jeremy, their foster mother, Sharon, and her daughter, Camilla. I got a Pepsi and pizza for Judy out of the vending machines. She was a nervous wreck. I asked her how she was feeling about telling the children that she was facing a date probably in the next year? Then I added that they might already know.

"They won't believe it until they hear it from their mom," Judy was adamant.

Then we prayed for God's peace to be within and around each of us. It gave a sense of calm.

During most of their time together, Judy held Jeremy and April's hands. When they stood, Judy put her arm around April. They had a hard conversation about the appeals process, and Judy gave no hint that she didn't want her death sentence commuted to dying in prison. Her children didn't ask.

They moved to easier subjects. April said her granddad spoiled her. If he had a Tab, April wanted a Tab, and she got it. Grandma, Jeremy recalled, made them do a chore, such as straightening up the living room, before going on to what they wanted to do.

I joined the conversation about the adoption of their younger brother, relaying what I could about my conversation with the woman who'd adopted him. She wanted no contact between him and his biological family since he didn't know about them. April wanted to write, but I discouraged that.

Then the conversation moved to teenage issues. Jeremy got an excellent report on the tidiness of his room. Camilla and April shared a small room, and tidiness wasn't a goal. The two girls were enjoying each other.

Their foster mother, Sharon, exhibited an effective blend of parental authority and loving guidance. She arranged with the police and the twins' school principal about media if a date was set for Judy's execution. There was to be no interaction.

April was energetic during the visit, but as we talked outside the prison after the goodbyes, it was as if April had gone into herself; her buoyancy had left. It helped that I had a box of gifts Judy had made for the twins—painstakingly painted Christmas figurines. April wanted to open the presents immediately; Sharon said she could unwrap one.

I felt privileged that April showed me a picture of her and her friends. She said she wanted to show it to her mother but wasn't allowed to take the picture in.

I wanted Jeremy and April to know that the "I love yous" expressed by their mother weren't glib. "She loves you more than her own life. It's what keeps her living."

April's comment came out of her existential situation. "The only trouble I have is boys!" That seemed to break the mood of despondency.

In our conversations Judy characterized family discussions as superficial. "If anything painful is mentioned, it's glossed over. Change the subject to something safe. It may be emotionally difficult for a few minutes, but never for long."

We were talking on the phone and then cut off. Judy telephoned again.

I said, "I hear an edge in your voice."

She said, "You were saying something before we were cut off."

"I'll get back to that. What's going on?"

I could hear her grin as she reacted. "You are the one person in my life I can't get to change the subject. Everyone else will let it slide."

"I am a challenge."

She agreed. "You're a pain."

"I want to be a pain."

Even the discussion about avoiding difficult conversations was a clever side-stepping.

Willow Weep for Us

September 1999

Judy's meetings with some of her siblings and other family members took place on another planet of sorts—near her death row cell. I wanted to experience Judy's kin in their space away from the restrictive setting of a prison, so I contacted the Tennessee family. My interactions with them had been cordial and, of necessity, on the surface. I wanted to continue broadening my understanding of Judy by having them fill in the bigger picture of the growing-up family. How would they describe their father, their mother? What had been their experience of Judy's husband? How did they feel about her crimes? They were agreeable to our meeting.

Three of Judy's siblings would gather at Davey's home, south of Nashville. Then I would drive to see April. She'd been working on her twin brother so the three of us could visit. My phoning Jeremy always got the following response: "We are sorry, but the line is being checked for problems." Judy's family affirmed that, "Whatever April says, Jeremy will do." It looked promising.

Sunday morning, I arrived in a new subdivision at the

home of Judy's brother, Davey, his wife, Amanda, and their children. Trees were sparse, lawns ample. The terrain was flat, and with the near drought, it looked starved for rain.

Amanda greeted me at the front door at 9:05 and invited me in. Little Bit descended on the scene, barking louder than her size. Two children appeared, tow-headed Corinne of three and Jordan of six years in his Garfield T-shirt. "Brian is asleep upstairs."

"I didn't know you have a third child."

"Yes, he's eight months old. Davey was so good to me. He brought me milk all the time." Amanda smiled. "I got sick of it. But we had a ten-pound boy!"

At my initiative, Davey and I exchanged a polite hug. It was hard not to feel I'd already met him through pictures and stories of an earlier, happier time. The house felt comfortable, the furniture amply cushioned. We settled in the living room with the large television screen. I seemed to be the only one distracted by the larger-than-life country music singers.

"Is Bill coming over?" Amanda asked.

"He better be!" Davey said. "I didn't drive thirty minutes to wake him up this morning, not to have him show up. I called Dottie, and she hadn't even gotten up yet. If Bill doesn't come, I'm gonna beat his butt." Davey redialed Bill's number. "No answer; he better be on his way."

I relaxed in a living-room chair and got out a few sheets of hotel stationery. "I think you know that Judy has asked me to write something about her."

"I wish she'd quit worrying about what people think about her!" Though chiding, Davey wasn't critical. Judy had told me that he disliked the idea of a book.

"If you think of anything I ought to include, I'd love for you to write it down and send it to me." I handed Davey the

155

paper and an envelope addressed to me.

Amanda and Davey became absorbed in dividing the Waffle House breakfast he'd picked up on his return from his "wake-up Bill" run. The food got rapt attention from the children.

Davey touched on his childhood. "I was four when my father died. It was tough financially. Home was rough and wonderful. Mama let us do what we wanted to, just not hurt anyone. Judy looked out for me." Then he moved onto a sore subject. "Alvin was a nice guy; he covered well. I was just a kid, but I knew things weren't right. Everyone was uneasy in the room when he was around. He was a fat guy, down on his luck. Judy was heavyset, didn't feel attractive. He robbed her of her life. He was into all kinds of stuff, like forging money orders. Then he forced her to do stuff." Davey added, "He's like Charles Manson."

He didn't linger on those memories. They told me they were going to an airshow in Smyrna. "It's for charity," Davey explained. "I figure if pilots can come down here on their own money, I can give them a few dollars to support the charity."

Davey stewed over Bill's absence, and a second plan developed. They'd lead me to Bill's place. I accepted the hospitality.

Introductions to Bill were quick and informal. His almost wolf-like dog was cordial. "It's the best dog you can have around children. He'll protect them."

Bill and I stood on the sidewalk facing the porch where his young solemn-faced son remained by his mom, Sandy.

"He scares me," Bill nodded toward his son.

"Scares you?" My mind was too nimble.

"Yeah. He's so mature. You can sit down and carry on a conversation with him. He's always been like that."

156

That was a scare I could handle.

Davey joined us.

"You know"—I had to keep saying it—"Judy wants me to write about what happened." Bill and Davey's expressions didn't change. "You probably want that as much as"—I floundered—"a dump truck unloading on your foot." They didn't react to my clumsy analogy.

"It's a good neighborhood," Bill said. "It's safe. But we're between two rough neighborhoods."

We wandered over to one of Bill's rebuilt cars. He talked about his long hours of work. "I fell back asleep in the chair this morning. I was tired; they've been working me hard." He seemed to be explaining, but not apologizing, for the missed reunion, calling forth a more vexing issue. "I told them they could have it; I quit. I got plenty of work here to keep me busy, and I can make more money. Repairing cars. I've been taking cars apart since I was twelve."

The conversation waned. "I want to get a picture of you two brothers," I said.

The two Adams siblings appeared to have outgrown their childhood tussles that drew Judy's interventions.

"We love one another. We may not have much, but we have each other. My children are more important to me than anything else."

The goodbyes were elaborate between the families as two of Bill's children were joining Davey, Amanda, and their children for the airshow.

"Bill, go in there and comb Jordan's hair; he looks like Buckwheat." While hair combing was in progress, the children edged closer to the van. The goodbye ritual began with hugs. When the two boys dashed off, Sandy or Bill called them back. "Oh no, you're not!" One more "bye-bye," hugs, and "gimme fives" finished their leaving.

Bill pulled out his wallet. "If the kids want something to eat—"

Sandy picked up the thread. "Get them a souvenir; yeah, get them a souvenir."

Bill handed Davey some ones.

I walked toward the rented Malibu and looked back to see Bill and Davey engaged in an exchange that appeared serious and private. I wanted to be there. What was so absorbing?

As we got into our cars, Davey called out, "I won't lose you." And he didn't as he led me out of town toward the next stop.

Dottie's accent was thick Tennessee. Her chattiness put me at ease. Across the room, her husband, Dean, sat immobile, watching a show on animals and anthropology, the sound muted. Dean and Dottie's daughter, Josie, was quiet. It was past noon; their older son, James, was sleeping. I didn't flatter myself that he cared about seeing me, but I wanted to be able to report to Judy about all her kin.

Dottie and I fell into an easy rhythm. She told me with pride that she regained her driver's license. For four years, Dottie's driving was curbed after her license was taken away for driving under the influence. She knew she'd asked a lot of her husband since it was extra on Dean to drive her everywhere. "Now I watch every sign and obey every law; I don't want to get stopped again."

After a while, she went to check on James.

Josie and I struck up a conversation about the possibility of their moving. There was talk of buying land from Dean's father, and Josie was concerned about changing schools—not an unusual source of anxiety for a mid-teen. I wondered if she was expressing that to her parents. I didn't know if the quiet demeanor was typical of her personality. I liked that she'd dyed her hair maroon. One way or another, she was expressing a growing sense of identity.

"What do you remember about Alvin?" I asked Dottie.

"Controlling."

Dottie described Judy's behavior and the evidence of abuse. "I could see her face puffy from crying when she came out of the room. He'd call for her, and she'd rush back in. She'd take off his shoes and socks, massage his feet, bathe him. I knew there was trouble. If she were tried now, her punishment wouldn't be as severe."

"I think you're right. But court-appointed attorneys don't always present much of a defense. For the ones who are diligent, the resources from the county or state are minuscule, reducing the capacity to investigate and interview witnesses. For the indigent, there is nothing level about the playing field."

Continuing with my endeavor to get pictures of Judy's family to give to her, I asked Dean if I could take a picture of him. When he agreed, I asked where he wanted to stand.

"By my truck," he said without hesitation.

Dean was proud of his dump truck from work. "'98 model. All the latest technology; not much more effort to operate than a fully loaded automobile," was his description. I liked his sudden vitality.

As the visit neared its end, I was surprised at what Dottie broached.

"When Davey, Bill, and I went to Florida with them …"

I knew the sorry saga of Alvin's coercion of Judy to convince Dottie to have sex with him.

It was my last opportunity to see James. A few days before Christmas in 2016, he was hit as he crossed a highway in Tennessee. He was forty-one. Friends wrote of his gentle and sweet spirit.[150] I sent Judy a card expressing my sorrow at the loss. She told me she'd never before received a card of condolence.

On my late afternoon drive to see April and her fiancé, Eddie, I passed through undulating terrain. Changes in the earth's orbit lit up stretches of land and caused deep shadows beyond the hills. Leaves caught the sun's waning glory. I felt a disconnect between the observed beauty and the harshness of reality.

Against the backdrop of a pro wrestling match on television that Eddie was watching, April and I covered basics. I knew she had to go into work at Applebee's that evening, and I felt an urgency of limited time. She reassured me that she had let them know she couldn't work because of my visit and a paper due for a college class the next day. She was to identify and examine psychological issues raised in a book of fiction.

April helped me understand more about her family. She told me that Uncle Benny took her and Jeremy to see their dad in prison, but April never met her two other uncles.

"How long has it been since you last saw your dad?"

"Not since the fifth grade."

"Do you want to see him?"

"No, not really. Although he was always joking around on our visits."

"Your mom's concerned that she'll poison you against him."

"Well, I've never heard anything good about her from him or his family."

Eddie worked as a manager of a branch mortgage company. He'd moved up quickly. During a television commercial, I asked him if he ever thought a person shouldn't get a loan, even if the person could afford it.

"Yes," he replied. "But I learned early not to put my emotions into it. I've heard every excuse in the world for missing payments. My bosses don't want to hear the excuses. They want their money."

April and Eddie became engaged on New Year's Day and planned to get married in the fall of 2000. She had one more payment on her wedding dress. It had long sleeves because she wanted to wear it when it got cooler.

When I asked if I might take a picture of them, April said, "If you like sunsets, you need to see this one." We went outside for pictures.

Although I desired a family reunion that day, how the day unfolded had a positive aspect. I looked forward to seeing everyone together, and the interaction would've been fascinating. However, as I went house to house, I found advantages to visiting with the families, who welcomed me into their respective locales. Davey and Amanda led me to Bill's. From there, they made sure I found the highway to Dottie and Dean's home. Each of them rearranged their schedules to spend time with me and tolerated my attempts to drill deeper into the dynamics of their years as children.

I focused on the quality of engaging the Adams families and remembering everything I could. Most of the conversations were about life's everydayness: children in and out, dogs and a kitten, televisions playing, and hourly rearranging plans. I hoped the revelations and insights would be just as illuminating as my times with Judy. It was unfair and unrealistic to presume that during a few snatches of conversation there would be the level of trust that Judy and I had fashioned over fifteen years. I couldn't decide if I'd missed the opportunity to be more an interviewer and less a friendly courier of Judy.

Monday morning at the motel, I had a few hours before returning to Nashville for my flight home. Walking outside to the front lobby for the breakfast buffet, I enjoyed the cooler air after record-breaking temperatures for September. I had paper and pen—just in case words started coming. And they did. Back in my room, I sat at my laptop and strained to capture the words and images.

As the flow waned, I looked outside at the placid scene of a small pond. I saw trailer after trailer stretching into the background. My gaze moved, coming to rest on a tree—one of my favorites because of its graceful branches. "Willow, weep for me," musicked into my head. My nose burned; sadness filled me, then stung and watered my eyes. Willow, weep for all the children of the world, the abused and neglected who have no one to weep for them.

Nothing moved outside that window. It could've been a painting. Nothing pushed that tree or blades of scrappy grass to give a suggestion of life.

It was two-dimensional—paralleling my ability to grasp nuances and secrets.

From Life to Death

I admired Warden Shirlie Lobmiller's work ethic and values. Her posture and demeanor comported discipline. Idle chit-chat wasn't part of her day. She let me know in one conversation that when she arrived at work, that was her frame of reference. Nothing about home or the world she inhabited before arriving at the prison or after leaving was to bleed into her professionalism. Several times, through personal tragedies, she proved that to be true.

She could surprise me. One occasion in 1995, she asked me to be present for the visit Judy was to have with her children, the first since she'd been on death row.

I checked in with the front-gate officer, handing over my car keys and driver's license but keeping a pair of sunglasses. The officer said I was not permitted to have the sunglasses. I explained that I'd been having trouble with light bouncing off surfaces, hurting my eyes, and told the officer I needed the glasses. We'd be outside in the visiting yard, and the concrete would spell trouble for my vision. He didn't relent.

Shirlie, who was standing beside me, said, "Do what the officer says."

I promptly, though not happily, laid the sunglasses on the ledge of the officer's window. Warden Shirlie took them. When we passed the third gate on our way to the visiting yard, without a word, she gave them back to me. Typical Shirlie: follow the regulations and then break them when human kindness is a higher value than the rule. While she showed respect for the officer and his following Department of Correction rules, she understood my predicament.

That complex personality met one of the crises of her career.

Warden Lobmiller rode in an ambulance with a bleeding death-row inmate. A few hours later, she called to tell me about Judy's suicide attempt. She wanted me to know before it hit the papers. And hit the papers it did! Judy's near death was catnip for critics.

The front page of the May 1994 *Montgomery Advertiser* blared: "Condemned killer Judith Ann Neelley attempted to cheat the electric chair in a suicide pact ..."[151] The day after the event, another headline, though not as prejudicial, was perplexing. "Even on death row, Judith Ann Neelley hadn't given up on living."[152]

Most readers never knew there were significant inaccuracies in the reporting.

Although the errors may have sprung from incomplete or conflicting accounts, the mistakes intensified the lurid news. "Guards at the prison making routine rounds found Neelley on the floor of her cell, lying in a pool of blood. She'd been on the floor for about fifteen minutes before she was spotted." Error count: four.

She wasn't found in a routine round, and she wasn't on the floor. The officer checked on her at the order of Warden Lobmiller. He went into the outer cubicle of the unit, saw her on her bed, and asked if she was all right. She quietly said she was. He left. He reported that nothing appeared out of the ordinary. Acting on instinct, the warden discovered Judy's mutilated arms. Judy had been cutting for at least ten hours, not fifteen minutes.

In a visit with Judy sixteen years later, there was a moment of remembrance. Her demeanor changed when she talked about that day in 1994. "My left arm was cut to the bone. I was mostly cutting with my right hand. Every time I woke up, I would make more cuts. When I cut with my left hand, it was harder to do."

The futility of existence had been present in Judy since she was a teenager. A chance meeting, exchange of letters, a photograph, and lengthy phone calls came together in a way to end the despair. On a narrow ridge of mental health, Judy slipped and fell.

1993–1994

Deborah was a volunteer in Tutwiler Prison in the nineties. She facilitated a battered women's group and heard about one battered woman in the institution: Judy Neelley. Deborah wanted to meet Judy and pestered officers to let her into death row. She finally got her way. During the exchange through the grille of Judy's cell, Deborah mentioned Reggie, a man who had a terminal illness and felt cut off from friendships. Maybe Judy offered to write him. Maybe Deborah asked. It was an interaction that led to obsession and death.

Correspondence began between Judy and Reggie. He accepted her collect calls. They felt a kinship with one another. His erratic behavior, probably due to a mental illness, produced a lifetime of rejection. They found common ground in the feelings of being judged and misunderstood. The next morsel innocently slipped into place. Reggie's young adult daughter, Melissa, was intrigued by a picture of Judy she'd sent to Reggie. Melissa was disappointed when he told his daughter that Judy was straight. Nevertheless, Melissa wanted to talk when Judy called.

Early in their conversations, Judy sensed Melissa's insecurities and loneliness, coupled with sweetness and a quick wit. To dispel the sadness in Melissa's voice, Judy took on the role of encourager and protector. Melissa told Judy that she was a lesbian, a fact that strained family relations and increased her sense of marginalization. They bonded over a mutual and perilous need to be loved. Unconditionally.

Judy became the most important person in Melissa's life, and over time, that was reciprocated. They developed a fierce and exhilarating devotion, talking for hours and hours as their worlds narrowed to those windows of connection. In the summer of 1993, Melissa began driving through the parking lot of the prison. Although separated by several fences, an outdoor visiting area and razor wire, they were able to wave to one another. If she saw no one in the parking area, she blew the car horn, and Judy put up an "I Love You" sign. It became a nearly weekly ritual.

The relationship moved in a direction Judy didn't desire, but she wouldn't rebuff Melissa. To Judy, it would've been a betrayal. She understood rejection and knew of Melissa's hurts.

Melissa wanted to meet Judy, but requests to have a person put on a visitors' list are scrutinized. The number of people, frequency of changes, and the relationships allowed are limited. Judy made an application for Melissa to be added.

Their introductory visit came on Christmas Eve, 1993.

Judy detailed the day. "I was frustrated because we couldn't touch except to hug. That's allowed when a person comes and when the person leaves. They're very strict. Officers monitor interactions until they see what the relation is between the visitor and inmate." Even before the visits, Judy knew that the intensity of Melissa's feelings was outpacing hers. She spoke with the prison psychologist, "trying to figure out how to right the boat." But Judy was captivated. Melissa's unconditional acceptance of Judy coupled with Judy's fear of hurting her vulnerable friend made for an insoluble dilemma.

"I was constantly trying to slow down," Judy told me. "'Give me time; I'm not ready.' I didn't want her to think it was her, to take it personally. When she first started telling me, 'I love you,' I said, 'I love you as a friend.' I was caught up in a rushing river; no way to stop it. Nothing to grab hold of to slow me down. Eventually, I let go and let the river sweep me away, a rushing river—that was the relationship."

In the prison, Melissa's and Judy's sexualities were gossiped and judged. Religious folk warned Judy that she was in spiritual danger. She made clear her disgust at their homophobia and the hurt she felt from their condemnation. When Melissa visited Judy's family, her siblings were accepting. Melissa was astounded at their response, having experienced rejection in her own family.

Judy knew I support loving relationships between same-sex couples, but I was troubled by the intensity of the bond they'd formed.

They took advantage of the cost of phone calls to and from Montgomery. They could talk for $1.75 with no time limit. Calls might last twelve hours as they shared secrets and mundane conversation. A few times, one or both fell asleep while talking; the line stayed open and didn't cost an additional $1.75.

Then came the bombshell telephone bill.

In April 1994, Melissa was notified that she owed more than seven hundred dollars. The monthly bill had been between thirty and forty dollars. Melissa's job was minimum wage, and Judy had little money to offer. In Judy's words, they freaked; they panicked. Their worlds had been contracting for months. People had been turning against them. Others who cared weren't privy to the depth of their involvement.

"It wasn't just a one-way street. I've never been so loved, so cherished. I never had anyone put someone else ahead of themselves." She smiled in an understated way. "It was hard to get anything done, in terms of doing something for the other one. It was a twenty-four hours a day job trying to avoid hurting her. It was healthy and unhealthy."

With one foot in idyllic attraction and the other admitting that each of their lives, in differing ways, was truncated, they fantasized about the home they'd buy. It would be space to be themselves, untouched by censoring minds.

Melissa and Judy were in danger.

From December to May, between phone calls and seventeen visits they agreed on a day on which they would attempt suicide.

On May 15, 1994, Judy began swallowing the pain pills she'd been hiding. She called to tell me not to come for the day's scheduled session. Whatever explanation she gave, I accepted it, giving it no further thought. Then she started cutting.

I received a letter from Judy on May 18. It was dated April 26, 1994.

> *I just wanted to write and thank you for all that you've done for me. Thank you for caring.*
>
> *I must apologize to you. I know I'll be letting you down soon. Please know that it is not because of your lacking in good advice or counsel. I'm just tired of everything. I give up.*
>
> *There are so many things going on. I can't deal with it anymore. I want out. So by the time you read this, I hope to be just a memory.*
>
> *Thank you for the years of friendship and support. You are a good woman and I've admired you greatly. Please keep working to help offenders and victims. Your work is usually unappreciated, and often unwanted. But I think people need more understanding in this world. You're performing an invaluable service. Don't give up.*
>
> *I wish you all the best. Take care. I give you and your family my love and prayers. God keep you.*

A handwritten note at the bottom was from May 15.

I just got off the phone with you. Forgive me for
the lie, please. I needed the extra time to prepare.
I'll do it tonight. I'm sorry for lying.
* I love you, my friend.*

As with Alvin, Judy was stuck in a closed system isolating her from rational alternatives. With Alvin, meaningful options were occluded. With Melissa, the potency of unconditional love was the elixir.

In our first visit after I was allowed to see Judy, she admitted that if I'd seen her, I would've known she was teetering. "I wanted to tell you of Melissa and my closeness, but I kept everyone in the dark until it was done. It's like going to the doctor and not telling symptoms, in part because you don't want to hear what the doctor says if you're truthful."

Perhaps that was said to assuage my conscience that I hadn't intuited the danger in the entanglement.

The day after her suicide attempt, Judy was returned to the prison and locked in the Green Room for a week, an area of the infirmary where she would, by necessity, be watched like a bug under a microscope.

Seven days later, she was served with a major disciplinary, Rule #62, "Intentionally Creating a Security, Safety, or Health Hazard."

> *On 5/16/94 inmate Neelley did create a security*
> *and health hazard by self-inflicted wounds ... Due*
> *to this behavior, officers had to leave their post to*
> *get medical attention for her. Our duties and the*
> *operation of the institution was halted for four*
> *hours.*

I was shocked and angry. They'd labeled Judy as a hazard to the institution, disrupting the prison's daily routine. How dare an inmate take pills, cut her arm, and almost bleed to death! How dare she inconvenience the staff, causing officers to do their job! They had more urgent duties than saving a person's life. Maybe—how dare she try to cheat the state from putting her in an electric chair!

Judy disputed the charges. "I wasn't trying to create any security hazard. I wasn't trying to create any problems for the prison. I was only trying to stop the pain."[153]

An accused inmate may request a witness at the hearing. Judy asked Dr. Helen Thompson, the prison psychologist, to attend. Judy listed two questions. "In your professional opinion, should I, Judith Neelley, be held responsible for my actions on May 16, 1994, given my mental state at the time? Is it your opinion that I intentionally created a disturbance for the staff?"

Dr. Thompson's answers were written one day before the hearing and attached to the report. She opined that Judy lacked culpability. No she should not be held responsible. "She was in a severe state of depression (despondent, hopeless, etc.) and was not responsible ... She was incapable of conceiving of or carrying out a planned disturbance." She further added, "FYI: Neelley continues to be very depressed. Imposition of further sanctions/restrictions at this time would be detrimental to her mental health."

At the disciplinary hearing on June 2, Dr. Thompson wasn't a witness because it was inaccurately reported that she wasn't present "during the incident." Then "shoulds" follow. "If her state of mine [*sic*] was such that we should have expected this, Dr. Thompson should have reported this prior to the incident."[154]

Dr. Thompson's voice was swallowed up in the wilderness of a penal system. Judy was sentenced to "30 days disciplinary segregation to include the loss of all privileges."

In cramped letters, Judy contested the statement that Dr. Thompson wasn't present. Judy remembered Dr. Thompson's being there and stated that she was incapable of comprehending the effect of her actions and that penalties would work against her recovery. She questioned being a threat to security; she was so weak from loss of blood she passed out as she was trying to move to the wheelchair to be transferred to the Health Care Unit.

She filed an appeal. Denied. Later, it was overturned; however, the damage had been done. When Judy's need for unconditional support was crucial and would've been most effective, it was withheld.

Back on death row, despite her instability, she expressed empathy for her neighbor. The constant checking on Judy was intrusive and meant no privacy for either of them. As part of the punishment, she was under administrative segregation, such as the number of days she could shower and limited telephoning to persons who supported her.

In her letter to me, she stated indignantly, "I don't know when [a visit] could be approved. They're not letting me see anyone right now. 'Security' overrides my need for emotional support. No surprise there." Under the guise of security, her bookshelf and cabinet were pulled. She couldn't have television, or a canteen—all tactics, she argued, were working against a more stable mental state. Then she added with resignation, "Are they making life worth living? Not hardly. But it doesn't matter."

Her handwriting was tight and in small cursive, the style she unconsciously used when depressed and anxious.

Judy was working out the unintended impact on her children and others. She wrote me.

What I did hurt them a lot. I didn't mean to do that. They don't even know me. I didn't think it would much matter to them. But I promised them (along with Mama, my family, my lawyers, and some friends) that I'll never try to kill myself again. And I'll keep my word.

I'll live for my kids. We were just trying to get away from all of the pain, and be able to be together … We wanted it over. We didn't think anyone would be too hurt. I guess we were wrong.

Now it's even worse. She's gone. Chaplain Johns, I need her. I can't believe it came to this. I don't really know how it happened. I just know that part of me died with her. I don't understand why God would let me live but let her die. It's not right. People tell me not to question God. But I do. And I admit I'm angry.

Judy described her state during the visits by the psychologist. "Dr. Thompson would usually see me crying like a baby. I can't stop crying." Dr. Thompson said Judy was better, but she didn't feel better. Her appellate lawyer, Barry Ragsdale, went to see her. On one occasion, he was accompanied by Tim, Barry's assistant. She was allowed to speak by phone with her twins, who were in foster care in Tennessee. But her small world had become smaller.

I was impatient to see Judy, confident that I could "bind up her wounds." It was almost a month before I was permitted a visit. Given the strict limitations that were placed on her, it

172

was a sign of trust that I was allowed to resume our sessions. The first lasted nearly three hours. I got permission to take in Play Doh, hoping she could express herself nonverbally. The most enthusiasm she could muster was to say the Play Doh was interesting.

After seeing Judy, I went into overdrive in shoring up Judy's precarious sense of purpose. After consulting with her, I wrote to the twins' foster parents, requesting more contact between Judy and the teens. I'd met the Chief Medical Officer for the Alabama Department of Corrections, Dr. George Lyrene, and knew of his empathy in caring for the inmates. I wrote him and raised questions. Stitches had been removed from her arm, but it hurt to extend her arm fully. Did she need physical therapy? Crying was incessant. She'd requested pain medication, but it was withheld. Why not medication in a liquid form? It couldn't be stockpiled.

I wrote Warden Lobmiller—always asking for something! This time it was clearance for Judy to have origami paper and a few items returned to her cell. "Because she ruminates incessantly, an idle mind is not in her best interest. I cannot ascertain what is appropriate, but a television and her cabinet might be starters. She has replayed her actions a thousand times and thought about how it has affected others ... But obsessing is not healthy."

In July, the list grew. Judy wanted to have one picture of Melissa and family photos that had been cleaned out of her cell. In retrospect, I question my judgment about a picture of Melissa, but photos of her family would've reminded her why life is held dear. No picture of Melissa.

I wasn't finished. I asked for authorization to bring in art supplies for therapeutic purposes. This was my improbable list: several large sheets of white paper; red, yellow, white, and blue powdered tempera; paintbrushes; three plastic containers for mixing the paints; and newspapers to cover the work area. I was astonished that each item was allowed. I must've been an unwelcome challenge for security.

Drawing on my knowledge of depression, with a tad more confidence than may have been warranted, I reported to Dr. Thompson that Judy was losing weight, had no interest in daily activities, no energy, uncontrolled crying, and sleep disruption. Somewhere, the order for an antidepressant was dropped. No medication was dispensed.

I reached out to the Department of Corrections psychiatrist, Dr. Robert Markush, who treated patients at several prisons. A return telephone call from Dr. Markush was to discuss Judy's treatment. I felt reassured that Judy had not been relegated to a basket of irredeemables.

Almost four months after Judy's attempts to dispel the depression, she wrote about picking up paint and paintbrush.

> *Had an interesting time painting yesterday. It was fun, really. But the things I painted made me realize how depressed I am. Tangible proof, I guess you could say. (As if the pencil sketches were not enough to show my frame of mind.)*
>
> *But in truth it sort of scared me. I saw the rose and butterfly with nothing but contempt. There was no pleasant feeling. No peace. Anger and contempt. That scares me.*
>
> *Why? I don't know. It's just unsettling that pretty, gentle things mean nothing to me. I guess there's so much pain inside that all I see/feel are blackness and depression …*
>
> *Thank you for your visits. It helps me very*

*much to be able to talk to you. I can trust so few
people.*

There were fair days and cloudy days in Judy's struggle to
find meaning in a mean world.

It took six months before she was approved for regular
visits and making limited calls. Blocking her from phone calls
or seeing friends felt cruel and wasn't a cure. Compassion
can cure.

Melissa's death and Judy's failed attempt hung around her
like a mildewed towel. Three months after that loss, Judy's
mother died. She was fifty. Her last year was filled with pain
from cancer, and at first, she couldn't afford morphine patches.
That weighed on Judy, along with the reality that she wasn't
free to give her mother emotional or personal care.

Judy was troubled about the expenses of her mother's
funeral: $3,000. One of Judy's pen pals was Dorothy Wilson,
who belonged to a Church of Christ in Florence, Alabama.
Every month, the church sent five dollars and a book of stamps
to thirteen inmates, including all on Tutwiler's death row. After
the funeral, she contacted Dorothy and asked if the church
would be willing to send the five dollars Judy was receiving
each month to Woodfin Funeral Chapel in Murfreesboro,
Tennessee. A small amount, but at least Judy felt she was
doing something.

The response was positive. Along with the five dollars,
Dorothy sent ten dollars personally. When she could no longer
afford the ten dollars, she was contrite. Judy responded with
gratitude for all Dorothy had done. Each month, Woodfin
Funeral Chapel sent Judy a receipt for the payment. With no
explanation, the receipts stopped. When Judy mentioned to
Dorothy that receipts hadn't been received in months, Judy

received a quizzical response. "She told me to thank Mr. Lowry at Woodfin, and that she did what she did because she wanted to give me peace of mind." Judy was mystified.

She wrote to Lowry and asked why she was no longer getting updates on the bill. She got a receipt. Nothing was owed.

Judy explained:

> *Dorothy paid Woodfin $2,000.00!!! I don't know if it was her money or the church's. Probably the latter because Dorothy does not have that kind of money. Either way it just blows my mind. Two thousand dollars! My brain cannot grasp it. The remainder of the bill had been $2,475. Dorothy paid $2,000.00. But on top of that, Woodfin actually canceled out the last $475. The bill is marked paid in full.*
>
> *Can you believe it? I can't. I just keep shaking my head. Total strangers have paid a funeral bill of almost $3,000. How on earth can I possibly thank people for doing such things? I get kicked in the teeth on a daily basis. Even a small gesture of kindness here is an extreme rarity.*

Anticipating her execution, Judy declared, "I'm going to make sure that my own cremation and everything are paid for before I die! There will be no funeral. My family's expense will be gas money to drive to Alabama to pick up my ashes. That is all."

Going to her mom's funeral was out of the question, but she could picture the plot where her mother was buried. As a child, Judy's mom had taken her to see the gravesite of the mother's best childhood friend, who was named Judy. The child was abused in her family, and her anguished cry to be loved resulted in an accidental death by a self-inflicted gunshot to her stomach. Now that childhood friend and Judy's mom lie about fifty feet apart in a Tennessee cemetery.

~

Interaction with inmates in the general prison population is limited for those on death row. An exception is when an inmate from segregation is in the segregation exercise area next to death row's "patio." Then Judy might have a passing conversation. In February 1995, she spoke with an inmate about her relationship with Melissa. The confidant was inventive. She concocted a novel from a tantalizing short story. In addition to salacious gossip of surreptitious lovemaking, a lie started circulating that Melissa had smuggled in a pocketknife for Judy to cut her wrists, and in the words of an inmate, "They could die and go to hell together."

Another inmate had a suggestion for Judy's revenge. She should grab the inmate's "hair through the fence and smash her head against the fence several times, then come inside and play innocent." Judy decided psychological warfare was the best retaliation. But the lies hurt deeply. In small and tight letters in her journal, Judy wrote about betrayal. "Is the world like this prison? Is 99% of the population in America untrustworthy? God, please tell me it's just the prison life and the people I've lived around. Don't let life be like this. And don't let me grow hard and cold."

At Judy's request, I began the process of contacting Melissa's mother, Allison. Judy offered to answer any questions Melissa's mom had and to send pictures of Melissa as a child that she had given Judy. I found the name of her pastor and sent him a letter with a letter to Allison. I had two reasons for not sending the letter directly. First was that she might be disturbed that Judy had her home address. Second, I trusted in her pastor to have knowledge of the appropriateness of hearing from Judy. Would Allison be comforted by the offer or further harmed?

I wrote, "Essentially, all of Judy's appeals have been exhausted. She estimates in two to three months there could be a date, or the execution. One of Judy's concerns is that Allison may have questions that Judy could answer about Melissa from the short time they knew each other."

After many calls and letters, I was instructed to send the pictures to a friend. She would give them to the mother when appropriate. I sent them, but we heard no more about Judy's offer.

As Judy approached the first anniversary of Melissa's death, her remorse deepened. Questions about God's existence joined her mix of feelings. She worried unnecessarily about my reaction when she expressed doubt. "I don't want you to stop liking me, and I don't want to disappoint you." But she wanted to be true to herself. "It scares me to think of a god in control, and it scares me to think there isn't a god." Then, in her ability to mock herself, she added, "Make up your mind, Judy."

Melissa was the subject of Judy's dreams as she romanticized their relationship and was haunted by the loss. Dreams gave her comfort that evaporated on awakening. On the second anniversary of Melissa's death, Judy composed reflections:

> *While listening to our old songs earlier this morning, I sat on my bed with my eyes closed, holding a possible instrument of death. I realized that I was fiddling with it much like people do in the movies, messing around with a gun before they put it to*

their head and pull the trigger. Contemplating. Considering. I put the razor down. Will I use it before the day is out? I doubt it. I can't be 100% sure about it. Besides, I figure when my time is up I'll die and not before—no matter how hard I try. I pray for death to come soon, can't possibly be soon enough for me. I wonder why I'm still here. What could possibly be the reason God lets me continue to draw breath and take up space? Is it that I have not been punished enough? I continue to live in order to suffer? Miss you Melissa. Two years ago love died. No one has ever loved me as you did, Angel.

On the third anniversary, Judy noted that a song they shared or even the blowing of a curtain would make her "catch her breath in remembrance. The pain is fleeting now. I admit that with a certain amount of guilt. It's as if I love her less because I don't hurt so much. I hope she would understand and forgive." A few paragraphs later, she acknowledged that the hurt wasn't fleeting.

It is still so painful. I do not try to focus only on the good memories to avoid pain. I think about the good and bad. I try to be an objective observer, to analyze the entire situation ... Healing. That's the word that comes to mind. In some ways I welcome it. In others it makes me very sad (and guilty) because I equate "healing" with "letting go" or "forgetting." Leaving behind. Moving on. I don't want to let her go. She meant so much to me. Literally more than life itself. Truly I had never realized how alone I was until she came into my life. A part of me died

with her and I'll never get it back.
My passion, my zest for life is gone. I have happy
times, the happiest being with my children. But it
is never enough. Will I ever want to fight for life
again, raging against life's injustices? I doubt it.

During a March 1998 visit, Judy was wistful. "When I attempted suicide, and I was lying here in this bed, and I thought I was dying, there was this … relief, freedom when nothing else mattered; all of this was going to be over. Although I was aware of everything around me, it was like …" Judy looked beyond the walls of her cell. "I can't put that into words." Her left hand made a small circling gesture as she closed it. "It is like a memory I can't fully hold. There was no more struggle. Everything was fine. The world will go on. I don't have to fight anymore. Someday, my family would accept and go on." Judy's focus returned to the cell. "I was wrong.

"It wasn't a case of it doesn't matter anymore. I reached that in the hospital. Lying here, there was no fear, no second thought that I shouldn't be doing this. It wasn't so much I desire death. I desire peace and an end to the suffering. I know that there's suffering in life, but it's not supposed to be unrelenting. That has been my life."

I held her words undisturbed.

Judy looked at me, "I hesitate to tell you those things; it may sound like I'll go there again. It wasn't a fearful experience. I remember it fondly; emotions were sweet. It sounds strange and twisted. Maybe some of that was due to medication. I'd taken a lot of stuff." Her ruminating tone changed to one of determination. "I don't want you to think I'll do it again. I'm not suicidal. I'm just tired."

Years later, as we talked, she untangled the forces at work

at the intersection of their lives. "At first, I was trying to help. Then it moved into more. I blame myself for it. I'm co-dependent; I'm unhealthy."

"It's good that you take responsibility," I said, "but you mentioned she'd made a suicide attempt before you met."

"Oh, I have no doubt she would've succeeded, eventually. But I'll always blame myself. It's on my shoulders. I can't negotiate relationships. I'll stick by that. I don't expect that to change. I don't have any counseling to help me figure this out."

Pills and Blood

Fall 2010

I took advantage of being in Birmingham for a sabbatical to visit Judy. But I ran into roadblocks. Because my husband and I had moved to New York, I was no longer on Judy's visitor's list. Attempts to be approved to see her were going in circles. I spoke with Shirlie Lobmiller for advice. Finally, I got on Judy's list.

Shirlie began at the prison in 1981 as assistant warden, a title later changed to deputy warden. She retired from Tutwiler in 1996, after serving as warden. I was chaplain for six years during her tenure.

After the visit with Judy, Shirlie and I met for lunch at the Hog Rock Bar-B-Q in Wetumpka. Then we adjourned to the tranquility of Gold Star Park. Set along the Coosa River, the small park invites people to slow down and wander the riverbank and listen. Birds sang the entire time Shirlie and I talked at a picnic table. The peacefulness of setting and sounds contrasted with our conversation. Shirlie and I had never talked about how close Judy came to killing herself. Sixteen years after Judy longed to end her life, I heard the story of that day from a unique perspective.

Shirlie was accustomed to being interviewed and recorded. At times, her recounting was detached and unvarnished. When she moved to editorializing, her opinions were not all flattering. Her low, southern accent was measured and unhurriedly fluid. In her usual attire, nothing was out of place in dress and demeanor. She spoke officiously.

"I am Shirlie Lobmiller Jensen, former warden at Julia Tutwiler Prison for Women."

In a formal and cool tone, she told of Judy's pending arrival in 1983. "We'd been expecting this inmate, because there was a lot of publicity with the high profile of crimes that were rehashed daily in the newspapers. Her attorney was well known.

"She'd put a lot of reliance on her attorney and him becoming, I would have to say, infatuated with Judy. I don't know, but there was a connectivity in her experience. She said they had a way of connecting by mental telepathy at an arranged time; she'd hold a certain object and think of him, and he'd hold a certain object and think of her. This is coming from her, not coming from her attorney. I'd have him thoroughly searched when he came in. I don't know why I didn't trust her attorney." She laughed heartily. "That was a strange relationship, according to what Judy conveyed to me and all that came out in public record in newspapers."

I agreed that the interactions between them crossed lines of lawyer-client. "My guess is he was trying to break her attachment to Alvin. Maybe there were genuine feelings on her part, his part. I think she was looking for male affirmation."

Lobmiller nodded. "It could have been, but Judy was a very attractive lady at that time, outward appearance. Mr. French would have to answer for himself. Judy would have to answer for herself. Mine is from a strictly outside observation as an authority person in charge of her care, custody, and control, and her well-being during the time of her incarceration."

She turned to the relationship between Alvin and Judy. "But the internal part of Judy had to be as corrupt as there ever was to allow the manipulation of a man in her life to make her feel that she was obligated to do these things for him. Somehow, she believed she had a commitment to him to do such heinous things. And then whether she'd want to lay all the blame on him or to accept the fact that those were some of her feelings, that she had animosity, or those anger feelings."

Without a verbal connector, she segued into an institutional crisis. Her tone held no hint of what was to come.

"On one memorable day, I was in my office and got a call from the Sheriff's Department in North Alabama in the Lookout part of Alabama." The date was May 16, 1994. "The sheriff had a letter in hand that indicated Judy Neelley and the young lady who befriended Judy ... had an agreement to simultaneously commit suicide. Judy was to do it by one method, and the person in the cabin or the cottage in another manner. He indicated that the suicide note was found by the body, or the letter was found among the things that belonged to the person who'd shot and killed herself in the cabin. He was trying to find out if Judy Neelley had done anything that morning.

"At that point, I called for an officer, a male, and sent him down to the death-row unit to check in on Judy Neelley, to see if Judy was okay ... The officer went down. He walked up to the iron-grille door and spoke to Judy. She was lying on

183

the bed. She was covered with a white sheet, according to the officer. He asked Judy how she was, and she said she wasn't feeling good this morning. So he said, 'You are okay?' She said, 'Yes. I'm fine.' He reported back to me that he figured she might be lying down because she was on her monthly. The officer didn't disturb her further."

Shirlie informed the sheriff that she'd also go and check to see if she found anything in Judy's cell indicating her intention to commit suicide. Shirlie hastily asked the prison psychologist, Dr. Thompson, to go with her. Then, with an officer as back-up, she had him open the inner door into Judy's cell.

Shirlie found her as the officer reported, with the sheet pulled up to her chin. "When I walked into Judy's dormitory room, I asked her, 'Are you sure you're okay, Judy?' and she said, 'Yes, I'm fine.' But her voice sounded weak, different from what Judy's voice normally would sound, and so I said, 'We'll see,' and I pulled the sheet back. When I pulled the sheet back, there she lay in puddles of blood with both of her arms slashed wide open … She'd found something that she'd jaggedly cut with, and they were just horrendous cuts that reached literally from the top of the hand on the inside part of the arm all the way up to the elbow. There are scars on her body today. Why she hadn't already bled to death is beyond my human ability to comprehend with the amount of blood that was there, but no puddles of blood on the floor … But when she moved, the blood came out. There was all this blood … I said, 'Judy, what have you done?'" Shirlie's voice dropped lower and quieter. Her words were measured and tinged with sadness as she repeated Judy's words: "I tried to kill myself."

"At that point, I knew the compact agreement note was in fact true, and I immediately told the officer to contact health care and have them call an ambulance."

Instinctively, Helen Thompson started to go to Judy, but Shirlie stopped her. She was emphatic. "You can't go in there. It's a crime scene."

Shirlie and an officer rode with Judy in the ambulance to the local hospital. Prison regulations stated she should've been put in chains, but Shirlie didn't follow the regs. "How do you chain a person whose arms are split wide open and chain that to a belly chain which regulations would call for in the case of a death-row inmate being moved outside the institution to a public health facility …? There was no way you could've handcuffed her and certainly no need to put leg irons on her, because it would only have made it more difficult for us to move her to get her onto the gurney for the ambulance …"

Her inflection changed as she confessed artfully, "So I bear the responsibility for the public to know now and forever more, and the DOC also, through my public admission of the fact of this documentation, that I allowed Judy Neelley to be carried to the hospital without the leg irons on or the belly chain with handcuffs."

The hospital administered activated charcoal to counteract the overdose. I learned later that Helen Thompson had gone to the hospital and remained with Judy until she went into surgery to suture her wounds. The hospital's treatment for suicide was to stabilize. She was hospitalized for one day, during which security was posted every minute of the day and night. Long-term treatment was left to the prison.

I was curious about Shirlie's breaking the Department of Corrections regulations on chaining a death-row inmate. Knowing that regulations can override reason, I asked, "Did anyone question you at the time or just accept the fact that you were in charge?"

"Everybody accepted that I was in charge, because they

were so traumatized when they came and saw what I was already involved in. The officer that'd gone down previously and checked was just blown away that he hadn't gone inside the cell and made the check that I made.

"I probably orally reprimanded him for not making a more direct search of the person's being and body. He felt he was doing what was right. God, in his wisdom, sent me down there as quickly as he did after I hung up the telephone that her life was saved, and I didn't have to deal with that as an accomplished suicide on her part."

"Did she protest your taking her to the hospital?"

"Oh yes. She did. She didn't want to go to the hospital. She said, 'Just leave me alone. I want to die.' I asked her if she had an agreement with so-and-so to do this at the same time. She said, 'Yes.'" Shirlie's voice slowed. "I don't remember if I told her that the girl was dead. Knowing me, I wouldn't have blurted that out to her. But I'm sure," she said with a chuckle, "that I discussed it with her at length later, because it was something that had to be discussed. She'd held to her part of the bargain she was attempting to do, but the girl had gone ahead in taking her life."

Preparing to Die

"Kill me. I'm tired of hurting."

1997

With appeals down to two, Judy dreamed of a calculating merchant of death. She wrote:

186

*There was a man. Tall, white. I guess he was 6'4"
or so. Clean shaven. Baby face. The man had been
sent to kill me. I didn't know him.*

*I was in a large room. Officer Jones was there,
as well as another person.*

*The man who came to kill me didn't say one
word. He had a slight smile on his face, which was
rather unnerving. But he made no sound.*

*He kept trying to attack me, using slow moves
that I was usually able to dodge. He didn't rush
at me or yell. No fast punches. No weapons. He
intended to kill me slowly with his bare hands.*

*I was calling to Ms. Jones, trying to get her to
help me. She would look up at me with a smile,
then look away to continue her conversation.*

*The man grabbed me and lifted me off the
floor. He had me around the waist squeezing the
breath out of me. We were face-to-face. He wore
that Mona Lisa smile.*

*I kept hitting him in the head and face, but
my blows obviously had no effect at all. Didn't faze
him.*

*When I was about to die, he let me go. I stood
gasping for breath, trying to clear my head. He
waited until I could move, then he came at me
again.*

*The man was slowly maneuvering around me.
I knew I would die slowly in his hand. I knew I
had no help.*

*I didn't fear. I was frustrated at my ineffective
resistance.*

And no one cared.

I wrote Judy:

> *So much is troubling about your dream. 'He*
> *intended to kill me slowly with his bare hands.'*
> *A looming date, and then the time comes—the*
> *protracted process completed.*
>
> *All a slow death. The fact that Ms. Jones was*
> *present but disinterested reminds me of the way*
> *people can react to a prison execution. You were*
> *facing this death alone. "And no one cared." To me,*
> *those were four words of desolation.*

I wondered if the man was a mix of an unknown executioner and Alvin. Judy and others spoke of Alvin's engaging grin. The man's being clean shaven and having a baby face mirrored Alvin's chubby youthfulness. She noted the cool way the man went about his job, how he tempered his menacing movements. Alvin didn't yell at Judy, a disconnect with his behavior that was alarming in its methodical coldness.

~

In her journal Judy quoted Socrates:

> *"The hour of departure has arrived, and we go our*
> *separate ways, I to die, and you to live. Which of*
> *these two is better?"*

Her memory of the quote was accurate, omitting, "Only God knows."

She wrote:

I have no fear of death. To me it would be a release from this living hell of existence. Not just of life on death row, but mostly a release from the torturous memories and bitter regrets. Oh so many regrets. It would be over. Finished at last. Peace.

But what of my loved ones? How will my precious children deal with it? My siblings, aunts, uncles, cousins. My dear friends, of whom I am blessed with many. I don't want anyone to hurt because of my passing. How could I minimize their heartache?

On a visit in the summer of 1997, Judy spoke defiantly. "I want the people I love to be long gone from the prison before my execution. I want to invite the judge, DA, and Alvin Neelley for a final stand. I want to face Al and say with my eyes, unspoken confrontation. I'm not trying to hurt. I don't hold a grudge against Judge Cole; he did what he thought he should do. But I want all of them to see me. I'm not looking for a reaction. It's about my standing up, saying you've hurt me; you haven't broken me."

Her stoicism diminished but didn't disappear.

"I've done the best I can in terms of the crimes. Now I need to comfort and protect loved ones the best I can. It won't be much. If it's harder on the children to see me more often, then I don't want them to come. How many people get a chance to say goodbye? It's a unique opportunity. People who are terminally ill may be in too much pain, their mind not right to be able to say goodbye. I've been preparing for fifteen years."

Judy knew an appeal to the governor for clemency was ongoing.

"I won't take life without the possibility of parole. I have thought about it a lot. I can't imagine waking up in this nightmare having to live all the things that happened, can't be with children, siblings. Be as if someone had tied me like a bungee jumper hanging over a pit of crocodiles. Exhausting. It never ends: the day-to-day insanity of prison. It's not like a broken bone that heals.

"If my children needed me, if there were some way I could help them, I would take life without parole. Not for others. It's a choice I don't want to have to make. If I am deciding on what is best for me, then it would be death. If I didn't have children, there would be no hesitation. Now I am in limbo. A mother in prison the rest of her life? Part of me wants to know how they feel. Then, maybe I don't."

We worked on the letter to friends in which she explained that her appeals were near an end. I suggested that people might like to support Judy, that to receive such a letter and feel impotent would make it even harder. She asked for an idea.

"How about asking people to pray that you'll have strength?"

"I pray for others, but I don't think God much hears prayers for me. You know, I don't have any trouble being completely honest with God. I reveal everything to God. My problem is that I don't trust God to do anything for me—to answer my prayers. Not a healthy relationship, huh?"

I studiously looked out the door onto the exercise area, then gestured upward in despair. "God, I've tried to teach her better than that."

Judy's laugh was contagious. She tried to "undo" her statement a bit. But I continued to show mock hopelessness.

After the visit, Judy wrote me.

I thank you for our visit last week. You are the only one I can talk to rationally about my death to face this and not pretend that it will not happen. Everyone else wants to deny it, ignore it, etc. Of course, there is a small chance that I'll not be executed. But I need to prepare. You understand and allow it. How can I thank you for that?

I know it has to be extremely difficult and painful. I am very sorry for putting you through this. I feel that I am being selfish. Don't tell me that I'm not because we both know that I am. If I were decent I would handle this alone and keep you out of it. But I admit that I need you. I'm not strong enough to do this alone.

I just want to crawl into a hole and hide. I don't want the responsibility of trying to prepare everyone. I'm already exhausted and emotionally unstable … How can I deal with this?

I wanted to tell her: don't hide; don't handle it alone. I wanted to impress on her that solitary subsistence was an insane idea. I wanted her to realize that I was awed by her toughness and compassion. That wasn't what she needed. She'd let me know I was meeting her needs.

Awake. Watched. Sleeping. Watched. Awake. Watched. Judy was existing in a fishbowl. She wanted it all to stop. The sliver of hope she could muster was that people who cared for her would accept that she yearned for death to release her.

One request Judy had for her memorial service was to play the song "Broken Wing" sung by Martina McBride. Judy described the meaning. "It's about a woman torn down by a man, abused." Even with his degradation, her broken wing doesn't prohibit her singing or soaring as she escapes him. That escape is ambiguous: did she leave or commit suicide? Judy could relate to the music and find comfort and similitude in the lyrics.

Psychologically and spiritually, Judy wrestled with her failings and sniffed around the consequences of inner scrutiny.

On a visit in 1998, she asked, "Am I pretty messed up?" Before I could answer, she jumped in. "Don't answer that!"

"Do you want my response?"

In a lighter manner, Judy replied, "If you say, 'no,' then I'd say it's true. But if you say 'yes,' it would hurt my feelings." She sighed. "Just when I think I'm getting things in order, I realize I haven't dealt with it that much."

"I respectfully disagree; I see a big difference."

"To me, I am making progress. Then, when I think I'm halfway up the hill, I look and the hill seems steeper; more obstacles. The summit much further away. I know I've made a lot of progress, which I wouldn't have done if it weren't for you. It's like there's never enough: putting out this fire, got another raging inferno."

I told her about a time when I asked for a reprieve from doing God's will. "There was a day in the chapel when I complained, 'God, enough already. I need a plateau for a while. I can't keep on climbing all the time.' Something had happened that would require spiritual stretching in my response. I didn't want to stretch, and I wanted God to give me time off for good behavior. I'd get back to growing, just not at that moment."

Judy was philosophical. "I believe in my heart that life is beautiful and precious, and it saddens me people take it for granted. I see at the same time—hatred, endless misery. I don't want to live in a world like that; I don't see any value of living. I can't explain."

I asked, "Do you mean for yourself?"

"Not just me ... People so busy trying to make ends meet, so concerned about raising family, paying bills, they don't have time to visit a friend, or go for a walk in the country, just to breathe the fresh air, listen to children laughing. Am I making sense?" Judy rubbed her shoulder. "Some in my family won't accept that I'm not getting out, or that I'll be executed. No one knows what it's like if they haven't lived it."

"If I say something now, may I retract it later?" I felt like a traitor to Judy's family and friends. "I want to do what I can for you to die the way you want."

My assurance was crude. Judy didn't *want* to die by being strapped into a chair, "Yellow Mama" to Alabamians. Electrodes attached on the head and leg. Two thousand volts of electricity pounding the head to kill the brain. The second to incinerate organs.[155]

Judy's response to my inarticulate assurance was a soft, "Thank you."

Both of us were near tears. I took her in my arms, and we held each other. She cried for a long time. As I released her, I interpreted my rash statement, "Which means, I'll be with you."

"I guess I need to remember people's desire for me to live. You may change your mind later. It means a lot to know I'm not alone. I thank you for that. You support me as a friend, one who understands."

As a pastor and family member, I've been with people

who were dying. I try to be present in a way that affirms the person's life and supports the transition. Capital punishment, conversely, is a forced and grueling legalized killing. The state's actions are egregious. Always looming was my promise to be with Judy to the end. The ordeal horrified me. I had to be there. But I had no confidence I could be present in ways she would need. What would that even mean?

It would not be about doing, but about being.

The time for doing had passed. The time would come for shared tears and silent presence.

~

10.

Mercy over Judgment

*For judgment will be without mercy
to anyone who has shown no mercy;
mercy triumphs over judgment.*
James 2:13

Appeals after appeals were written, delivered, and denied. Judy was having conversations and disagreements with people who said they wanted to try for the impossible. Rather than the electric chair, clemency was a prolonged death sentence inside a prison.

Clemency doesn't mean a person isn't guilty. Clemency doesn't mean someone escapes repercussions for the offense. Clemency is mercy and is predicated on the offender's remorse and rehabilitation. The crime isn't forgiven. The act of clemency is a way to assert that there are reasons for leniency beyond a strict adherence to the laws. It's a form of justice that's often problematic for victims of the crime to accept.

~

As director of the Alabama Prison Project, Lucia Penland worked with inmates and lawyers to unearth mitigating factors in a person's crime.[156] Her focus could become laser-like, and when she decided it was time to put together a clemency packet for Judy, the strong personalities clashed.

Lucia knew resources and people who were potential allies in a campaign. National Clearing House for Battered Women. Amnesty International. Whatever was done, there had to be an effective campaign in Alabama to recast Judy's image. The executive director of the State Coalition Against Domestic Violence advised a campaign to reacquaint people with issues of domestic violence.[157] A public defender in New York advised a born-again pitch that was religious and chronological. Judy Adams the little girl to Judy Neelley the murderer to divorced Judy Adams. Although Judy initiated the divorce, and it was granted in December 1983, she couldn't escape the toxicity of the Neelley name.

Reporters could assist if they were impartial. Tom Gordon, *The Birmingham News,* covered the trial. A *Mobile Register* reporter did a piece on the execution of the second man in Alabama after reinstatement of the death penalty.[158] Talking to reporters was a nonstarter for Judy. She'd heard their pitch to convince her to give an interview—I want people to know the real Judith Neelley—and knew it was a ploy.

Names were tossed around, and Ruth Graham was mentioned as an advocate for an inmate's religious rebirth. She'd taken a public stance to save the life of Velma Barfield, a death-row inmate in North Carolina, because of her reported religious conversion.

As to promoting a conversion angle, that was also a firm refusal from Judy. The case of telegenic Karla Faye Tucker, sentenced to die in Texas, was generating full-scale media assault in 1998. If her religious redemption from a brutal murderer to a blessed believer didn't score clemency points, nothing Judy espoused would persuade a governor.

Judy made a distinction between religious and spiritual. "I know how spiritual I am, but I'm not religious. Whether or not society ever forgives, I know God has. That's enough. I still have to live with what I did. I'm happy Karla Faye has found peace earlier than I. Not even sure I have found peace."

The aversion Judy had to media coverage didn't hamper quiet efforts to strategize.

One name emerged with national standing to present a credible argument against the death penalty. She neither shunned nor sought fame or infamy. Sister Helen Prejean took the spotlight to advocate for humans caught in the machinations of a criminal justice system that puts people to death.

Sister Helen is a member of the Sisters of St. Joseph of Medaille in New Orleans. As part of their commitment to the disadvantaged, Sister Helen began corresponding with a man on death row, Patrick Sonnier. That led to her visiting him and becoming his spiritual adviser, giving her troubling knowledge of the dehumanization of persons in prison. Out of that awakening came her best-selling book, movie, and opera, *Dead Man Walking*.

Prejean was invited to Alabama in 1998 through the Alabama Prison Project. She was the featured speaker at First Baptist Church in Montgomery. The next day, she spoke at a clergy luncheon at St. Bede's Catholic Church. In my introduction of Sister Helen, I made sure I pronounced her name correctly. "Prejean" was no problem. It had become a familiar Louisiana surname. But her "first" name, "Sister", could be the gaffe. It was "Sista," as she pronounced it, straight out of her Louisiana heritage.

Sandwiched between those events were two other meetings: one with Judy at the prison, and the second with the legal adviser for Alabama's governor, Fob James.

The meeting with Judy included Sister Helen, Barry Ragsdale, Lucia Penland, and me. I arrived early. In response to my asking her if she was nervous, Judy typed on my laptop, "Yes. I've met famous people before, but not someone that I admire. Let's face it, Geraldo is famous, but not the least bit admirable. Ha. Oops. Nervous laugh. Ha. I think I shouldn't write today because I'm really not thinking straight."

Barry and Judy had an easy camaraderie. It wasn't long after his arrival that they jousted. Judy chided Barry for some insignificant lapse. "You're full of empty promises." To which Barry smilingly quipped as he turned to me. "Isn't it interesting? With you present, she plays the victim."

Judy countered, "Barry has a soft heart. He hides behind humor." Then, directing her words to Barry, she said, "You do care."

Soon, all had settled into a candid exchange. Prejean's caring, sprinkled with a lighthearted manner, put Judy at ease. "Judy, how long have you known each other?"

"I met Chaplain Johns when she became chaplain in 1984. In 1989, I took confirmation classes with Lucia. Then I joined the Episcopal Church in 1990."

Barry interjected waggishly, "I got appointed."

"That's true. But you stayed even after I screwed up." Judy

addressed Prejean. "Four years ago in May, I attempted suicide."

In her signature calm manner, Prejean observed, "I'm glad you didn't succeed. If you have to fail at something—"

Judy interrupted, "What surprised me was how angry people were at me for what I did."

I parried. "I wasn't angry. I was sad that I hadn't been more in tune with your needs."

Barry added, "You see, empathy is her business. I was mad! Here I am busting my butt to save you, and you try to kill yourself!"

"May 16. I tried taking pills. Then I tried cutting."

Barry revealed his concern while couching it starkly. "After being chained to a wheelchair, her arm looked like cuts done by an apprentice carpenter."

Sister Helen shifted the conversation. "You've got more friends than a lot of people I see, a lot of good friends. I have a feeling you're worth it."

Judy's rejoinder brought laughter. "I'll quote you on that, but that's debatable. To me, there are worse things than death. The main reason for not asking for clemency, outside of the chance I might get it, is I don't want to live like this."

Sister Helen probed. "What is it about life without parole that you don't think you can handle? How would life be different if you got life with no possibility of parole?"

"Many things would be different. Now I can't go to the chapel. I live in a single cell, except for the small exercise yard. As hard as that can be, I'm not sure how I would do in population. Prison is a never-ending ordeal: changing rules. I still have trouble dealing with what I did. My crime is horrible. Every day, I face condemnation from staff and inmates. I'm tired of getting beaten up." Judy was struggling to keep composure. "Some would like to be there to fry me.

I'm probably a little paranoid. I read into their expressions. I don't like being paranoid."

Sister Helen ruefully noted, "The death penalty is a freeze frame. You're the worst act in your life. That becomes who you are."

Redirecting the conversation, Judy brightened. "We have the privilege of growing vegetables. We've gotten big tomatoes and cucumbers. Can't get carrots to grow."

Sister Helen was astonished. "I've never met anyone who could grow plants; forget prisons! You can grow plants!"

Barry knew how rules could change. "Warden Jones: today tomatoes, tomorrow marijuana."

Judy raised a question. "How many people on death row, a rough percentage, deny guilt?"

Barry weighed in, "On death row, thirty percent say they didn't do it."

"Since reinstatement, about seventy-eight have come off the row because they were innocent," Prejean added.

Barry needed to know how to position his legal work. "If you had a choice today, would you choose life without parole?"

"If I have the choice of living a nightmare for forty years, let me go or execute me. I'd love to be free. Isn't going to happen."

Barry pushed for clarity. "You don't want to ask for clemency because you're afraid you will be given clemency? Fob James is unpredictable!" In mock relief, Barry asked, "Does this mean I don't have to write appeals?"

"Okay with me." With a grieved expression, Judy asked, "Am I being selfish? Not wanting clemency?"

After Sister Helen reassured her that it was her choice, Barry somewhat adroitly asked, "Are you working on getting mad at us for not agreeing?"

"I'm not getting mad. I'm scared." Tears came. "My

experience is that if I don't do what y'all want, you'll drop me." Quickly regaining her balance, she added, "I ought to get points for admitting that."

Barry gave her two points.

I wanted to know the number of possible points to which she should aspire. I laughed at Barry's unattainable, "Three hundred!"

Judy continued, "I over-analyze. I have a lot of time."

Gently redirecting the conversation, Sister Helen asked, "Do you have any family, Judy?"

Judy told of her siblings, but focused on her mother. "My mother died August 1994. I saw her in ninety-three. Barry paid for her bus ticket to come here." As Judy paused, I reflected on Barry's kindheartedness.

"My mom was a strong woman. She had cervical cancer. At the end, she was getting morphine.[159] I have twins. I would expect them to be angry, angry at the world. They've suffered a lot. They'll have a hard time; they may handle it better than I."

"Do you think it would be rougher for your kids?"

"Yes. They may think I'm choosing death over them. Kids have grown up without me. I have no contact with my youngest son. I wasn't with them. Even if I get clemency, I won't be able to be there. Endless waiting."

"I've been visiting in prisons for years," Prejean responded. "The best gift we can give is presence. If you're here, you can give them your presence, wisdom for whatever is going on in their lives. Consciousness is a gift. I've been with people who couldn't articulate. There is no acuity. It is a blind, dull thing."

Prejean empathized. "I haven't suffered abuse as you have; yet you're loving; you're intact. To me, you're like an incredible thing of God's grace. You tend to put your experiences down. I have a hunch if you change your mind, it will be because of your kids."

"It's my weakness. When they were here in November, I was afraid they'd come to ask me to try for clemency. When they were here in March, we talked about clemency; it could mean another fifty years. Dying is easy." Judy exhaled forcefully. "Life is hard."

Sister Helen contemplated the uncivilized machinery of capital punishment. "I've been through four executions. Once I'm gone, I go over it in my mind."

Barry wondered aloud if it was worse being at an execution of someone with whom you've worked or not being there.

I responded that it would be worse not to be there, even as the thought of it was repelling. In her writing, Sister Helen had said that after one execution she'd thrown up. I told her that was oddly reassuring. Then I suggested it was throwing up demons of death row.

"It wasn't quite all; it was a beginning," Helen conceded.

Lucia reiterated her offer to put together a clemency petition. Although unusual, it was possible that a judge, a prosecutor, juror, or other official could also be supportive of clemency.

Judy asked Barry, "Have you heard from Judge Cole?"

"Put yourself in his place? Would you call?"

"No. Of course we all know he overrode the jury, but I'm more angry with the DA. He attacked me! I would really like to see him. He was one of the major factors in my life. He was so opposed to me."

In feigned criticism, Barry said, "You have a handicap. You're too smart. The lunacy committee believed you were too smart to be abused."

Looking around at us, Sister Helen asked, "Why do they stick with you?"

Judy began cataloging. "Lucia is tenacious." Gesturing to me, "I don't know. I guess she loves me. She always comes on my birthday, June 7. With Barry, he lets me in on his life, tells me about his family."

"That's the nicest thing she's ever said," Barry quipped. "Just recently, in talking about clemency, she got angry. I'm working my buns off, trying to save her life."

Sister Helen's assessment brought out laughter: "All these people won't give up. It's just your luck."

"I realize I may change my mind. I haven't said absolutely no to Lucia about clemency. But I need to prepare for what will probably happen. I don't see how any of you have the strength of character to do this over and over. I don't know if I could walk with people to their death. I have an enormous amount of respect and admiration for you."

As time for the visit neared the end, Sister Helen told Judy, "I really appreciate getting to meet you." Then she turned to Barry. "Are those oysters on your socks?"

"I think they're paisley."

Prejean bent down and eyed them carefully. In her musical alto voice, she asked, "Are you sure you've got them on right side out?"

In 1994, Montgomery Attorney Julian McPhillips Jr. was in the Alabama Supreme Court waiting to give an argument for his client. The case before the justices was familiar to him: Judith Ann Neeley. Her lawyer, Ragsdale, argued that she'd been denied due process. The appeal was turned down, but Judy's story and the persuasiveness of Judy's legal case interested Julian.

I asked McPhillips to set up a meeting with Governor James during Sister Helen's time in Montgomery. The morning after visiting Judy, five of us gathered to speak with Jim Main, the governor's legal counsel.

We were in varying degrees of nervousness or composure. I was apprehensive. Lucia Penland, Sister Helen, Julian, my college-age daughter, Michele, and I made up the delegation. We underscored the governor's authority to grant clemency as a sacred privilege. It wasn't long into the discussion when Judy's case was raised.

Lucia asked about the importance of public approval for Governor James. The governor, Main said, didn't act for political reasons; therefore, he felt free to make decisions devoid of optics. James would weigh the facts and decide on that basis. Not public pushback. Main knew that capital cases were the most fraught of criminal cases, legally and politically.

Lucia said, "People know the crime. They don't know Judy." She was working logistics and needed guidance on the length of a clemency packet.

Twenty pages or fewer was Main's answer.

We spent about forty-five minutes on death and life matters. Main was gracious and said nothing to dissuade us, giving salient tips on how to proceed. We left knowing that no matter how passionate, knowledgeable, and conscientious we were, clemency was an elusive dream. And yet, we harbored hope.

Personal and religious connections might be providential to a plea for clemency: Governor James and Judy's trial lawyer, Robert French, knew each other. James's conservative Christianity portended receptivity. Bob French and Fob's wife, Bobbie Mooney James, had been school classmates. McPhillips had run for office and knew James. There were clergy who could speak to Judy's maturing spirituality: the Reverends Tom Crittenden, Massey Gentry, and Robert Miller, the Alabama bishop of the Episcopal Church, into which Judy was confirmed. I knew Jim Main's brother, Tommy. He was a member of First United Methodist Church in Union Springs, where my husband and I were pastors. Tommy was a kind, compassionate, and spiritual man. I had no reason to believe that his brother was different.

Lucia moved ahead in constructing a clemency petition. The arguments in the letters were legal, moral, and humanitarian. Although twenty pages had been recommended by the governor's legal adviser, the packet was over forty. The piece by Barry Ragsdale put clemency into a historical frame. There were letters from two Episcopal bishops, three pastors, one church vestry, three friends, Judy's four siblings, her daughter, and remarkably, the testimony of a woman who was almost a victim of Judy and Alvin.

Barry cited two governors who had commuted death sentences as they were leaving office. One was by Governor Celeste of Ohio who granted clemency for eight inmates, including a woman who'd been abused by her husband. Barry also listed reasons that were significant factors for mercy. Judy was barely fifteen when she met Alvin. He was a married twenty-six-year-old. Her home life was untenable; her mother was an alcoholic and had multiple sex partners in the trailer where they lived; necessities were scarce. Judy had become the homemaker, giving her responsibilities that a pre-teen and teen shouldn't have. She was an honor student, and prior to meeting Alvin, she'd never been in trouble with the legal system. After Judy ran away with Alvin, he began executing control by threats and beatings.

To be considered for clemency, those mitigating circumstances are critical. But what had Judy done with her life after being sentenced to death? Without remorse and rehabilitation, she'd be a threat to society. It was easy to find signs of her remorse. In letters of apology, she asked for nothing. Her love of learning aided rehabilitation. Within three months of the death sentence, she was awarded her GED. How absurd to get a GED while on death row! In the 1980s, she earned an Associate Degree from Central Alabama Community College.[160]

Letters from siblings were similar in themes describing Judy's sweetness and kindness, her being a good student, and suffering under Alvin's dictates. Her older sister, Dottie, said that parties were increasing at the family's trailer. Judy was miserable. She met a man who showed her all the attention she needed. He seemed nice, but everybody misjudged Alvin. He was slick about making Judy, at fifteen years old, believe anything. So he talked her into running away. Dottie wrote that he had guns, and they didn't. She told her mother to call the police and report the guns and have them removed from her property. But her mother was scared, and she didn't do it because her mother was afraid he'd think it was her and kill her. "He told Judy that if she didn't do that killing, he'd come and kill everyone in her family, starting with the twins." Dottie had no doubts. "He was a very mean and twisted man. If you want to call him a man. I don't. I call him a monster."

Judy's two younger brothers spoke of her fondly. One of them noted that the long hours their mother worked to support five children changed Judy's role.

Our sister Judy became sort of a mother hen to her siblings and made sure we were fed, clothed, and cared for while our mother was at work. She was the perfect sister for anyone to have, and I thank God for giving me a sister like her, and I hope you understand that what happened was not my sister,

but someone Alvin made the way he wanted her
to be. She does not deserve to die, although her
true spirit died when she met Alvin. Now she is
the same person that she was before they met and
should be aloud [sic] to have a chance to show who
she really is.

April, Judy and Alvin's daughter, composed a poem, "Mother of Memory." She imagined a mother's aching in the separation from her children.

Through the wired window,
she gazes at the sky.
Her thoughts begin to wander,
her eyes no longer dry

Memories sweep across her,
slowly she spirals down.
A little boy with bright blue eyes,
a girl with soulful brown.

The poem recalls a reunion. It was the first time April and her brother had seen their mother since they were two.

Her end is drawing closer
her heart still aches to see
the children she gave life to
and hurt unconsciously.

Unknown to her they seek her out
their mother of memory
whose gentle hands once held them close

and caressed them lovingly …

Bright blue eyes and soulful brown
draw her eyes at last.
Gently speaking, without words
they forgive her for the past.

A letter to the governor from a "potential pickup," a term used in the trial, contained surprises. Diane Owens was one of three such witnesses who testified in Judy's trial. Diane was twenty-one; a second witness was in her late teens, and the third was a thirteen-year-old. Their stories were similar. An unkempt woman asked them if they wanted to go riding. Despite the woman's persistence, each declined.

Diane said she was proud to have testified at the trial as it fulfilled her duty as a citizen of the country. She had no regrets and no doubts. "Not about what I said then, nor what I write …" Even so, "my defining association with the state differs greatly from that of sixteen years ago. That is to say, I no longer see value in what they propose. The state is petitioning for the death of Judith Anne Neelley; I propose they already have it."

The eagerness to speak for Judy came through Diane's scrupulous inventory of her life in 1998. That raised questions about Judy. She wondered if she'd been put to death. After exploring Judy's life since sentencing, she felt she knew the facts: Judy was on death row, she was a Christian, and she was about to be executed. Without knowing what to expect, Diane wrote to Judy. Diane stated that in the past sixteen years, as she searched for truth, Judy, she wrote, "had a firmer grasp on reality than I. Her cell had taught her well. She had wrapped herself around a truth I had only read about. She had truly been set free. I had only thought I was."

> *Mr. Governor, please don't allow the allusion of justice to negate the truth. Yes, Judith Anne Neelley committed those horrible crimes, and somewhere—hidden from our view, in a desert cell—over the past decade and a half—justice was served. Judith Anne Neelley died and the world became a better place. There is no need to kill again. No need to burrow out any secret sins. The truth has already done that.*
>
> *In fact, the woman that now lives, lives for the love of her family alone. It is not her voice you hear crying out. No, she has not pleaded for her own life. It is my voice you hear—her families, her friends, her loved ones—all those who cry out selfishly for themselves. We are not so noble, Mr. Governor. We do not ask for her life to be spared for her alone. We ask because we need her. She has brought to us what we cannot find for ourselves. A sense of settlement … Her spirit has been seasoned—cultivated by years in a cell … through an existence that to most would seem unconscionable. Hopeless, even. Yet, somehow, hope survived and grew into a woman that has dared to bring hope to us all.*

My clemency appeal dealt with the principles and rationale for clemency, rooted in Judeo-Christian scripture, and the merits in Judy's case. To dwell on an "eye for an eye" misconstrues the biblical intent. In the Mosaic Law, there are a minimum of twenty offenses punishable by death: adultery, blasphemy, violation of the Sabbath, to name a few. Those who take scripture as prescriptive of capital sins might want to ask for mercy.

> *Jesus refused the way of violence. He told his followers, "If another disciple sins, you must rebuke the offender, and if there is repentance, you must forgive (Luke 17:3)." Proverbs 24:10–12 warns against our feigning ignorance when someone is unjustly taken to death.*
>
> *To spare Judy's life will accomplish more than saving one life. Her twins, now eighteen, would not have to live with the awful reality of having lost their mother through an execution. Crime is cyclical in families. The twins are fine young people, but the anger over such a loss would have a highly detrimental effect on all members of her family.*
>
> *Today Judy is a loving, energetic, talented, and deeply spiritual person … If she is executed, she will appear before God and receive her judgment. I am confident of God's mercy for her. We do not need to lose her story and her journey of faith. Our society has in place a mechanism for redressing wrongs. That is clemency!*
>
> *The state has done its duty. The prison has done its duty. Judy has done her duty to God. She has made amends to victims, as she has been able. Her broken and contrite heart is the best sacrifice she can give. The community failed to see the road down which Judy was going …*
>
> *Now we have the final opportunity … I have been amazed at her capacity and eagerness to grow.*

I must speak out for saving her life …
   This is a solemn act for the executive branch of our state to make. I pray … for you, Governor James, that God will lead you to do righteousness, and to effect God's justice by giving deliverance to the needy.

According to the Old Testament, rulers were God's representatives. In Royal Psalms, the believer petitions God to bestow justice through the ruler, the emissary of God on earth to guarantee justice, principally for the poor. It went with the job! The psalmist prays that the monarch will be over other lands and rulers because the monarch is a savior for the poor and those without assistance (Psalm 72).

While James was in office, seven men were put to death by electrocution in Alabama. Bob Gambacurta, James's press secretary, described the governor's struggle with the death penalty. Gambacurta said the people who were executed increasingly weighed on the governor.[161] Commutation, a rarity, would be after a death date was set. No one in Alabama had had the death penalty commuted since the reinstitution of the ultimate judicial punishment in 1976.

Judy's appeals came to a halt on January 11, 1999, when the United States Supreme Court said it would not hear her case. In preparation for death, Judy had her hair cut short, so when they shaved her head, to make a better contact between the skin and electrodes, losing her hair wouldn't be too repellant—she hoped.

Gobsmacked

January 1999

Urgent, the message said. *Call your husband ASAP. He has good news.* The note on bright yellow paper was tacked to the seminary's message center. My husband was home in New York. I was in the Atlanta area for three weeks, working on a post-graduate degree.

He answered my call eagerly. "It's Judy." His voice cracked as he endeavored to speak. "I don't know if I can say this. But I have to."

I counted on the phrase "good news" to get me through whatever was causing his agitation.

"The governor granted Judy clemency!"

Incredulous, I asked, "Are you sure?" Then I inhaled sharply. "That's wonderful!" "Wonderful" was a paltry response, but impressive utterances are often written after they're ostensibly spoken.

The meeting with the governor's legal adviser had occurred months earlier. Since then, Dick and I had moved to New York from Alabama, begun new responsibilities, and I was back into my work for a Doctor of Ministry degree. A house full of boxes will muddle a mind; I hadn't been concentrating on the chances for clemency.

"How did you find out?"

"Lucia called."

It was January 15, 1999.

I wanted to tell someone. I wanted Judy to know I'd heard.

I also wanted verification that it was true.

I called the prison and spoke with one of the officers, a woman who could stare down a grizzly.

"Is it true about Judy?" My excitement got ahead of my better judgment to be restrained.

"What have you heard?" Her words bore no inflection.

"That she got clemency?"

"We got the message from the attorney general's office that her sentence was commuted to life."

If I'd heard that before, it had no reality until she said it. Not LWOP: life with no possibility of parole. Life. Possibility of parole. It was the strangest, yet heady, possibility.

"Will she be in population?"

"We'll have to work all that out."

"Judy has permission to call me in New York. But I'm in Atlanta now. Is there any way she could call me here?"

"Judy is going to lose certain privileges when she's off death row."

That was the prelude to her denying my request. But she promised to let Judy know I called.

Governor Fob James, a Republican, lost the election in November to a Democrat. One of James's last acts was writing the order to commute Judy's sentence to life. Her family, friends, and legal team were hysterically happy. The incoming governor and many others were outraged.

In between calls confirming James's action, I made an avocado sandwich while singing, "Freedom, oh freedom. Freedom is coming. Oh yes, I know."

I was ecstatic. I wanted to rejoice with Judy, to hear her joy.

Lucia Penland arranged a three-way call with Judy. As soon as I heard her voice, I said, "Praise God, from whom all blessings flow."

Laughing, Judy replied, "You got that right! This is such a shock. I think I'm okay. Reporters are everywhere."

We had a few minutes; I pushed past any effort to chit-chat. I knew Judy well enough to ask, "What are your fears?"

"I've never been on the hall. It's going to be a big adjustment. I don't think I can do it if I have to spend a long time out there."

"Maybe it won't be more than a couple of years." To myself, I thought, *a couple of years would feel like a lifetime to me.*

"I can do that," she said.

"Yes, you can. What do you want me to pray for?"

"I haven't a clue."

"I'll pray for you to have strength," I said. "And God knows what else you need. I'll see you next Wednesday."

I got a message to call Tom Gordon, *The Birmingham News* trial reporter. I left a voice mail for him. When Tom returned my call, he began, "I believe you left a message to the effect of dancing in the streets."

"Yes, I did. I'm so excited, but I realize that many others are saying, 'This isn't justice.' I'm sorry for that."

"There are some furious people!"

"No doubt there are. I believe there has been justice, although the victims' families probably aren't feeling that." I paused. "The occasion calls for saying something profound. Governor James has done that in granting clemency."

~

Diane Owens and I planned to get together while I was in Atlanta. I was eager to meet the writer of the poetic letter in support of clemency. Our connections for months had been letters, emails, and phone. When I called, I hadn't expected

Diane's exuberance. She was as excited as I was. "I just found out when I got home at 6:00 p.m. I ran up the stairs screaming. I've never received news so good!"

I repeated Gordon's reporting. "Some folks are furious."

"I refuse to allow their fury to change my excitement. Some are angry that it was handled with such decorum."

Eager to share our elation, we set up a time to meet the following day.

We were in a celebratory mood. Less than twenty-four hours earlier, we'd heard the stunning news. January sixteen is Diane's birthday, which added to the day's joy.

We went to Pastries A Go Go in Decatur, Georgia, for lunch and both ordered a loaded potato—greasy, cheesy, with peppers and tomatoes—and it was delicious.

We chose chocolate mousse for Diane's birthday cake and focused our eyes on the chef as he cut the pieces, heating the knife with a blue-hot flame. It felt decadent. Back in my room at Columbia Theological Seminary, we savored the mousse and hot tea. I improvised a birthday candle by ceremonially putting the broken end of a plastic iced teaspoon in the cake and then sang "Happy Birthday." The mousse was as delectable as it looked. We were high on all the present goodness of life.

Diane punctuated her words with generous hand gestures and a dramatic flair that I found appealing. She wore a white cap worn by many Mennonite women, and her face crinkled when she laughed.

"What I liked so much was the subdued way in which clemency for Judy was handled," she said. "You could just see the hand of God working. With Karla Faye Tucker, there were so many hands in it, you couldn't tell if God's hand was in it at all."

That took us into a discussion of Beverly Lowry's *Crossed*

Over, a story of Karla Faye Tucker's life. She'd been executed by the state of Texas almost a year earlier. Diane had a strong reaction to Lowry's dwelling on details of the crime. She saw it as having an alluring enticement for others to try the same thing or worse. Copycat crimes are well documented, but I hadn't reacted as Diane did. To me, the crimes were repelling.

From Diane's court testimony, I'd read of the day Judy attempted to kidnap her. But there were new facts. "Judy was very persistent in wanting me to go with her. There were children in the car. I thought later, *I'll bet she was a lesbian.* I probably would've gone with her if my husband hadn't been at home and was coming to give me a ride to work. The timing was providential!"

It was too much to absorb in a few moments how close events had come to making our meeting impossible.

The capstone of our hours together came when Diane said, "Fob James is a great man!"

I was more cautious. "I'm no judge of anyone's greatness, but I'm convinced he did a great thing."

Four days later, I drove from Atlanta to Wetumpka in a bubble of disbelief and anticipation. It was Wednesday, January 20.

After Judy was escorted to the visiting area, the officer took off the handcuffs. The change in her from Friday was alarming. She seemed flat.

"How are you?" I piped up cheerfully.

"Not good."

"By the time I leave, you'll feel better." My arrogance startled me.

She was suspicious, almost baiting. "Why? Do you have some good news?"

Her eyes grew vacant as she itemized the past days. "I've

been in extreme emotional distress since Friday. I was better yesterday. I was settling down, finding my focus. Then things changed. The warden said I could stay in the death-row cell for thirty days before going on the hall. That was such a relief. Then I was put in administrative segregation this morning. Suddenly, I had to pack. I didn't have time to adjust. They keep doing things." Her words broke apart.

I needed to set aside my joy and join Judy where she was, to understand her sadness and fears. The sudden changes triggered PTSD flashbacks. She'd gone from a one-person cell to the noisy and confusing environment of segregation. The perception of her as a cold-blooded killer preceded her. She was an island surrounded by a relentless hurricane. Judy had come close to making peace with her death sentence. Faith and repentance gave her courage. Then, without warning, she'd been thrown back into the hypervigilance and unpredictable existence she'd experienced with Alvin.

"Everyone is expecting me to jump up and down, but I'm in shock. It's hard to prepare for something when I don't know where I'm going. I'm happy I'm not going to be executed. This locked door is suddenly open, and I'm stumbling out. With my ex-husband, I had a gun at my head, knife at my throat; I was resigned to a brutal death. Now I don't know whether to run or cry. I'm lost."

I left the prison aching for Judy's complicated transition. For those who looked forward to the state's having the last word, there was ire. Happiness for one person may be sadness or even betrayal for another. Empathy for Judy tempered my happiness.

With the recent commutation of Judy's sentence and the strong reaction by people who get quoted in the press, being in Montgomery gave me occasions to speak about Judy. On the day of our visit, I shopped for a laptop. As the conversation with the salesperson wound down, he noted that people who buy a laptop for the novelty don't need a laptop. I told him I use mine for research and writing about a woman who was on death row. "You might have heard the name: Judy Neelley."

I didn't expect his response. He told me his thinking had changed in the last few months about the death penalty. "You may not agree with me, but I don't believe in abortion. If I think killing is wrong, then how can I sanction the death penalty?"

National newspapers picked up the story of Alabama's governor granting clemency: *Los Angeles Times, Houston Chronicle, Boston Globe, New York Times, The Atlanta Journal and Constitution.* The last of those stated, "In an unexpected legal twist, outgoing Alabama Gov. Fob James on Friday wrote the last chapter in the grisly 1980s murder of a Georgia teenager."[162] The last chapter? For family members and friends of Cathy Connolly, it may not be possible to have a satisfying final chapter.

The letter commuting Judy's sentence was typed on Thursday. Fob James signed it, but he wanted to give it further thought overnight. On Friday, January 15, he dated it. He walked out of the capital and left town.[163] He wrote the letter on his stationery with the barest letterhead. No personal names with addressees: only Alabama Supreme Court, its address, and the Circuit Court of Dekalb County, Fort Payne, Alabama.

> *Pursuant to the authority granted to me by virtue of Amendment No. 38, Constitution of Alabama, I hereby commute the sentence of death of Judith Ann Neeley [sic] to life imprisonment.*
> *Done this 15th day of January, 1999.*
> *Signed: Fob James, Jr., Governor, State of Alabama*

In fewer than forty words, James had caused a firestorm and saved a woman's life.

Inmate Z-429 on death row had a new designation. No longer was she at the end of the alphabet.

For a time in Alabama, it was a contest between vilifying Forrest Hood "Fob" James Jr. for his clemency order, or Judy, as the epitome of cruelty.

James was Alabama's governor for two terms. His first was as a Democrat from 1979 to 1983. In his inaugural address, he promised Alabamians that his leadership would be "free from racism and discrimination." His political acts were not easy to calculate. He integrated his cabinet during his first term and reinstituted chain gangs for male prisoners in his second.[164] For that term, 1995–99, he was a Republican. James chose not to attend the inauguration of his successor, Don Siegelman.

The headline of an article from *The Huntsville Times* announcing clemency blared, "James ditches rules to the end." James's press spokesman, David Azbell, delighted in his boss's style. "Fob is the last of the colorful Southern governors." He bolstered his assessment by describing James's public appearances. He might juggle apples for schoolchildren or tell Huntsville professionals that legislators behave like "trained seals" when they're around lobbyists. In business, he'd been a civil engineer and CEO of the manufacturing company he started. The self-promoting behavior of some politicians wasn't his style.

Fob James's values in office sprang from his faith. He and his wife are evangelical Episcopalians. They were known to promote conservative religious causes, congruent with many Alabamians. He was admired for an administration that was "largely scandal-free," contrary to a few of the governors following him.[165]

Rarely does a prosecutor agree with commutation. The incoming Alabama Attorney General, Bill Pryor, said he was ready to set a date for Judy's execution and was disappointed that he could not. Mike O'Dell, DeKalb County District Attorney, described the decision as "outrageous," "insane," and "insensitive." He said, "What this cowardly, soon-to-be-former governor has done is, he has unleashed a vicious killer on the citizens of this state." Then he referred to the report of James's going duck hunting after signing the commutation. "I'd be ducking too if I had done such a cowardly deed as this."[166]

The former district attorney, Richard Igou, was vehement. "To think that one man could stain his legacy with this (mistake). I can't understand it. He obviously didn't understand the facts."[167] The specter of her being near immediate release on parole was dangled before the public. Be afraid!

There was understandable criticism that victims, prosecutors, or the judge weren't consulted regarding clemency. It is not required. From the reactions, it's clear that there would've been strident efforts to block Governor James's action. He knew that.

My letter to James in April 1999 began, "It is a pleasure to write you and express my profound appreciation for your commutation of the death sentence of Judith Ann Neelley. I can see nothing other than courage in what you did." I expressed my regrets to him and his family for the vicious attacks leveled against them. I wanted him to know that Judy was making the most of her new life:

> *Judy has made a good, although predictably unsteady, transition to population. Perhaps you know of Kairos. It is an ecumenical, prison ministry sponsored by Episcopalians, United Methodists,*

Catholics, and others. Judy was able to attend Kairos at Tutwiler in March. She needed that spiritual strengthening. She is active in the chapel and utilizing her time well ... She has you to thank for that opportunity.

Many theories and accusations abounded about Fob James's granting Judy clemency. I mentioned that I hoped for an opportunity to speak with him at a future date. I needed to hear from James himself to confirm my belief about the reason for his action.

I located his address, to which I sent a certified letter. I let out a whoop when he granted me an interview.

Fob and his wife, Bobbie, were living at their hunting lodge, as a new home was being built south of Montgomery. The directions were precise. I was to go over a creek, onto a county road, run out of paved road and then onto a dirt road. If I saw a green mailbox, I was getting close. Down a hill, the next marker was a barn. Nearby was the hunting lodge where we were to meet. I expected to see security with a firearm positioned to stop my car, check my identification, and ascertain that I wasn't a threat. I saw no one. It was July 2000.

Fob greeted me graciously and relayed regrets from his wife that she wasn't present. She had an appointment in town. I expected to speak with James for an hour and be on my way. Our conversation lasted several hours.

Unhurried and relaxed, James asked about work as a prison chaplain. "Wasn't that an interesting job?"

I mentioned the challenge of balancing inmate needs with security. Many officers helped me negotiate that, but it could be frustrating. "My sense is that God called me to that job. Nevertheless, it wasn't a place I needed to stay. One of the things the inmates taught me was that more of them want to make amends than we think. And often they have no way to do that. The legal system is set up to keep accused and accusers apart. Judy is one of the inmates I worked with in trying to make amends with victims, to tell them how sorry she was.

"I saw her yesterday. I asked her if she had questions for you. She wondered if you'd gotten her letter. She wrote to tell you that she wouldn't let you down, not get into trouble. Do you have any recollection of the letter?"

"Oh, sure, I have the letter." James responded quickly. "It was very compelling. I didn't answer for two reasons. Number one, it was a difficult letter to answer. Number two, I don't know if the mail is scrutinized. It probably is. I thought anything I might write might be used in disfavor regarding her. So tell her that I wish her well."

"I'll be glad to. Mail is more scrutinized coming in. Everything is opened. The exception is if it's stamped, 'legal mail.' They're not supposed to open that. She said she'd love to meet you sometime, although she said she didn't know if that was likely."

After a moment, I returned to James's question about my intent in interviewing him. "I want to write about Judy. The clemency part is critical—in that specific act and also in the results of that act. From one day to the next, her entire future was changed."

"So you're asking how I got to the decision?"

"Right."

James looked down at his papers. "It was really simple in retrospect. I made some notes this morning. In Alabama, our statutes, as you know, the governor can't pardon. That was changed several decades ago. What the law does do, you can commute a death sentence to life without parole. That is the single, sole prerogative available to the governor. Of course, I read all the material I could get.

"Several things came through. Number One. The same DeKalb County jury found her guilty of first-degree murder and recommended life without parole. That was a signal. I know DeKalb County well. DeKalb County jury, in my judgment, wouldn't have reached that conclusion unless they had reasons. So on any case like this, I felt the governor's responsibility was to view the case relative to the legal proceedings. I've always been a believer in capital punishment, but you have the responsibility to ensure it was a fair trial, and as far as technical error, I didn't find any."

James considered his words. "So when you move beyond that, you try to put down and get clear in your mind several facts that are germane to the situation. And this first fact that was established, or that I came to believe, that here you had a fifteen-year-old girl-child that had suffered torture for an extended period of time. She was alone." He looked at me. "I hope I was accurate in that."

"Quite accurate."

"Then the second is, what is extreme torture? I defined, as best I could tell from reading, you had to look at military POW experiences to qualify that. It's severe physical pain inflicted on a person and a threat where that person is in constant fear of death or fear of death to a loved one … For POWs and like prisoners of apartheid, they believe in what they were doing. As best as I could glean from the record, her husband had shot his first wife; she carries that bullet to this day. From the time that Judy and Alvin were married, maybe a few months before, she suffered what you could define very accurately as extreme torture."

Fob's measured and modulated tone changed in intensity

and pace. "So … you go back and look at where we know of torture in the military. I was in the army; I never was in combat and certainly never been a POW, but in reading about their experiences and that of intelligence agents, they've said that the bravest of soldiers and agents, people that are highly trained and physically fit in their twenties and thirties, will sometimes break when subjected to torture, coming totally under control of their captors. This … was a fifteen-year-old girl compared to an intelligence agent or to soldiers. No training, little raising. I don't see where she could've had the mental or physical capacity to resist what was happening to her."

His next statement portended a later declaration. "If she had, she would've shot the guy."

My quick laugh of irony didn't interrupt his analysis.

"I sympathize, but those are the basics I determined to be the truth. Because of those, I believed she should be commuted to life. This is another subject; I don't know what happened to Alvin Neelley. I think he's in prison."

"He's in prison in Georgia."

"If she'd been my child, my sister, a relative or friend, I would have killed the man. Evidently, she had nobody to protect her. Nobody to come to her rescue." He shook his head in bewilderment. "Horrible situation."

"*He got it,*" I thought with pleasure. "I've met all of her siblings," I said. "Unfortunately, I never met her mother; she's deceased. Her siblings knew something was going on. They were passively concerned."

"She seemed to be totally alone."

"Yes, I agree."

Fob spoke of the forces that propelled Judy toward the violence. "The crimes that were committed were terrible.

224

Heinous. But from the evidence and the testimony, she was forced to do that. It didn't make sense." He continued in calculated speech. "Here's a fifteen-year-old girl who's never hurt anybody, and all of a sudden, she comes under the control or spell, whatever you want to call it, of a guy that's eleven years older than she is. Stronger than she is. Crazy! And abused physically in God knows how many ways. Then she had to live in constant fear of being killed."

My eyes burned without warning. "You have so much insight into this. Sometimes it's hard for people to appreciate what was going on in her life."

"It's all in the record."

I thought about the people who question the interpretation of the record. I sighed. "Yes."

James relaxed into his words. "I say in the record. Of course, all of it wasn't in the legal record, but in letters and corresponding information. It was all there. At least I thought it was there."

I mentioned a book written about the case. "It's from the perspective of Alvin Neelley, and he's pictured, I think the expression was, 'as just a lovesick slob,' completely under her spell. I guess it's one more case of how you see it, but—"

"I don't see how you can say that about a guy who shot his first wife. It just doesn't make any sense. No sense a'tall."

"It doesn't to me either. I'm a skeptical type. I keep wondering, what if Judy has manipulated me? But I've known her for sixteen years, and she has proved in a variety of ways that she was one of Alvin's victims." I moved to a core question. "One of the things that was tried in the press was whether clemency meant life without parole or whether it was life. Did you have in mind either one of those?"

"Number one: there's no alternative. There's no option.

The only alternative available is to commute, not pardon."

"You know there has been talk, the way your clemency statement was written, that there might be the possibility of parole for her after a period of years." I wanted that to be his intention because I feared if it wasn't, somehow straight life could be overturned.

"I think the wording of the law is life without parole. I never heard it expressed any other way. But you see, the jury found her guilty. Then the jury determined they had two choices: they could recommend execution, or they could recommend life without parole, and the jury recommended life without parole, and I imagine they came to that conclusion very much the same way I did."

"I find it amazing that with townspeople as upset and traumatized as they were by the child's death, the jury voted ten to two for life without parole," I said. "That speaks volumes to me."

James nodded. "The DeKalb County jury, in the immediate aftermath, determined that she should receive life without parole rather than execution. Believe you me, there were reasons; they wouldn't have done that without reasons."

I agreed. "In physical terms, Judy was mature at the time of the crimes, but psychologically and emotionally she was not prepared for Alvin's seduction. Getting to death row is a heckuva place to try and grow up."

"Well, I can see where she could've been in constant fear that he'd kill her." James shook his head. "And of course, the trump card of that was knowing what he was able to do to her with impunity; she heard his threats of harm to others, especially their children."

I asked him about his legacy. "I've talked with people who've said that because you granted clemency, you have a great legacy. Do you consider what you did in signing the clemency papers as one of the more significant parts of your governorship?"

Fob promptly replied, "They're incomparable. A pardon is in the line of duty, but you can't compare it to general work on better roads, or lower taxes, or better schools. It's a totally different issue coming down on what is justice and realizing that it can be very elusive and subject to error. I can't categorize. That was a decision about an individual named Judy and a life, and so, there it's essential to be right, if humanly possible to do so. When a decision is made for the state to take a life or not to take a life, the governor should do everything possible to have the facts." His voice lowered. "It was a simple right or wrong. From the information I had, both court records and others, there's no question that a twenty-six-year-old man treated a fifteen-year-old girl in a manner that was equivalent to torture. This girl was systematically tortured over a period of several years, and I believe the child was totally broken."

"That's why we have clemency in our laws," I said emphatically. "A head of a state as you were, that's an awesome responsibility. I'll admit I took great joy in the fact that you issued your order and sort of walked out the door. You didn't grandstand. It wasn't something you said, 'Hey, look at me; what a good guy I am.' You did it, apparently for reasons of morality and justice, and then let it be."

"Well, you take the oath of office to uphold the constitution of the law, and where life is at stake, it is essential that the law be upheld and justice be met."

"Do you recall being moved at all by any of the clemency letters? I know there was a poem from the daughter. There was a letter from a woman who was almost a victim, and other people. Did those …?"

"I read those letters. You can't help but be touched by them, but they aren't relevant to the decision I made. Justice cannot be just unless you have the facts. So really public opinion or letters or conversations are irrelevant to my duty. This can't be stressed enough: the *jury* in the heat of the day came down on life without parole."

I climbed onto my soapbox when we moved to prison overcrowding and the quandary of illegal drugs. "People think if you tear someone down, the offender will be motivated to stop offending. My premise is that retribution itself doesn't change people's lives. People need to be penalized for criminality, but then you've got to move into a mode of helping rebuild. The prison culture should find ways to rebuild them. Inmate self-esteem is scarce. They've got all kinds of issues, masked by unhealthy behavior. We should help them take responsibility for what they did and provide the kinds of emotional and spiritual help to rebuild their lives. Then we might make some progress. We've got too many people in prison to do that effectively."

Our conversation brought to mind a drug bust in which James was involved while governor. He smiled as he told the story. "When Alabama was growing a lot of marijuana, we would take planes, and you've got surveillance equipment. And you can literally destroy that stuff from the air. You can sweep down. We've got insecticides. In one drug raid, we caught a DC3 coming in, and that thing was absolutely *full* of marijuana, cocaine. And I went on that raid, and we caught about thirty of them who were coming to get it, to distribute across the country. And the reason I remember it so well, a guy, I was standing there, and he said, 'Hey, number twenty-three, it's been a long time.'" The governor explained that they knew each other from playing football in college. He didn't mention that he'd been a standout in football, a sport close to a religion in Alabama.

I'd arrived mid-morning, and after a few hours of talking, James offered me lunch that his wife had prepared. I valued spending more time in conversation, so we sat at a counter on stools, enjoying the summer lunch. It gave me the opportunity to ask what I'd been wondering. "Do you have security?"

He laughed. "That's just an excuse to have a chauffeured car. I did some research. Few governors have been injured. There are a few exceptions: George Wallace, Huey Long."

"You're quite a student. You study what you want to know more about."

"My father was a historian. I suppose I get it from him."

The governor's congeniality and relaxed manner put me at ease. He had no intimidating scrutiny of security.

I felt euphoric when I got in the car to leave. I had interviewed the man who'd been vilified and extolled, and he gave me permission to tape the interview. I let out a long breath, relaxing my body. When I looked at myself in the rearview mirror, I burst into laughter. A dab of toothpaste sat on my cheek. The entire interview I'd sat across from the former governor of Alabama with the hygiene error on my face. My pride plummeted. But I had the interview. Audio. Not video.

Dueling with God

Sing to Yhwh, you who love God!
Praise God's holy Name!
Yhwh's anger is fleeting,
but God's favor endures forever.
There may be tears during the night,
but joy comes in the morning.
Psalm 30:4–5[168]

To accept God's forgiveness meant making room for unconditional love. Judy couldn't go there, because in her assessment, she saw nothing worth loving. Her hands had blood on them, and she knew there was always a residue even with repeated scrubbing. She'd shown no mercy; she deserved no mercy. Her journey had been one of fleeing from genuine love and chasing a form of it that didn't validate her worth. She didn't deserve forgiveness from God or anyone else.

Yet she questioned the harshness she felt from a god that paid no attention and kept heaping on more punishment. The god she read about in the Bible didn't seem to match the god who was either deaf or in another part of the galaxy. She trusted that God would hear her prayers for others, but stated that God had no interest in paying attention to her needs.

Our visits ended with prayer. Possibly, in Judy's mind, God paid attention to my prayers on her behalf. Judy would have nothing to do with being the pray-er. I encouraged; she declined. As the time came for one visit to end, we took hands. I said, "I want you to do something this time. I'll start the prayer with 'Dear God' and then pause. I want you to say a short prayer, one word, a phrase, or a sentence: that's all."

I expected resistance. Her expression said no, but she didn't voice it. She looked more frightened than resistant. "I want you to trust me," I said. I can't explain my conviction that this was the appropriate time to urge Judy to pray, except to say that I felt God was leading me.

As we were about to begin, I told a funny experience to reduce tension. "This past week, a close friend of mine and I were praying. She was asking God to help my husband and me as we were moving to new pastorates, to say goodbye to that which was past and be open to what lay ahead. Coming to the end of the prayer, I expected to hear, 'Amen,' but my friend inadvertently said, 'Bye-bye.' It cracked both of us up."

Judy did her best to smile. Then we bowed our heads. I took a deep breath and began. "Dear God—" I stopped, and after a few seconds I heard Judy laugh. Nerves, I thought.

She hesitated, pushing the words out. "I want to thank you—" she began, but she couldn't continue. What I thought was laughter was the beginning of sobbing.

I released her hands and took her in my arms, then picked up her prayer. "I pray Judy will know that you surround her with your love. Keep her in your care. Amen."

We held each other for a few seconds; her crying subsided. Whether Judy had heard my "Amen" or not, I didn't know, but she said "Amen" emphatically.

"I'm getting you all wet," she said as she released her arms from around me.

Tired from sitting on the hard mattress, I stood up.

Judy followed suit. "I don't want to say goodbye."

"Yes, I know. Neither do I."

As Judy's faith developed, she moved into unraveling what

a desire for payback does. "I don't want to hate Al anymore. It's not for Al's sake. My hate doesn't hurt him. It's for my sake."

I asked what that was doing to her.

She gestured toward her chest. "When I think of all the people he hurt, it's hard not to hate him. It eats me up. Tears me up inside."

"Do you think if you don't hate him, he doesn't get what he deserves?" After her response of "Yes," I pushed on. "Does it help to think that God is angry at Alvin for what he has done?" I was drawing on Old Testament prophets on their channeling God's anger at unfaithful people.

"No, it doesn't help. I know God forgives and may already have forgiven Al, since if we ask for forgiveness, God will do it."

A few days later, Judy told another inmate that she was trying to forgive Alvin. The inmate's reply was blunt. "How long will it take? You don't have an endless time."

After Alvin's death in 2005, Judy expressed her sorrow. It wasn't for his death, but for the loss of an unlikely hope. She wanted him to say he was sorry for what he'd done to her and many others. His death was a reminder that forgiving Alvin was spiritual work independent of any action taken by him. He had not killed her soul.

Trusting God when it's so dark you can't see your hands or feet tests the agnostic and saint. That test came for Judy in January 2014. When she called, her voice was strained. Nearly choking as she began to cry, she tried to tell me about a letter she'd received. Julian McPhillips, a Montgomery attorney who had taken an interest in the case, wrote to explain that his legal load didn't permit him to work on parole. He'd give the case to an associate in the practice. Judy was distraught.

"What am I supposed to think? My Bible says that God

will give us life and give it abundantly. I'll be fifty years old in June. Just when I think, hey, something good is going to happen, then this. Really?" Her voice catching, she pushed out her words. "I just don't know what to think. I'm tired of fighting this. I don't know how much longer I can hold on."

I spoke with admiration. "I don't know how you've had the courage, the tenacity to get this far, even to get up every morning, living in a place that barely values life. I'm not sure I could do what you've done. Your resilience is greater than even you realize."

After a long silence, Judy's voice quieted; she spoke in a whimper. "What do I do? How do I deal with this? How much longer am I going to function, to stay relatively sane? How much longer before I break? You know I have before." Tears returned. Her voice was muted. "I'm scared."

The despair was heart-rending. I intuited that Judy's reaction to the letter from Julian was as much about feeling cast aside as it was about legal hopes. "I renew my promise to you. I will not abandon you."

After a moment, in a near whisper, Judy said, "Thank you."

My promise and her words held us.

"I want to remind you of conversations we've had about God and punishment." To soften Judy's anxiety, I began with, "Remember, I have no pipeline to God. You already know that. Unlike God, the punishment dished out by humans can be harsh and unrelenting. Yes, scripture passages warn of an avenging god. But God's offer of forgiveness and open arms are what I live by. I don't believe God is doing this to you. To me, it's like saying that what Alvin did to you, God caused that."

Judy's tone was like a stifled wail. "He didn't cause it, but he allowed it to happen!"

"That's true, the awful thing and the great thing about

233

choice. We make terrible choices, and we make good choices. And sometimes events are foisted on us. God allows things to happen. God doesn't step in like superwoman. God doesn't zap or vaporize somebody. It doesn't mean that God doesn't love you, that God isn't with you during this time."

Judy lamented, "I'm struggling. Part of me wants to say, 'Okay, God, I trust you.' Part of me wants to say, 'I'm so mad and tired, and he continues to allow it.' I understand I made choices that led to what happened. This is more than thirty years later, and I'm still suffering the consequences. When is it going to be enough?"

"It's already enough."

Her voice sounded dispirited. "Apparently not."

"Sadly, some will always believe you're a dangerous convict. Judy, you're tough and have fought bigger fights than this. Think about what it took for you to live through all Alvin's terror and abuse. Somehow, you survived that. You were sixteen years on death row. You came off. You were in shambles. I saw that. In 1994, you tried to stop the pain by suicide." The intensity of my words subsided as I said quietly, "I know you have plenty of reasons to be angry."

"The anger is about being given false hope. I told Julian five or six years ago when he volunteered, 'Don't give me hope if there is none.' I can deal with what I've got to deal with, but don't let me hope. I am not mad at Julian. He said he didn't have time." Then she made a statement of discernment. "I feel abandoned and resentful. Anger isn't my major emotion." She spoke with resignation. "I'm just tired."

"I hear the exhaustion in your voice."

We let silence offer solace.

Trying to be the bearer of good news, my next comment took us to God-surprises. "I put twenty-five dollars on your account." She thanked me and with a slight laugh said she had thirty-five cents on her Tutwiler ledger. "Penny candy costs eleven cents! I don't know what made you do that, but I am very grateful to you."

"God nudged me."

"Thank you, and I thank God. But I'm mad at God. I don't know what to do."

"Talk to God. God can handle it. If what I'm going to say isn't right, I hope God will correct me. Rather than turning away, God wants us to express our anger. The psalms are full of people railing against God's seeming inaction and injustice, but by the end of the psalm somehow, they move to praise.

"Often our petitions aren't answered as we want; it feels like God is either acting against us or is passive in hearing our pleas. If that's our measure of God's action on our behalf, we may miss when God shows up anonymously. There seems to be no DNA evidence of God, yet something happens unexpectedly that's good. To me, those are God-moments."

I returned to what Judy had told me earlier. She'd gotten two letters on the same day. The first was from McPhillips. It overshadowed the more important letter that Barry Ragsdale had written. He asked if she wanted his help on filing for parole.

"When you told me about getting those two letters from Julian and Barry, I thought of that as a God-moment. I hope you can see other evidence of God's love and care for you. It may be as simple as someone being kind or not being unkind! It might be an officer who treats you or someone else with consideration. It could be a gorgeous sunset or time free from the pain of arthritis. I believe God does fancy footwork, finding ways to be present without nullifying our will."

Judy conceded that the timing was opportune. "I haven't heard from Barry in years. One letter saying, 'I can't help you,' and the other one said, 'Can I help you?'"

"What are the chances that those two letters would come in the same day? Watch for God. Be on the lookout."

"I'll try."

Living has a way of surfacing thorny questions. What should Judy be doing to atone for her crimes? Is confession and contrition enough? If restitution is required, what possibilities did she have? We discussed Judy's reservations about whether the death of Jesus could atone for the sins of all humankind, including hers. We looked at scripture and how it has been used to justify what we want to believe.

She mused about whether I was insane or a saint to visit her and work with others who were incarcerated. I assured her my insanity was more probable than being near sainthood. In a playful and serpentine response, I wrote, "Although you can't believe, because I believe, remember the faith that you question is the faith that causes my insanity!"

Humor that isn't at the expense of others can be beneficial. I'm relieved Judy appreciates my attempts, such as in a letter I sent on July 4, 1997:

> *I am wondering what special perks you got today that I, as a mere citizen, didn't get. I am sure you were taken to the beach and had a cookout ... probably got sunburned a little. Or perhaps truckloads of sand were brought in and artfully placed around the Olympic size pool, and you spent the day sunning and swimming laps. All on death row were given a private showing of Batman*

… complete with popcorn and Pepsi. Then after working on your Nordic Track, you sat at your desk and composed limericks. So here I am, with no perks!

If none of that sounds familiar, then maybe our fine leaders haven't tried to duplicate the country club federal prison system.

(I've been in country clubs and federal prisons, and I would never get them confused.)

I laughed at her response. She reported:

The sand around an Olympic size pool was a blast. Nordic Track, then compose limericks at my desk? I think you've been sniffing paint thinner again. I'm sorry you had to suffer through the fourth without perks.

The Judge and the Lawyer(s)

September 2003

I was in Fort Payne, in northeast Alabama, getting a sense of the county seat town, the site of the trial of Judy Neelley. Twenty years had passed, but the residents' memories remained acute.

The trial transcript leaves the impression of Judge Randall Cole's even-handedness. He showed courtesy for every person who came forward, making no distinction between the accused and the accusers. He expressed appreciation for the jury's service. He exerted authority in a way that engendered restraint from a gallery that wasn't well mannered in the beginning.[169]

Judge Cole agreed to see me. The conversation was brief. When I asked about his thinking in sentencing Judy to death, he said, as he'd already explained to the media, that the severity of the crimes rose to the level of ultimate punishment. I disagree with his override of the jury's recommendation, a moral difference to me, not legal. That does nothing to take away his earning the address of "Your Honor."[170]

Without my asking, he made sure that the county clerk's office was available to me. The women working in that office were helpful in numerous ways. I sought conversations with residents of Fort Payne. For those who'd lived in the town during the trial, memories were vivid. For newer arrivals, they'd had many opportunities to hear stories of the crime and the trial.

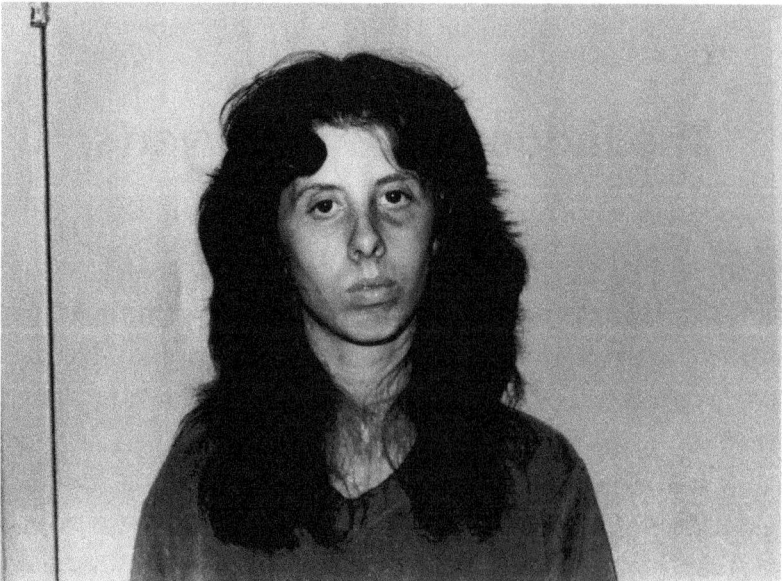

Judy Neelley, 1982 Mugshot

When Judy was arrested, her appearance revealed mistreatment, poor hygiene, and scatter-shot nutrition. Her hair was long and dirty, and she wore a t-shirt with no bra.[171] The mugshot shows a woman with a blank stare, dark circles under her eyes, and bruises: a freeze frame of a tangled life.

For the trial, Bob French re-made her. She wore clothes from Bob's secretary: demure and feminine outfits. Her long hair was styled and makeup applied. She was transformed, at least in appearance. Not everyone was impressed. I heard, "French dressed her up, dolled her up. They went overboard."

They were equally disgusted with Fob James's clemency. "It really burned people up what James did. That's the reason people didn't vote for his son. He was the lowest scoring person in the primary. He didn't get his plane off the runway."

Fall 2010

When I made my plans to return to Fort Payne, I could not have guessed or hoped for the wealth of conversations I would have and the evidence that would be placed in my hands. My first goal was to get a list of jurors. I asked for that in the circuit clerk's office. It was elusive. In fairness, the case was twenty-seven years old. There were no digital records. A list might be, I was told, in the basement. I wasn't the first, nor probably the last, to come looking for credible details or salacious bits. The clerks may have had Judy-fatigue. There were several suggestions. "Call up the judge and get a court order." "Go up to see Mr. O'Dell; see if he has a list."

O'Dell was deputy DA during Judy's trial. As I was heading toward his office, he came into the hall. I introduced myself and asked if I could get a list of jurors. He bristled, telling me forcefully that he didn't want someone making trouble for jurors who'd served on behalf of the people of DeKalb County. "I don't want anyone harassing them or praising them."

Even though his presence and words were intimidating, I tried reassuring him. "I'm not interested in judging anything about their service. I want to hear about their experience in a challenging case."

My words fell to the floor.

"Don't go anywhere near any one of them!"

One flight down and back to the clerk's office, and an offer came. One of the women mentioned that someone had recently asked about evidence from the trial. She thought it was a film company. "We got some stuff out for them. I don't think it's been put back up."

"So what happened to the film?" I asked as I followed her.

"Don't know. Nothing. I guess."

She showed me pieces of evidence in disorder, stuck in a closet. A box of letters caught my attention.

"Here are some letters Judy and Alvin wrote to each other."

I didn't mind showing my excitement. "May I read them?"

"Sure, I don't see why not."

She gave me a desk in a corner, and I found over sixty letters scattered in the box.

They were boring and tantalizing, indicting and innocuous. I knew there might be a nugget in the letters that would produce an insight then or later, but I didn't get to read all of them because I had an appointment with a Baptist pastor in town.

The pastor and I were almost finished talking when he asked if I'd met Bob French. I told him I'd written him years ago to see if I could speak with him. Since he dismissed that earlier request, I didn't relish trying again. The pastor knew him through business dealings and was gently encouraging.

It was about 5:30 p.m., and I needed to get on the road to La Fayette, Georgia, where I would spend the night. It was easy to dismiss his idea.

The next morning, I was to meet with a relative of Cathy. In the afternoon, I planned to go back to Birmingham, where I was living during a sabbatical. By Monday evening, I was questioning my plans. Why not revisit Fort Payne, read a few more letters, and drop by French's office? I was sure he could help. I had nothing to lose. My new itinerary was a return to Fort Payne to examine more letters and try my luck with French.

The request I made in my letter to Judy's lawyer in 2001 was because I wanted to broaden my understanding of the woman he'd defended. Would he be willing to talk about his experience and how the trial had affected his legal career? I wasn't confident he would write back, but it came within the week. I'd written, "Has your assessment of Judy changed? Can she be rehabilitated, or has she been rehabilitated to your knowledge?"[172]

I felt chastised by his response that Judy didn't need rehabilitation. I felt it must mean that in his estimation she was beyond help. My brain had gotten ahead of the letter's contents, however. He said that all she needed was to get rid of Alvin Neelley, that she was Alvin's slave.

Nine years later, after that initial contact with Robert French, known as Bob, I looked across the street at his office. French had recovered from financial disaster after representing Judy. He was minutes from the DeKalb County Court House. The brick facade and teal shutters framing the windows of his law office invited clients. Nothing ostentatious.

I wanted to meet the man who'd become infamous as the face and force that defended the child murderer. Sensational stories about French abounded. "He was in love with Judy." "He was having an affair with her." It kept tongues busy and reporters hungry.

I didn't want to meet Bob French. Once appeals were out of his hands, the newly appointed attorney had to uncover legal arguments for reversing the death penalty. He did, and they were imprinted on my judgment. Barry Ragsdale, JD, argued up the appellate process. Hearing some of those arguments tainted my impressions.

I would not, I should not, like him. He'd deceived and beguiled Judy, and that meant no loyalty or admiration of him from me. Pity for Judy. Yet again a victim of a man.

Pushing aside conflicting feelings, I showed up in the receptionist area of the law firm. I gave the receptionist my card, identifying myself as a pastor who'd been chaplain at Tutwiler Prison.

"Do you have an appointment?" she asked me. I hoped the secretary wouldn't ask why I wanted to see Bob, and she didn't. She took the card and disappeared down the hall. A few minutes later, she returned to tell me Bob would see me.

He extended his hand and said he was pleased to meet me. I quipped, "You may not be pleased after I tell you why I'm here."

"I used to get reminded of Judith Neelley just about every day," the conversation began. "Now it's more like once a week. You must be it for this week." I found his sardonic humor appealing.[173]

We got past that and had a good conversation of about fifty minutes. We talked about everything from getting his theological writings published to his resistance to take Judy's case. He was drawn to theology, having written extensively on the Gospels. His ancestry included pastors.

I'd decided to focus on two facets: getting names of the jurors and reading more letters. I knew his law practice had meticulously researched the venire list. It was a joint effort in the firm, gleaning political persuasions, membership in civic clubs, hobbies, religion, relatives, neighbors.[174] My goal was to speak with several of the jurors.

Yes, he had a list, and I could see it. He might have the letters in question, but the files with letters and those juror cards had long ago been put in storage.

He reminisced about the case he tried to dodge and the personalities involved. "Alvin's mother gave me all Judy's letters that Alvin had kept. His mother and I were great friends until she found out who I was. There was no love lost between Mrs. Neelley and Judy."

After showing pictures of Judy before, during, and after the trial, he generously said, "If you write a book, I'll let you make copies of these pictures."

In one, he looked haggard and thin. "That's what the trial did to me," he said.

"You look older in that picture than you look now."

He told me about the death of his wife in 2001. He knew the length of time between the cancer diagnosis and her death: seventy-six short days. The loss he felt was evident in his cadence.

I stepped outside of my original, limited goals. "What did you think when you met Judy?"

"I didn't like her."

In his book about the trial, French said the first time he saw Judy, she appeared to have been beaten around her mouth and had bruises. Her appearance was dismal. "I looked in her eyes. There was nobody home. She had no affect ... no facial expression ... and she seemed to be in a trance."[175]

French couldn't have known then that he was in the presence, not of Judy, but of Alvin. Two bodies. One identity.

The reluctant lawyer recounted stories that circulated. "Rumors got started about an inappropriate relationship with Judy when some TV person asked me about how it was to work with Judy. I told him, 'Well, if you can't love the unlovable, then there's not much good to your Christianity.' From there, people took it that we were having an inappropriate relationship. Anyone who would think that has never been in a jail. It's not possible. There's always an officer present."

He circled back to a phone call. "The judge called and said, 'Bob, I need you to take the Judy Neelley case.' I told him I wouldn't do it."

The judge's reply hadn't been what French wanted to hear. "You're the most qualified." The judge knew it wouldn't be French's first death-penalty case.

Again, French said he wouldn't do it. The judge said he'd call another lawyer, and if he wouldn't take it, he'd be calling French back.

"The judge called back," French told me. "He said that the other attorney said he didn't have enough experience."

The standoff continued. Again, French told the judge he wasn't going to take it.

"Then, Bob, I'll have to issue an order," the judge said.

French submitted. "Save yourself some ink and penmanship. When did she confess?"

"Eighteen hours ago."

"Thanks!"

The call ended.

I detected pride that he'd taken a stand against defending the teen he named the "booger woman." He paid for it by losing clients, facing pickets in front of his office, declaring bankruptcy, and being told by a few members of the Sunday school class he'd taught for years that he ought to step down. He didn't.

As I stood to leave, I thanked him for his time. "It has been a pleasure meeting you. You saved Judy's life."

"I don't know about that. Maybe she saved mine." The trial and its aftermath provoked a reexamination of his life and spirituality. Then he added, answering my unasked question. "I don't ordinarily talk with people about the Neelley case, but I decided to since you're a minister."

I drove back to Birmingham that evening.

I wasn't counting on Bob's offer that he'd wear jeans the following day and go into the basement to see what he could find. The next morning, the phone rang at about 9:15. The voice was deep and resonant. French had found four filing drawers full of the case. Although he hadn't spotted the juror info, I was welcome to come back and dig through things. If I found something of interest, they would make copies of what I wanted.

After his offer, he stated, "People have never forgiven me for defending her!"

"People need to move on. You have a present, not just a past. Although," I added, "I am aware there is an allure to the crime."

"I was the eleventh best-known name in Alabama. I was notorious. I had my fifteen minutes of fame, and I didn't enjoy it. But I stayed with it."

The call ended, and I sat immobile, astonished by Bob's efforts to assist me. Then I let out a muted yelp, not wanting to startle the other hotel guests.

On Friday, I was in Fort Payne in jeans and a sweatshirt. Because of mold, I was not thrilled with hanging out in the basement for hours, but I knew it was worth my temporary allergic reaction. Bob had set up a small table at the back entrance of the law offices on the first floor (a busy thoroughfare) with a pen and pad. He told me I could copy anything I wanted. I bounced between the basement and the first floor to make copies.

I worked from 10:30 a.m. until they closed at 4:30 p.m. I read letters and material relating to the defense's preparation of the case. I made copies, trying not to impede the legal work.

Bob was gracious and helpful. He didn't want to get back into the case in detail, and I didn't ask for that. But he was willing to assist me. He told me to contact him if I had any questions.

Reading the transcript revealed a skilled defense attorney. French could feign self-deprecation before the jury. Humor momentarily broke the strain of hearing details of repellant acts. In the trial, his soliloquies to the court were imaginative and entertaining, sprinkled with historical references. Like spokes on a wheel, he would lead the listener to the hub of his argument: Judy was the victim of vicious battering. Then he would return to the outer rim with broad illustrations that were to lead those whom he was trying to convert back to the hub. Some of his history lessons were more elliptical than helpful, but I admired his instincts and tenacity.

I never found a list of jurors, although I gleaned most of them from the trial transcript. I decided their identities were bronze, and the material to which I'd been given access was gold. The work of the jurors was exhausting. They'd done their best as citizens. The photos, physical evidence, and testimonies that they had seen were sickening. Without hearing the lurid details of Judy's life with Alvin, most citizens rooted for the electric chair. And yet, ten of them said, "Don't kill her. Keep her in prison for the rest of her life." There were others in the community who expressed anger at their lesser recommendation. The jurors served faithfully. That was enough.

11.

Crazy as Usual

Judy's daughter, April, sent me an urgent email with troubling news. On the thirty-first of January 2002, she wrote that her mom was in segregation.

> *They won't tell her why they put her in there ... only that she's under investigation. She can't make her one phone call. I think they even read the letters she sent us; they were taped shut before being stamped. She's feeling very down and asked for our prayers.*

Eight days later, I received a letter from Judy. Mystery solved as to what had happened, but not why or by whom. Judy apologized that the letter was written in pencil. She had no choice; in segregation, she wasn't allowed a ballpoint pen, a potential weapon. Her nine-page letter began as usual with a cheery, "How are you all doing?" Then she said things were okay with her, although a "little crazy, but that's not unusual."

An officer taunted Judy as she was being taken to segregation, saying that whatever she was accused of, she was guilty. The assistant warden told Judy she was under investigation. When Judy asked for a reason, he was nonchalant. "I may stroll through here one day and tell you." He didn't.

On the fifth day of her confinement, the Investigations and Intelligence Division of the Alabama Department of Corrections interrogated Judy. The rationale for being "arrested" (that is, put into segregation) was a letter purportedly written by Judy sent to Alabama Governor Don Siegelman. She described the letter as disgusting, "filled with cussing. Vile." The writer threatened the lives of the governor and his family if Judy wasn't released. She offered a sample of her handwriting. Not necessary. They'd already made the comparison with a letter she'd written. Not a match.

The investigators asked about enemies Judy had, starting first with the possibility of a girlfriend relationship gone sour. Nothing there, Judy told them. She said she wasn't aware of anyone who hated her enough to send a letter, then added, "But obviously someone despises me." They raised questions about specific individuals in prison with whom Judy had had conflict. Three years earlier, one inmate, Judy told them, just wanted to kill her. Judy saw their present relationship as being without rancor.

What about a lie detector test? Judy offered at least four times. One of the agents said that it wouldn't be necessary.

One rumor circulating was that Judy had been put in segregation because Georgia authorities were on their way to take her into custody for the additional time she had. Two more letters were written from inside the prison with Judy's prison identification number. They were complaints against a third shift officer. Judy noted one upside of prison life: short attention span for gossip. An embellishment or new rumor bumped the last. But I knew an old story could be dusted off and recycled if needed.

Hostility and Boredom

Few people have their résumés burnished by a stint of incarceration. Assumptions are made: inmates are stupid, crazy, drug addicts, and of course, cheaters, liars, manipulators, and psychopaths. Inmates are the lowest in a hierarchy. It's a short trip to move from seeing inmates as people to seeing inmates as things.

Prisons dehumanize. They're also tough places to get due process. Filing a grievance against an officer is a chancy proposition. Even if the inmate is believed, the power of a badge provides ways for payback. The presumption of good cop and bad inmate justifies assigning guilt. Even so, thousands of officers go to work each day with the attitude that all humans deserve civility, and when there is a need, help should be forthcoming.

Every inmate has her or his stories that go from maddening to frightening to inane. Judy shared a few with me. One incident was amusing. I could imagine Judy facing the officer with her defiant and shrewd response.

"The other day, Officer Sabin was trying to get me to go off. He was messing with me. He was talking about prejudice, calling me a 'white girl.' I'm prejudiced against stupid people!"

In another incident, she lashed out at a male officer who

triggered vivid memories of domestic violence. "I got upset when a male officer was harassing a female officer. I don't regret opening my mouth. If they were playing, they shouldn't be doing it around me. I don't play about that."

Judy told me about a warden's terse pronouncement. "An officer may look at you in the shower, on the toilet. But if the officer stares, he'll get 'the officer's ass out of here!'" Then she related an incident. "An officer stared at me during my shower. He said, 'I'm going to do my check, and as far as you are concerned, you didn't see me.' I could report him, but I want to deal with it myself. I don't want to run to daddy. I have no respect for him as an officer. He disrespected me; that check wasn't required."

Working with emotions was a challenge for Judy. Frustrations and arguments led to anger. Other times, she pulled in and longed for solitude and the privacy to cry. Impatient with herself and with others, her battering thoughts shattered concentration and indicted her conscience.

Life in a prison is monotonous, and that contributes to disciplinary issues. Same uniform. Same feuds. Same tedious jobs. Same mindlessness. Same potatoes.

Judy fought her brain atrophying. Not satisfied with serving time, she made time serve her quest for more knowledge and more self-understanding. Once she was off death row, her opportunities and mind expanded. The choices of courses are diverse, such as relationships and self-discipline, Bible classes, and college courses through Alabama's Auburn University. Many courses have excited her: "Evolutionary Botany: Plant Adaptations," "Introduction to Biology," and "Printmaking." Since clemency in 1999, she has taken over one hundred twenty courses.

Despite plans for classes or work, a day can become a

chaotic heap of clothes and people.

Judy was writing a letter when a commotion erupted. "The jump-out boys came in. AKA 'Men in Black,' 'Goon Squad,' etc. They're the CERT team. Correctional Emergency Response Team. They wear all black and carry large clubs. They don't mind busting heads. I rather think they enjoy it." Any prison has to take it seriously when someone says they saw a gun. Even when the inmate is well known to be a liar. Such was the case this time.

"The jump-out boys shook down every inmate in this prison. They tore through locker boxes and laundry bags. Everything we had was thoroughly searched and left in a wreck. We don't have much property. I have one locker box and one laundry bag full. They wrecked me. It took two hours to set everything to rights.

"Every person was also thoroughly strip searched and walked through a metal detector. All this activity started around nine o'clock in the morning. It finished around midnight. No gun was found. They did find some drugs in other dorms. I went to bed around midnight and got right back up at two." She concluded. "Everyone was traumatized."

Being strip searched is routine. It can happen several times a day, for example, returning from classes in trade school. Squatting and coughing is part of the drill. Breasts must be lifted. After every free-world visitor, it's another degrading strip search.

~

Medical care in prisons can be professional or calloused, inept or competent. In a dorm full of double bunking and shared facilities, spreading germs is inevitable. Judy had been sleeping across from a woman for several months when she was diagnosed with tuberculosis. She was immediately put into an isolation unit. All in the dorm were tested; three women were positive for tuberculosis.

Gynecological exams precipitated flashbacks for Judy due to repeated violations by Alvin. While she was on death row, her legs were shackled, making the exam more agonizing.

Over the years, she lost teeth while in a prison dental chair. It seemed easier to pull teeth than to fill cavities. Jaw teeth were gone on the bottom. One dentist made the appointment as painless as possible. After three shots, she was well numbed, which lasted for hours, and she didn't mind a bit. The dentist's mission was to drill out an old filling and replace it.

She remarked, "His gentleness even helped to ease my newly acquired fear of the dentist. For that, I am very grateful. The worst part of the experience was having to remain handcuffed while I was there. The indignity of prison life is sometimes almost too much to bear. But I made it through."

At the end of the 1999 conference, "Religious Organizing Against the Death Penalty,"[176] I went with eight people to Texas's death row in Huntsville. We spread out, trying to see as many of the 462 men the state intended to kill as we could. A pleasant thirty-something African American was using the toilet for a chair as he listened to his radio through a headset. After introducing myself, he spoke softly and shyly. He never moved closer to the bars from the back of his cell. He said he had a visitor the day before, the first in about fifteen years, then for two days in a row, he was talking with free-world folks, neither of us family. He'd become so accustomed to a solitary life that with two visits in two days, he couldn't quite find his "feet."

The most energetic men with whom I talked were busily

working on their cases as best as they could. They were the newest on the row. The long-timers appeared passive. The light had gone from their eyes. They knew they were disposable.

I spoke with one man, but he didn't follow what I was saying. With a few words of Spanish, I tried again. He came closer to the grille and told me he was deaf. When he got to death row, the noise was so intolerable that he used a ball-point pen or pencil to puncture his eardrums.

To Louisiana and Back

My husband yelled to me from upstairs. The phone had rung. I was in the middle of washing dishes and could barely hear his anxious announcement. "It's Judy. From Louisiana."

It wouldn't be Judy. She'd called recently. But even if she called so soon, it couldn't be from another state.

"Who?" I asked as I hurried to answer.

"Judy."

By then, I was at the phone. With incredulity, I asked, "You're in Louisiana?"

Judy laughed. "Yep. I'm here."

Upbeat, she described the support inmates had given her to apply for transfer. Van after van had transported female inmates to a private prison in Louisiana to comply with a federal order to relieve dangerous prison overcrowding. No one, Judy believed, would be moved who had a detainer due to the sentence in Georgia. But abruptly, in early January 2005, she was told to gather her belongings for a ten-hour bus trip to an unknown location. For security reasons, the trip was unannounced and an all-nighter.

The bus driver shortened the ten hours to eight and a half hours with several near misses. But it was a change of scenery for Judy, who hadn't been out of Tutwiler for ten years. Even after the hair-raising driving, she was animated. "They nearly killed us," she reported and laughed easily.

She knew she was in Basile, Louisiana, not far from Texas, but anything else was a geographic blur. My computer was on, so I searched for Basile. I told her it looked like it was about ninety miles west of Baton Rouge and double that for New Orleans. About one and one half to two hours from the Gulf of Mexico. None of that changed the isolation of the privately operated South Louisiana Correctional Facility, which was just what the owners want.

Judy ran down the pluses, minuses, and unknowns. The dorm housed fifty-four women. Smoking was allowed. Tutwiler had cracked down on smoking several years earlier. The telephones were in the smoking/television area. You could call anyone collect for $4.54 for the first minute. Each additional minute was fifty-nine cents. Anyone could send money. Visitation was the same. Receiving stamps wasn't allowed. A roll of toilet paper: $1.09. A bottle of water: $1.16. She said the tap water was bad! A church could send envelopes, paper, and ink pens.

"It sounds as if you're liking it."

"Some." The excited edge in her voice modulated. "Pray for me."

Private prisons are for-profit prisons companies. Their first duty is to shareholders. I could have shared with Judy my reservations for such prisons, but I checked my impulse; Judy was benefiting from the change.

Six months later, she got two disciplinaries. It's easy to be written up for a rule violation in prison. Judy had avoided them, except for a few. The incident at South Louisiana Correctional Center bordered on the absurd. One infraction could garner two strikes, she was told. One recorded in Louisiana and the same disciplinary in Alabama. The misadventure was "destruction of property." Judy and two other women were sitting on their locker boxes. Nothing was broken. Judy was upset and talked with the captain. She reassured Judy not to worry about it.

"Maybe it was just a scare tactic. It worked! I bet I don't sit on that locker box again (smiley face)."

She remained at Basile one and a half years. Then Judy and other Tutwiler women were shipped to J. B. Evans Correctional Center in Newellton, Louisiana, another for-profit prison.[177] By October 2007, she was moved to the Montgomery, Alabama, Women's Facility. Then back to Tutwiler.

Unmerited Compassion

There was a strange twist in Judge Randall Cole's overriding the jury's recommendation of life without parole. Had he followed their lead, there would've been no clemency. Almost certainly, Judy would die in prison. Off death row, there was the slim chance of parole. But first, she had to have a parole date. She accepted that parole in Alabama meant time in Georgia, due to the plea deal for a life sentence she'd struck with the court in 1983 for the murder of Kay MacRae.

One confusing element to sentencing is that "life" does not mean a person is being sentenced to die in prison. "Life" varies from state to state. In Alabama, life means a minimum of fifteen years. The nearly six thousand days on death row didn't count toward a life sentence. The clock was reset. Judy's earliest date for consideration was January 2014. However, parole eligibility is not a given.

To the surprise of many, the parole board signaled that Judy was to be considered as soon as she'd served the fifteen years.

The most surprised were Alabama legislators. They thought they'd put Judy away for good in 2003 when they passed a law, often called the Judy Neelley Law. "Any person whose sentence to death has been commuted by the governor shall not be eligible for parole" and "the operation of this act shall be retroactive to September 1, 1998."[178] The public drew a sigh of relief. Judy would die in prison—one way or another.

The parole board read the law as being inapplicable to Judy because "the retroactivity clause reached back to 1998 and the crime was committed in 1982."[179] But the board contacted the attorney general for his legal read. He was unequivocal. She wasn't eligible. After months of rising hope for a chance to be paroled, Judy received a crushing letter from the board. She was barred.

Attorneys Barry Ragsdale and Julian McPhillips doggedly picked up the challenge. They argued that the 2003 law was passed *ex post facto*, after the fact. James's commutation took place before the law was on the books. No success in the district court. They said Judy Neelley failed to file within the two-year statute of limitations, which was by 2005. Ragsdale pursued the fight to the United States District Court for the Middle District of Alabama. The decision of the lower court was reversed and remanded in 2018. Judy was eligible to be considered for parole.[180]

Quickly, the date was set for May. I wondered if the rapidity of the hearing was an effort to minimize mounting support for Judy. In a letter to family and friends, Judy asked them not to attend the parole hearing, because she feared reprisals. That applied to me as well. "I don't want you to be there. I love you. It's going to be bad. I'm scared for you. People strike out. They will try to hurt anyone who tries to help me. You'll be a target for the rage and wrath people have."

I'd been having conversations with people who confirmed that it could get dicey. However, I saw the threat as minor. To me, the graver danger was her welfare if she were paroled. I was afraid for her. She was an "it," the object of hate for many. I deferred to her plea.

A representative of the board went to Tutwiler to assess Judy's readiness for parole. He was encouraging: at least sixty percent of those who went for parole were granted. Judy scoffed. He asked about her crimes. She didn't hesitate in admitting responsibility.

Cathy Connolly's family gave interviews and spoke on camera. Concerned for the welfare of the child's family, Judy reconsidered the hearing and wrote to the board:

> *Although I am grateful for the opportunity to demonstrate how much God has changed my heart and life over the past 36 years, I know that now is not the right time. In order to spare the … family the pain and trauma of having to attend the hearing, I have agreed to waive my right to be considered for parole at this time. I will continue to pray daily for God's forgiveness and for peace for the … family.*[181]

Not everyone was impressed with Judy's offer. The state director of the Victims of Crime and Leniency (VOCAL) called her letter a "dog and pony show" of waving her parole hearing so victims wouldn't be further traumatized. The "family is prepared to fight for justice … by speaking out and protesting at Neelley's parole hearing … Let the voices of the victims be heard."[182]

The board replied. She had two options. Proceed with the hearing or permanently waive her right to a future parole date. Judy chose the former.

Judges in Alabama are elected: from probate courts to district and circuit courts, the Court of Criminal Appeals, all the way to the Supreme Court of Alabama. District attorneys and attorneys general are also elected positions. Most serve the public's highest interests, not their political aspirations. But if it's a notorious case in which the elected official has authority or power, those officials may take a posture they believe plays well in the press and in the voting booths. To be tough on criminals.

The governor of Alabama appoints parole board members. Governor Kay Ivey informed the board. "Under no circumstances should Judith Ann Neelley be granted parole. Her crimes … include acts of unspeakable brutality. And her character includes a disturbing tendency to manipulate others toward her own, violent ends."[183]

In the May 23 hearing, one who protested Judy was in a runoff for attorney general.[184] Another pronouncement was from the DeKalb County district attorney who had been second in command in Judy's capital murder trial. He reminded the receptive audience of his thirty-eight years as a prosecutor and over two hundred murder cases. He was merciless and uninformed. "I have never prosecuted one other defendant who murdered for sheer sport. She loved killing." He was emphatic in denouncing "brainwashing" as a defense. In a quick gloss, O'Dell stated that defense was rejected by the jury and all through the appellate system. But the jury's recommendation of life without parole signaled that they accepted the impact of coercive control. Erroneously, he declared that Judy "is still not willing to take responsibility for the acts."[185]

If some of the accusers had read the report filed by the man from the parole office who interviewed her, they might have gotten a glimpse of Judy's remorse. If the parole board had met with her, they could've learned that the teen in 1982 bore little resemblance to the woman in 2018.[186]

Because Barry Ragsdale had a conflict, Julian McPhillips agreed to represent her at the hearing. He wanted everyone to know that she was a changed person who admitted that she'd committed the horrific crimes. "To say that Ms. Neelley was brainwashed is a vast understatement. She was more like a zombie, no independent mind, no rational mind of her own, coerced by her husband." He had a suggestion. Alabama could send her to Georgia and let them pay for Judy's upkeep.[187]

The board's deliberation took about one minute.

Judy heard the decision on the twelve-noon local news.

Denied.

Letters of Remorse

Keep loving each other like family.
Don't neglect to open up your homes to guests,
because by doing this some have been hosts to angels without
knowing it.
Remember prisoners as if you were in prison with them,
and people who are mistreated as if you were in their place.
Hebrews 13:1–3[188]

With Alvin, Judy had been in a perpetual stance of heightened awareness—of him. It took all her energy to survive. On death row, as that anxiety diminished, she was able to focus on what she'd done. She began to take a moral inventory and almost buckled under the strain of guilt.

During one of our visits in 1998, Judy spoke of her yearning to let victims know that she was remorseful. This wasn't a new idea, but its urgency at that time was apparent.

Judy told me, "I'd like a chance to talk with family members of my victims before I die; I really, really want to do that. Even if I'm not executed this year, I want to do it ASAP. I know it can't bring back loved ones, but I want a chance to tell them face-to-face how sorry I am."

Judy knew about the Victim-Offender Reconciliation Program I started in Montgomery in the early nineties. Facilitated by a mediator, the process is to promote healing in the victim, to hold offenders accountable relationally for what they've done, and to agree on restitution that can assist in the healing.

Her grief and contrition could have stayed within, poisoning her in the way self-abasement becomes toxic, spiraling into self-pity. Until she communicated sorrow to the people most affected by her crimes, her remorse was half-born and an abdication of a moral duty. The longing is spiritual, not temporal.

Finding families of victims can be challenging. If a victim agrees to speak with a reporter, or a nosy person, those can be unruly exchanges. It requires reliving the victim's ordeal. It took years, a variety of sources, including friends, Judy's attorney, and a few cold calls to get in contact with family members.

Judy's first effort to express her sorrow was to staff of the Georgia Department of Youth Services in late 1983 or early 1984. While in jail, she was allowed to make a call to the Rome Center. Although she wasn't able to speak with Linda Adair or Ken Dooley, victims in September 1982 of a fire bombing and having shots fired into their homes, Judy asked the receptionist, whom Judy thought of as kind, to relay her regrets.

Years later, I sent Judy's letters of remorse to Department of Youth Services staff, Dooley and Adair:

> *I am sorry to intrude into your lives again. I am writing simply to apologize and explain. It has been more than 13 years and I do not wish to stir up painful memories for you. But there are some things that need to be said, and this is long overdue.*
>
> *Al was extremely abusive and possessive. He always hated anyone who was kind to me ... He wanted me dependent on him one hundred percent. My respecting or admiring anyone was absolutely unacceptable to him. I do not know how to explain it further. I know it makes no sense at all. But Al*

did things that made no sense.

She considered the compassion and competency of the staff and the efforts they'd extended in numerous therapeutic ways. Judy described Linda Adair as having a "heart of gold." She described Dooley as funny and smart. His teaching the students the alphabet in sign language had stayed with her. Dooley helped Judy realize that her perceptions of men were skewed. He reignited her love of learning.

I spoke on the phone with Ken Dooley and found no hint of bitterness in his intonation or the content of the conversation. He'd forgiven her and was willing to receive Judy's letter of apology. His kindness had been repaid with meanness. His main question was why?[189] After I told Judy about the "why," she wrote him:

> *I do not understand it fully myself ... I wish I could describe in detail the extreme physical, mental, psychological, and emotional abuse I experienced at the hands of Alvin Neelley ... Maybe then you and Mrs. Dooley could understand that I was broken. Shattered. I did exactly as Al told me to do.*
>
> *It didn't happen overnight. It was a process. Bit by bit he broke me. I do not try to justify my actions because there is no justification. I'm just trying ... to make amends somehow.*

In that conversation with Ken, he told me that fourteen years after he was erroneously accused of sex crimes at the center, he had the impression that the police remained suspicious about his alleged behavior. Ken said he'd take her letter to the investigators and show them what Judy had written.

That piece of the conversation upset Judy. She felt her letter to Ken wasn't sufficient. She wrote two more letters. The first was to Ken, expressing dismay that he remained under suspicion. At the trial, she'd vindicated him. She assumed that in telling the truth, there would be no doubts as to his innocence.

> *I cannot make up for the fourteen years you have suffered. But I can do whatever is in my power to clear your name, to make sure the truth is known. Enclosed you will find a letter that I hope will help. You can give copies to whatever authorities you deem necessary ... I am sorry, Mr. Dooley. If there is anything I can do, please let me know.*

Judy expressed gratitude for his "precious gift of forgiveness," although she felt it was undeserved and humbling. "I have done a great deal of harm in my life, which I regret more deeply than you know. There is a measure of relief to know that I am forgiven by some. But I will feel a bit better when you are cleared of all suspicions."

The letter to the police read in part:

> *I am writing this letter in regard to Mr. Ken Dooley and in the allegations I have made in the past to Mr. Dooley's misconduct, sexual or otherwise. It is my desire that the truth be known and Mr. Dooley be cleared of any alleged improprieties.*
> *I met Ken Dooley in 1980. At that time, he was a teacher in Rome, Georgia's Youth Development Center. I was a resident of the center. Mr. Dooley never once behaved inappropriately. He was a kind*

264

and compassionate teacher. There was absolutely no misconduct of any kind sexual or otherwise.

In 1982 I placed calls to authorities in Rome, accusing Mr. Dooley of sexual misconduct. The accusations were complete lies, fabrications of my now ex-husband Alvin Neelley. I was forced to make those calls. I deeply regret it ... During my trial ... I testified to the truth. I assumed that Mr. Dooley would automatically be cleared of all wrongdoing. Only last month I learned that I was wrong ... Had I known before now Mr. Dooley was still under suspicion I would've written this long ago.

Alvin's jealousies and his conviction that she had sexual liaisons with the staff were fuel for payback.

To force me to "confess" Alvin would beat me severely. It didn't take long for me to "confess" to any indiscretions he alleged—anything to avoid the beatings ... I had no idea that Alvin would later try to destroy these innocent people ...

The murder for which I am on death row now is vaguely connected to the previously described insanity. As payment for my alleged sexual indiscretions I was forced to procure females for my ex-husband ...

Alvin forced me to call the police to confess to these two murders, exonerating Alvin completely. In my confession I was to explain that my motive for killing the 13-year-old was to protect her from rape and sexual abuse that she would receive in the

youth centers …
> *If you have any questions … I will do whatever*
> *I can to help set things right and I do so with the*
> *knowledge and encouragement of my attorney.*

Letters to families of the two she murdered attempted to strike a balance between taking responsibility and stating how she lost agency. "I want you to know that I did not want to participate in those crimes. I had no choice. The idea was my ex-husband's. But I did participate, and the guilt is equally mine."

She offered to answer questions that had nagged them. If she could help them heal, it was worth the shame.

"I know an apology changes nothing. It is far too little, too late. Nonetheless, I want you to know how deeply sorry I am. It is all I have to give. I do not expect your forgiveness. You suffered more than I can imagine in a terrible crime."

She reassured the recipients that their addresses were not known to her. Judy closed the letters. "My prayers remain with you all. God bless you and give you peace."

Surrogates for Judy

Many who have intersected Judy's life have stepped forward when needed. A North Georgia resident, Janice McFry, is one of those.

Janice read about Judy's case and decided to write to her. They became pen pals. She called me in the fall of 1998 to see how Judy was doing. In the conversation, I said it would be beneficial to make a trip to Rome to talk with victims and family members of victims of Judy and Alvin. Janice offered to set up meetings with whomever I thought I should see. I found one free Saturday between then and moving to New York. It was a good decision. It made sense.

I was feeling stress from many angles. I dreaded telling Judy we were moving. Another abandonment. Separation anxiety. Although I knew visits would be few, I tried to lift her mood. "Whether you like it or not, you can't get rid of me that easily."

The closer I got to the Rome trip, the less sense it made and the more I dreaded taking the time from other jobs elbowing me. Even so, in the week of November 15, I contacted Janice to confirm my coming on November 20. She'd been running interference for me, but midweek Janice said there was a hitch. Several of the women with whom I wanted to speak were leery of trusting anyone after their negative experience with an author.

I emailed Janice my purposes in desiring to speak with them. I promised not to reveal what was confidential. Finally, considering the likelihood of Judy's execution in the near future, I stated that my goal was to offer her remorse in their ongoing healing.

As I traveled to Rome with no guarantee of seeing anyone connected to Judy, except Janice, I felt calmed with a sense of God's guidance. I prayed about every aspect of the trip I could imagine. God was making a way out of no way.

Janice and I met for supper at Patterson Feed Mill. Before the meal, I prayed. "Thank you, God, for the efforts that Janice has made. May our spirits be in fellowship with one another as you are in fellowship with us. Amen."

My reasons for speaking with people were sufficient for Linda Adair. She asked that I let her know when I got to Rome.

Her husband wanted to come; therefore, we set a meeting for that evening. I was grateful for the presence of Gary Adair. He came as supporter and protector of his wife. The Adairs, Janice, and I met in my hotel room.

They described the investigation into the firebombing as one in which they were treated rudely, and that it lasted much longer than the emerging facts warranted. It was stressful for their family and the Youth Development Center.

After the murders, Linda was again summoned to the police station. A story had circulated that Judy was going around Rome in a blond wig, impersonating Linda. The police wanted the boyfriend of a victim to identify Linda. The logic of that eludes me. When I asked Judy about the impersonation story, she was astounded. It never happened.

Linda told how she felt about the author's showing up at her front door. She'd made it clear she didn't consent to an interview. The author promised that she and her husband would see what was in the book before it was published. They heard nothing. "Finally," she stated with a mixture of frustration and anger, "I started looking for the book, but couldn't find it. I came home one day, and a friend had a copy. He read the first page to me. I couldn't believe it; he'd put in personal information!"

I thought about how vulnerable they felt. Revictimized.

"We had nothing in writing. I talked with some lawyers, but they said without a written agreement, there wasn't much that could be done."

Linda's mood lifted as she said she had to tell me about the dog. "It was like God had sent something to protect me. Our neighbor's St. Bernard stayed at our home until Judy and Alvin were in jail in Tennessee."

One night when the neighbors were away, Linda heard

her godsend yelping. "It took a lot of courage for me to go out. He was still crying. I didn't know if he'd been hit by a car, but [since] his owners were gone and he was too big for me to handle, I went back in and got a gun and sat outside with him for an hour and a half." The next day, the neighbors took their dog to the vet. "He had cancer in his legs; they had to put him to sleep. I didn't feel safe after that."

Like aftershocks from an earthquake, victims can experience reverberations for months and even years. I admired the resolve of the Adairs to speak with me, because events from sixteen years ago were hovering in the room.

They mentioned that they felt an unsettling threat from Alvin and even from Judy, although markedly less from her. They were disturbed by the lack of information they had on Alvin's status. Was he coming up for parole? Would they be notified if he were paroled?

I urged them to make an official request for information regarding Alvin's status. Fortunately, Adair knew the attorney general from his work as an insurance investigator for the state, so he said he'd see to that. Janice gave Linda the name of a victim-service officer in Rome who would help.

Linda Adair said she wanted to acknowledge Judy's letter of apology, but she didn't know what to say. I encouraged her to write and let Judy know how the crime had affected their lives and to ask questions. Even though it would be difficult for Linda to write and Judy to reply, she was eager to make amends.

When Judy was at the Rome center, she told Ms. Adair about her family. Judy said before her dad's death, they were a healthy family. I said her father's untimely death accelerated the decline that was already in motion. Ms. Adair observed that people can tell what they believe someone else wants to hear, not necessarily the entire truth. A prettier story is an attempt to make more tolerable the inappropriate shame and self-reproach the child may carry.

We talked for about two hours. Linda's persona was calming. She said she'd prayed for Judy and forgave her. Having read some of Alvin's letters to Judy, she had insight into his mental state, and that had guided her as she tried to get through to Judy.

Linda commented that talking about all that happened was healing. When I asked in what way, she explained, "It helps to talk with someone who understands what I'm talking about." Even so, it was stressful to relive wounding memories.

The most troubling revelation of our time together was when Linda said that if the police had given them more information, she believed the two deaths could've been prevented.

Later that evening, I turned my attention to Saturday. Janice McFry and I were to meet the mother of Kay MacRae, Betty Morrow.

Kay was Judy and Alvin's second murder victim.

Only a few days after Cathy's death, Alvin dispatched Judy to procure another girl. After many hours, the one victim Judy could snare was a woman of twenty-three. She and her boyfriend were walking home, and Judy used a practiced line, asking directions. Or she extended an invitation to go riding. Whatever the enticement, Kay and Steve were hesitant, but got in Judy's car. Soon they met up with Alvin, who'd contacted Judy on the C.B. They spoke ostensibly as strangers.

They drove into the country with Alvin in the lead, searching for a remote area. At their first stop, Alvin changed the seating arrangements. Steve would go with him. The twins would go with their mother (Alvin couldn't get them to quit

270

crying), and Kay would remain with Judy. Back on the road, Alvin told Steve they were looking for bootleg liquor. Finally, Alvin pulled over where there weren't many houses and gave Judy precise instructions. When she approached Steve, he saw the gun in her hand. She told him to walk down the dirt road and into some weeds. He complied. A few minutes later, Judy shot Steve in the back, and he crumpled to the ground. It's fortuitous that Alvin was shouting to Judy to hurry. She ran back, not knowing that Steve was alive.[190]

The three of them—Alvin, Judy, and Kay—left the scene of that crime and went to a motel, where Alvin abused and raped Kay. Then came the decree: Judy was to get rid of another witness. The next morning, they took Kay to a rural area of northwest Georgia. Judy obeyed. Alvin watched while she shot Kay three times.

Steve's testimony was invaluable in beginning to unravel the identity of the couple who'd abducted his girlfriend and him, and it became the key to solving a murder in Alabama. Despite the suffering, his testifying carried no hint of the lifelong scar he bears. His responses were respectful and patient with the repetition of lawyering. He was an able witness.

Janice McFry and I went to the home of Kay MacRae's mother on a Saturday morning, November 1998. The sky went from cloudy to sun streaked and overcast again. Janice said we should go about 9:30 a.m. to catch Betty before she got out.

"Don't be surprised if she greets us in her pajamas. She doesn't know all the social skills."

I asked, "Should I wear mine under my raincoat, to make her feel comfortable?"

"Sure," she responded.

I imagined myself visiting in pajamas and laughed.

We arrived at the Greystone Apartments, a renovated

downtown hotel for low-income residents. Betty had intellectual limitations, but she made the best with what she could do. Housing had been one of her challenges, but finally, she had a warm, secure apartment.

We stood outside the glass doors, and Janice punched in numbers on her cell phone. Security was tight.

I listened impatiently for Janice's "Hello."

"Betty, good morning. This is Janice. We're here. Is it all right if we come up and see you?"

There was a pause. I wouldn't be sure it was going to happen until she allowed us into the apartment building. Why would she allow me into her home? As part of the victim-offender program, I'd been rejected by victims who wouldn't talk with me in far less serious crimes.

"Yes," was Betty's quiet response.

"Good. Can you come down and let us in?"

It was going to happen!

The time moved quickly. I saw a white-haired woman, short and heavyset, approaching the door.

"Is that she?" My question was in the air when she opened the door.

We skimmed over social amenities. Janice had prepared Betty to expect both of us and explained that I had a letter to her from Judy. Betty led us into the elevator. As we entered her apartment, I noticed a puzzle in progress.

"Oh, you like puzzles," I said, impressed with her hobby. Puzzles require analytical ability.

"Yes." She invited us to go into her bedroom, where she had others, finished, and sealed with puzzle glue to preserve them.

Just as quickly as we'd gone into her bedroom, she directed us to take seats in the living room—a small area that merged into an eating area that merged into the kitchen. Nearly every space was covered with figurines. No doubt each with a special history. We settled into two chairs. Betty directed Janice to sit beside her on the small sofa and me to take the chair at a right angle to the couch. Betty lifted one foot to cross her legs. She wore house slippers, and her ankle and foot were swollen.

"So how are you?" Janice began.

"Pretty good."

I knew I'd need to pay close attention to Betty. She used speech patterns with which I was unfamiliar, so I found her words sometimes unclear to my ear.

Betty described her daughter as a gentle person who was helpful to her. The memories were sweet and matched Betty's demeanor.

When I sensed the time was appropriate, I asked if she wanted to hear the letter of apology that Judy had written to her. She agreed. Ms. Morrow listened closely.

When I finished, she said, "She writes well. I can't write like that."

I said, "Everybody is good at something."

She laughed. "I'm good at fussing."

Betty's responses to the letter and to our meeting revealed a caring heart. She had no questions or concerns. Then, unexpectedly, she asked if I wanted to speak with her sister, Sylvia. Almost before I agreed, she dialed the number. Sylvia didn't hesitate to talk with me and was as accommodating as her sister.

I gave the letter to Ms. Morrow. She said she would read it again.

It was a remarkable weekend made possible by extraordinary people: Betty, the Adairs, Janice, Sylvia. Heroic, forgiving. Each an instrument of healing.

The God-News of Forgiveness

August 2009

People exist who are adept in empathizing with sorrow and joy in other's lives so they can be our guides for a time. They are God's human messengers. Physical appearance and ethnicity are irrelevant. Age or gender identities, economics or political party are not factors. When they enter our lives, they offer discernment. Their presence is God's spirit in human clothing. The guidance is often challenging; we can reject or accept it. I base my conviction on experience and Genesis 1:27 that we are created in God's image. That makes it possible to follow God's lead. When we trust the Spirit to lead us, we become messengers for others.

Cindy Silva accepted the challenge of forgiveness and is a messenger. After years of intermittent searches to find a Connolly family member, I read a newspaper article that provided the lead I sought: Cindy, a cousin who lived in Georgia, north of Atlanta.[191] I discovered the article ten years after it was printed. This was my first solid connection to anyone in the victim's family to ask about receiving Judy's letter of apology.

In August 2009, I sat in the sunroom of the parsonage of St. Mark's United Methodist Church on Long Island where my husband was pastor. Late afternoon rays suffused the room. I prayed for God to govern my thoughts and for Cindy to be receptive to the Spirit's leading. A modicum of trust had to occur in the conversation to convey the empathy I felt for the family's suffering. Every word mattered.

I dialed the number I'd found, hoping I'd be able to speak with Cathy's cousin. A woman answered. I introduced myself as a pastor in New York and that I'd had a connection with Judy Neelley over the years. I asked her if she were the cousin of Cathy Connolly. She said yes.

She didn't hang up.

"It's so ironic you called. I ran across something about Judy a month ago. I go to church. I teach Sunday school, four- and five-year-olds. I'm an avid worker for the Lord. I know you have to forgive."

Cindy was emphatic that forgiveness is expected of all Christians. She had relatives who were murdered. She'd had too many occasions to learn to forgive.

Her voice was warm and Deep South. "I believe God forgives everyone. I started doing research in the Bible and found out that Paul was a notorious killer. We live under the grace of the New Testament. I don't think we're supposed to take life. That's not up to us; it's up to God.

"I've often wondered why Judy would do what she did. She has been on my mind. When it happened, I was barely eighteen years old, married with a new baby. Judy was eighteen or nineteen."

"She turned eighteen that summer."

Cindy's tone grew wistful. "It hit me hard. Cathy and I were almost like sisters; she spent nights with us. Many times, we took things to Cathy's family. My dad was a truck driver. He loved his older brother." Referencing the night Cathy was kidnapped, Cindy observed, "All Cathy wanted to do was get back home."

Pain in Cathy's family stifled good memories. With sorrow, I said quietly, "That was a tragic crossing of paths." After a moment of silence, I said, "I want to explain the purpose of my calling. Several years ago, Judy asked me to write about her life. I'm not trying to justify anything Judy did. But inaccuracies in the public's perception fuel spiteful words. She trusts me to be fair."

Cindy could relate to the desire to share a cautionary memoir. She said she was writing about her life with the help of a relative. "If I could save one teenage girl from mistakes I made, it would be worth it. I was seventeen when I got pregnant. I didn't marry the child's father. What I did was wrong. Sometimes God requires things we don't understand. Part of healing is understanding the other side. When you get into God's word, things are revealed to you. Every time you read it, there are new things."

"You sound to me like someone who lives what you believe."

"You have to. And you have to give from the heart like the widow in the Bible who gave everything. We must learn to forgive."

"As hard as it is, I agree." I returned to the purpose of my call. "I delivered Judy's letter of apology to the mother of the woman killed in Georgia. Her reception of the letter was inspiring." I considered my words. "Would you be willing to receive a letter of apology from Judy?"

Cindy didn't hesitate. "Of course."

I was elated. "That's courageous. Judy will be very grateful." I took a beat to absorb Cindy's response. "How should Judy address the letter? To you or to the family?"

She anticipated ire over her decision to accept a letter and chose to have it addressed to her home. I advised that it is generally better for the offender not to have direct contact. Others may not want Judy to have the address of anyone in the family.

Cindy described the impact of Governor James's order of clemency. Some family members were angry. A sheriff reassured her by saying that even if Judy got out of the Alabama system, she'd be picked up and taken to Georgia to serve a life sentence. Cindy's nuanced reaction was her belief that God should be the arbiter of when people die. Her easy laugh and downhome accent made for an enjoyable conversation. She opened another door for Judy's apology. It would be a linchpin in her restoration.

Working with people can be messy, and it can be astonishing, both happening simultaneously. My insides were a jumble at the impossibility of what had occurred. Cindy's unexpected compassion touched me. Those thirty-seven minutes were like seeing the first sprouts of a crop. God had been preparing Cindy, even as God had been nurturing Judy.

The next evening, Judy called. I held back my news, allowing me to gauge her mood. She described a recent visit with family, its high and low points. Her voice held an edge of irritation.

I waited no longer. "I have good news. I talked with Cathy Connolly's cousin yesterday. She's agreed to receive a letter from you."

Silence. When Judy spoke, her tone was quiet and determined. "I do want to do that. A chaplain's assistant said I need to find someone to help me make peace with the past. Maybe the timing is opening the door a little. How could I not write? If it were me, I don't think I would ever want to hear from someone who killed a family member."

A few days later, Cindy called to report on the reactions of some in the family. "Everyone was shocked. I told them if Judy writes, I'll write her back. It's not a matter of how you feel. It's a matter of doing what is right."

Judy wrote to Cindy the next month on the twenty-seventh anniversary of Cathy's death. Every year that September date glared at Judy, accusing and merciless. In writing the letter, Judy recognized a seed of kindness—planted not by her, but by a member of the victim's family.

Hours after finishing Cindy's letter, Judy reported for work and waited in the dining room to get supplies for her dorm. The area began filling up as others waited. "More and more crowded. Hotter. Louder. The crowd kept pressing in on me."

She fled, trying to speak but only managing a stutter as she struggled to regain equilibrium—an anxiety attack.

She wrote to me. "I was shaking, crying, couldn't breathe. I was beet red, which I didn't know until later … I truly thought I'd handled writing the letter well. I thought I was okay. I was apparently wrong."

Judy's letter to Cindy and family covered five handwritten pages.

"I am sorry … for every tear … for every drop of rage, anger, every feeling of hopelessness, helplessness, fear. I am sorry for all the dreams destroyed, every frustration at the injustice. For every birthday, Christmas, Thanksgiving. I pray for your family every day."

In the letter, Judy anticipated disbelief that she didn't willingly kill Cathy. Judy recounted life with her husband. Abuse in 1979 "was a shameful secret." Alvin's mother responded to Judy's tales of beatings in varying ways, with laughter, with silence, with disinterest. If Mrs. Neelley didn't believe, having seen the cuts and bruises and having heard the fights, then who would?

"I hasten to tell you that I am *not* excusing what I did. I am simply explaining as best I can. I never wanted to hurt anyone. But I did not stop it, so I am as guilty as Alvin Neelley." Her contrition was fulsome, but she didn't seek forgiveness from Cathy's family.

She offered the family what no one else could give: full transparency. If anyone had questions, she would strive to answer them. She wrote with gratitude of God's unmerited forgiveness and "relentless love" despite her incapacity to receive it fully.

The letter came to me. By my mailing it to Cindy, her address was not known to Judy. She had a request. "Please pray over it before you send it. I do not want to say *anything* wrong. They've suffered more than enough. I don't want to add to it."

Nine years later, the circle of reconciliation widened to include another relative of Cathy. Judy's avenues to convey remorse were expanding in small measures.

May 2018

Soon after Judy's parole hearing, a friend told me that a member of Cathy Connolly's family was interested in speaking with Judy. The friend asked if I could facilitate a meeting. After I said I'd be happy for the opportunity, he provided what I most needed—a phone number.

I collected my thoughts and made the call. We talked about victim-offender mediation as an opportunity to express feelings and ask questions that were unanswered in the legal process. I assured her that Judy's goal wasn't to have anyone in the victim's family support parole for her or offer forgiveness.

I mentioned that I was writing a book about Judy's life to lay out the breadth of the abuse by Alvin and how that dominated her behavior. No concern was expressed about my close association with Judy and how that might impact a mediation.

The conversation flowed and remained courteous and at times passionate. I said that arrangements at the prison would require patience and persistence.

In a follow-up, I wrote to the Connolly family to detail the thorough process. A mediator meets with victims to hear their needs and questions. The mediator then speaks at another time with the offender. If the mediator believes a meeting will be productive, a time is set to bring all parties together. My assumption was that I would be the mediator. A Department of Corrections official said that I could neither mediate nor be present.

In Judy's letter to Cindy Silva almost a month after the parole hearing, Judy expressed the impact of forgiveness.

> *You will always be special to me, Cindy. You forgave me when no one else would. You reached out to me with love and encouragement, suffering the outrage of others in doing it. You love me as Christ instructs us to do. So much easier said than done. I don't think you understand how much your forgiveness has affected me. I don't even know if I can explain it. I will try.*
>
> *What happened was a horrible, unacceptable thing. I know the reasons. But I was unable and unwilling to forgive myself for it. I could not move forward, no matter what the Bible says. I could not let it go. I loathed myself and listened to the endless lies of Satan.*
>
> *Then you forgave me. You opened a door within me. One that I'd kept bolted shut for years. One I had been unwilling to even consider opening. How dare I forgive myself and move forward? How dare*

I hope to receive forgiveness from anyone—even God—after what I'd done?

But you, with your sweet spirit and unconditional love, simply forgave me. You did not allow me to be less accountable. You simply let me feel loved. … You forgave the unforgivable. You quite literally changed my life.

As time has passed, I have slowly walked this path of forgiveness. I have been able to forgive myself and accept God's forgiveness. I am able to forgive others for what they do, or have done to me. Had you not reached out to me, I don't know where I would be today.

12.

Marking Time

listlessness
mistrust
clout

emptiness

blank days
blank seasons
dissolving decades
family bonds hollow ...

grief
guilt

bitter taste of bars

282

At the end of long days I walked out of the prison. I carried hurts and anger with me, the sense of hopelessness, the hopefulness of hoping. But I didn't have to queue up to take any prescribed medication. I wasn't locked in my bedroom overnight. I wouldn't be awakened by an officer or someone screaming from a bad dream. There wasn't cardboard for food where I lived. I didn't have to face another day of deadening and tedious work.

A penitentiary is where one does penance. Even the women and men who have changed face employers conducting background checks, and that is one of dozens of barriers to becoming a law-following citizen. For those who are not guilty? What do they learn? People believe prison is a place to be converted. A convict goes in, guilty as sin, and comes out transformed. But incarceration sucks out character traits that are wholesome and fills the void with ego defense mechanisms. It reduces humans to survival mode. Mothers and fathers don't emerge as better parents. Older people stumble out the gates into the gloomy fog of a precarious future. The young may feel emboldened, but with no job training, untreated mental illness, addiction, failure to mature, and families who have moved on—the temptations to fall back into destructive acts begin to feel like the solitary option.

Judy and I talked about the impact of decades of imprisonment.

"My life is not rainbows and butterflies. It's not as difficult as it has been."

"Are you willing to unpack that?" I asked.

Judy teased me for asking knotty questions to which she often responded with hard-earned wisdom.

"I'll always feel guilt. The rage and pain are still with me because of what Alvin did to me, but I've largely worked through that. Forgiveness is an incredible thing. Some family members of victims have forgiven me. It's powerful. I also know the strength of hatred. It's heavy to carry. Those who hold on to hate don't realize the prison they're in. I never thought I would forgive Alvin. I must remind myself when feelings of anger sneak in. 'You've worked on that. You don't need to pick it back up.' That's hard work—and worth it."

Reflecting on Judy's rehabilitation and wildly divergent implementations of justice, I asserted, "Our so-named justice system is a roller coaster of emotional challenges and legal machinations. To the degree it could and should, it does not serve victims or offenders well."

Her voice hardened. "The justice system is so messed up. 'Justice' is bought and paid for. There are innocent people in prison, often because of ineffective counsel."

I added, "It's tragic. And we know that guilty people aren't always incarcerated. A boatload of skilled attorneys and community clout can make years vanish. I've never heard of a wealthy person on death row. The saying that the rich get richer and the poor get prison is illustrative of class disparity. Apparently we aren't willing to deal with it."

A COVID Birthday Party

By the summer of 2020, COVID-19 took over daily life. Settings of higher density, such as nursing homes and prisons, are playing grounds for any virus. Someone in Judy's dorm became infected. The warden quarantined the dorm. No roaming the halls. No trips to the cafeteria. Soon Judy felt ill.

Loss of the senses of taste and smell, extreme fatigue. Because she didn't run a fever, she wasn't tested for COVID-19. Resentment simmered among inmates and anxieties grew.

Judy's birthday came as her body's defenses began to overcome the virus. One of Judy's friends in the dorm found a way to lessen the tension. She spent weeks constructing props from cardboard to make a jukebox, Victrola, microphone, and more. On the day of Judy's birthday, they were the scenery on the small smoke yard where about thirty women crowded for a karaoke session that lasted two hours. Along with blowing bubbles, the karaoke was a good stress-reliever given their lockdown status. Judy observed that some of the music, such as "Gunpowder and Lead" might not have been the best choice, since the song's solution to abuse and injustice was further violence.[192]

The birthday menu, created by pooling food resources, was inventive. A heated tortilla shell was the base. Then the layers: cheese, refried beans, summer sausage, spam, pickles, jalapeños, all smothered in ranch dressing. The birthday cake was a pie made with whipped coffee creamer to which was added powdered lemonade, then poured over a graham cracker crust. Judy's sense of taste and smell had been hijacked by the virus, but she enjoyed it vicariously.

Judy's fifty-sixth birthday was that rare time when she felt valued. The women experienced camaraderie and lightheartedness. Bickering was set aside. Petty animosities were left on bunk beds. The limitations of the environment and the anxiety of COVID-19 paled.

Judy summed up the day. "We had a blast!!"

Since the past weeks had been of illness and fears of dying, I was happy to hear of an extraordinarily good day. Few occasions can be described as joyful in Judy's life.

I decided to include the birthday party in this book as a sign of resiliency and hope. Judy's reaction to reading the story was unforeseen and contrary to that intent. She said it was as hard to see the party described in print as reading an autopsy of three years with Alvin. The party's fun disintegrated.

Despondently, she told me, "Somebody is going to read this and say I have no right to one moment of happiness." She paused and added matter-of-factly, "They would be right. I don't deserve to be happy."

I couldn't negate the appraisal that there would be angry reactions. Even though some would be glad for her day of festivity—especially having weathered COVID-19—a vocal segment would bristle at her temerity to have one good day. I wanted to say she'd paid for her sins in God's court, that God's mercy opened her to joy that no one could steal. The voices of denunciation were trying to muddle God's grace. Instead, I relied on Judy, who had survived pits of darkness, to find her way back to affirming that contempt is defenseless against love.

A New Address

Early 2022

During the length of Judy's imprisonment, her security designation has gone from the most restrictive to minimum. She entertained the idea of going to another facility with fewer people and the coveted possibility of air conditioning. At Tutwiler, brief respites from the heat of summer only came with floor fans, wet t-shirts and towels.

She put in the paperwork for a transfer. The steps for eligibility were medical, psychological, and security level. She was approved. The next hurdle was finding a facility where a bottom bunk was available, a must to mitigate arthritis.

After months of waiting, she boarded a van to a place she'd never seen. Though nervous and excited as she faced the unknowable, passing scenes quieted her. She felt she could breathe as she gazed at evergreens and oaks on sloping hills. Her eyes moistened. She was transported to being a child again, exploring the woods, running freely. and talking to cows.

The ride was too long and too short. When she arrived, a friend from Tutwiler gave her a welcome gift: a banana and a stick of gum. Other inmates helped her get settled. The air conditioning was working. Fresh fruit was a rarity at Tutwiler; she was delighted to find out they had bananas at breakfast.

Less than a year later Judy was stunned, "Pack your things." She was being returned to Tutwiler. No explanation. I got a quick e-message telling me of the change. The trip to a different facility seemed idyllic compared to the return trip. The landscape she had seen before, as one of unfettered freedom, now looked desolate and gray.

Within a few days I got a call. "This is a collect call from ... Judy ... an incarcerated individual at Alabama Department of Corrections. This call is not private. It will be recorded and may be monitored. If you believe this should be a private call, please hang up and follow facility instructions to register this number as a private number.

"To accept charges and consent to this recorded call, press one. To refuse charges, press two. If you would like to permanently block your number from receiving calls from this facility, press six. For balance and rate quotes, press seven ...

"Thank you for using Securus. You may start the call now."

Judy was puzzled and angry. No amount of questioning prison officials provided an explanation for the transfer. Perhaps it was because she was coming up for parole in May, or someone had protested her being in a less secure facility. There were no answers.

~

May 2023

Five years had passed since the last time Judy's name was on the docket of the Alabama Bureau of Pardons and Parole. The day before the hearing Judy was in "utter dread" over publicity. The possibility of some reporter finding any of her children and grilling them compounded the dread.

In 2018 a circus of interviews and angry speeches against Judy and even the whiff of parole preceded and accompanied her case. Decades after the crimes, Judy's case continues to spark media coverage. The 2023 hearing stirred less interest. Judy was grateful.

I considered traveling from Virginia to Alabama to attend. Given the number of people on the docket—forty-three on the day of Judy's hearing—board members have to be prepared to vote prior to the speeches. I also knew that if I spoke, it would draw more attention to Judy and potentially interviews of me by reporters. The less exposure the better.

I opted to write to the Board, hoping a letter could have an impact. I didn't mince words about the crimes.

Judy Neelley committed horrendous crimes. Her murder of Cathy Connolly is still shocking and should not be forgotten. My writing in support of Judy's being remanded to the Georgia DOC in no way lessens the harm she did.

Nearly forty years ago I met Judy when I became chaplain at Tutwiler Prison. We have stayed in contact over the years. I have not been mesmerized and conned by Judy. I have questioned what she says. I have consulted with psychologists. I have combed the trial transcript. All of that scrutiny has brought me to the conclusion that Alabama DOC and Judy's efforts have rehabilitated her.

I believe the pain of victims and families of victim can be assuaged in part by lengthy sentences. But when someone has been murdered, no punishment of the offender brings back the loved one. Properly administered, incarceration can rehabilitate the offender and return her or him to society as a law-abiding citizen. Rather than being a threat to society Judy has the capacity to give back to society through her intelligence, lessons from her life, and a desire to do good.

I facilitated a restorative process between Judy and a cousin of Cathy…. Judy is willing to meet [with members of the victim's family] and takes responsibility for her crimes. She has not asked for forgiveness. She believes it is her moral and spiritual obligation to offer what she can: absolute remorse.

I concluded with a money saving suggestion. If Judy were sent to Georgia, the state of Alabama could save around $30,160 a year.[193] They must not have been impressed. Reset date of May 2028. If points were given for the most speakers on that day to object to parole, Judy would win. Eight protested her release.

On the afternoon of the hearing, we talked after we'd learned of the denial and reset. She hadn't expected to be sent to Georgia, so the decision was no surprise. I asked about reaction of folks at Tutwiler. Women in her dorm had been encouraging and expressed sorrow at the outcome.

Her voice was calm. "I'm not resigned to being here. I am eager to know how God is going to use me."

~

Even as she attends to the ways God can use her, Judy's confidence in the sanctity of God's purposes weighs on her. She has questioned why she continues to live. Or why she hasn't been released. She has atoned for egregious sins. Imprisonment served its purpose in changing the course of her life from crime. Then why does she remain in prison?

She grapples with the way she's depicted by the media, by legal authorities, and on occasion, by inmates and staff. For them, she remains the eighteen-year-old who killed two people. Those facts are irreversible. But she is no longer that lost teen.

If you question why Judy remains a prisoner of the state of Alabama, if you wonder why anyone who is not a danger to society is in prison after 14,800 days and counting, I join you.

If you expect a happy ending, a final chapter announcing she is released and living a productive life, it has not been written. Judy scoffs at the suggestion that one day she will read the words "Judy Neelley" and "paroled" in the same sentence. Events and people have rearranged her expectations. If hope is based on the belief that she'll one day be free, then she is without hope.

I can leave you with the knowledge that Judy lives each day with dignity, continues to learn through life experiences, and counts only on the mercy of God.

Afterword

Seek wisdom to temper justice with compassion.[194]

Judy Neelley has been characterized as devil-possessed and evil. She was labeled in an online post as an "inhuman slug." One person writing about Judy said that we kill animals and then added ominously, "Chop. Chop." There is no debate about the horrific actions taken by Judy and Alvin. A civil society responds with a resounding indictment, but holding a person responsible and the way that is done can create a chasm of injustice.

From the first interaction between Alvin and Judy, through the trial and sentencing, the major figures in her life were almost exclusively male. I have found no record of her interacting with a law enforcement official who was female. Her lawyers were male. The prosecution team was male, as was the judge. By 1982, the women's liberation movement had been building momentum. I can attest, however, to its not having crossed the state lines of Alabama with widespread success. Patriarchy was in play, and it didn't serve Judy well. Everyone knew that females have their wiles for snaring innocent men. They are the victims. Women are the offenders. That gave Alvin Neelley the responsibility to control Judy.

I believe that Judy should have been convicted. Yet demonizing her in the courtroom, in the press, and in the general public has hidden a more complex truth. Judy needed intense psychological therapy to break Alvin's power over her, not a death sentence.

Restoring people to the community who are no longer a threat should be the goal of a just legal system. A few states have passed laws that acknowledge the legality of coercive control as a defense. The dialogue earlier in this book titled "Interlude: Moral Complexity" presents several reactions to the argument that a person can be reduced to acting against that person's moral compass. For many, that's a ludicrous notion. A difficult conjecture to comprehend does not, however, make it invalid.

The treatment of Judy Neelley is indicative of the cynicism of people who won't examine the validity of coercive control. It's also about the moral superiority assumed by authorities in the criminal justice system. You do wrong, you are to be punished, ostensibly to convert the sinner. There's skepticism if someone says she or he has been rehabilitated. We send people to prison in order to change them, but then deny that that's possible. In practice, we treat the offender as being beyond redemption.

Are prisons designed to rehabilitate or warehouse? Proof that the brain of a teen is not fully developed and that many offenders "age out" of criminal activity is often not considered. They are treated as static entities. Judy's incarceration, like many in this country, is too long to be effective and too punitive and cruel to facilitate rehabilitation.

Lawbreakers are humans. It seems a needless statement, but it's easy to treat someone as depraved, based on the worst act the person committed. The moment we speak of a person in a degrading way, we are attempting to make ourselves superior and the other person inferior. That gives us the false permission to abuse with impunity. It swings wide the door to violence and normalized aggression in all its forms.

Even when a perpetrator has been found guilty and sentenced, more than one victim has experienced a hollow victory. How can someone pay for a crime? Although the question is unanswerable, it must be asked again and again. Our responses define who we are.

The criminal justice system in the United States is designed to be logical and fact-based. It is also adversarial. There are two sides. One is as right as the other is wrong. Advocates for the accused and for the accuser face off. The state is the victim, the injured "party," because the focus is on the law that has been violated. The victim and the defendant are several steps removed. As offenders become backdrop for the drama, so do victims. Prosecution portrays the accused figure, seated at the defense table, as evil in the flesh. Defense scrambles to erase that image and to present the defendant in ways that humanize.

The system is limited by laws and rules that inhibit restorative justice, which can heal all parties. Each step in restorative justice brings together our communities in a mutual vision. Justice is ephemeral and never, in the strictest sense, attainable when there has been injury. You can't unsay a word; you can't reverse the motion of a fist finding its mark. But when justice is viewed and sought as fundamentally the quality of our relationships, we can be healers. Justice is most viable when relationships have equal weight with legal proceedings.

Retribution, not redemption, is the premise of many public officials and the core of countless institutions in the United States. Law without mercy undermines humanity and contradicts the objective for change and growth.

Too many inmates and too few resources place correctional personnel in the unwinnable posture of being both cop and counselor. Trading favors and bargaining are all in a day's passage throughout a detention facility. An environment of reciprocity rather than goodwill is the norm, as people bargain for food, sex, drugs, and more. Treating people as humans and not commodities fosters a sense of worth, a bedrock of healthy communities.

If we are a society that cares about every person, we will be audacious enough to admit to the failures of misguided punishment. We will have the hard conversations necessary to tear down what imprisons us so we can build a more just society.

Crime splits communities. In the wake of a crime, communities can collide over demands and engage in finger-pointing. Or we can come together to create spaces where people thrive. That is not attainable without multiple partners and the willingness to hear one another by seeing the inherent good in the other. We'll disagree and keep working together. Out of our diversity and richness of ideas, we will weave a social fabric made of equity, reverence, and restoration.

Is that the world in which you want to live? What are you willing to do to make that world a reality?

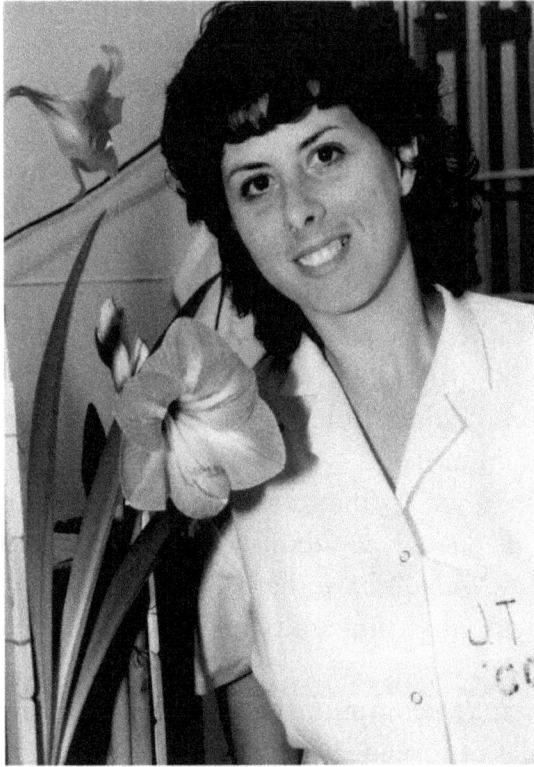

Judy Neelley in 1995 while on death row. The amaryllis
was a Christmas gift. Photo by Melissa Springer.

Please visit my website to explore issues raised in this book. www.LouiseStoweJohns.com.

Sample question:

Do we always have free choice? Or are there circumstances in which we cannot do what we believe we ought to do? If there is coercion, where does responsibility lie?

Acknowledgments

I am indebted to hundreds of people in the decades-long effort to bring this book to life. This is an effort to express my thanks. I regret any omissions because my memory or notes have failed me.

I extend my gratitude to—

Tutwiler Prison for Women: Wardens Kathleen Holt, Jean Hare, Shirlie Lobmiller. Psychologist: Helen Thompson. As the first female chaplain in the state of Alabama, I was fortunate to work with strong women who believed that those who are incarcerated are to be treated with respect within an environment of appropriate discipline. Prison staff, inmates, and volunteers: in varying ways they worked for the betterment of others.

Legal and professional: Barry Ragsdale: answered every question I lobbed at him, sent me the entire trial transcript, and has gone far beyond the obligation to represent Judy, all with skill and dry wit. Governor Fob James: for his life-giving act of clemency and his hospitality to me during our interview. Julian McPhillips: interest in Judy's case brought willing facilitation of connections and legal acumen. Robert French: extended me the courtesy of an interview and then provided unlimited access to files from the case. Jim Main: legal counsel to Governor Fob James. Court Officials of Fort Payne, Alabama: Randall Cole, District Clerk's Office. Melissa Springer for allowing me to use her 1996 photograph of Judy.

Those who exemplified the power of forgiveness: Cindy Silva, Linda Adair, Ken Dooley, Betty Morrow.

Residents of Fort Payne, Alabama: shared a range of honest feelings and helped in my research.

Community, church, and institutions: reporters and newspapers that printed them, especially Tom Gordon. First United Methodist Church, Amityville, New York, for its supporting and nurturing me while I was their pastor. The Lilly Foundation for awarding me a three-month minister-in-residence program at Claremont School of Theology, where I interacted with students, faculty, and staff: Kathleen J. Greider, Bill Clements, Karen Dalton, Jackie Bates, Sharon Thompson, Marcia Doss, Betty Clements, Elaine Walker, Laura Yavitz, Danny Soewito, Olga Morales, Ruth Northrup, Alan Wirth, Jack Coogan, Charles Wesley Jordan, Kathy Black, Mark Hobbs, Jon Hooten, Laurie Crews, Iona Dickinson, Marilyn Black, Janelle Raup, Catherine Tuell, and others. A sabbatical grant from Samford University, Birmingham, during which I had conversations with Michael Wilson, Linda Dukes Connor, Caroline Baird Summers, Fisher Humphreys, Larry Thompson, Shirley Richards.

Friends: Linda Mary Thompson and Robyn Hyland: the kind of friends no one deserves but is privileged to have. Those who read and critiqued my manuscript: Sue Gilmartin, Gail Jeffries, Marionette and Ed Jones, Linda Thompson, and The

Page Turners Book Club. Liza Nehring: helped in tracking down historical material.

Family: Dick, for his sacrifices of my time away, whether it was for three months coast-to-coast separation, times when I was visiting Judy, or mentally distant as I thought and wrote about this book, along with critiquing my writing. My daughter, Michele, who visited Judy with me and who has never grown tired of my stories; Christopher, my son, who expertly supplies technical support, listens, and stores that listening for future feedback to alert me to a concept I hadn't considered. Barbara and Alex, who see the value in working for justice wherever it is needed.

People who made it possible for you to read this story: Tahlia Newland, Managing Editor, Rose Newland, Book Designer and the rest of the team at AIA Publishing (Awesome Independent Authors) who improved the quality of my writing and met every question or roadblock with a steady hand and precise information.

About the Author

Louise Stowe-Johns is an ordained elder (retired) in the United Methodist Church. She served congregations in Alabama from 1992-1998 and in New York from 2000-2015.

She was an adjunct instructor in the Department of Religion and Philosophy at Huntingdon College, Montgomery, Alabama from 1974-1992, teaching courses in Christian education, Bible, and criminology. Louise served as chaplain in female and male prisons in Alabama, 1984-1990, and taught American Christianity for inmates through Central Alabama Community College.

After resigning from chaplaincy, she became the spiritual counselor for Judy Neelley. Louise created the first regional victim-offender reconciliation program in Alabama and has mediated criminal cases from nonviolent to violent, done community mediation, and consulted on cases outside of Alabama. She is also the founder and was the executive director for "Epiphany," a program for youth offenders, which operates in eleven states.

In 2001, Louise completed her Doctor of Ministry degree in restorative justice from Columbia Theological Seminary, Decatur, Georgia, and in 2022 she was a TEDxWarrenton (Virginia) speaker on the subject of Crime, Punishment, and Redemption. She is also the author of *Climbing Jacob's Ladder: Twelve Steps in Your Spiritual Journey*. She and her husband, the Rev. Dr. Roger Dick Johns, live in Virginia and have two children.

Appendices

Works Cited

Associated Press. "Neelley Fears Jailed Wife: Says Allegations 'a Show.'" *The Advertiser* (AL). November 2, 1984.

Benn, Alvin. "James Spares Inmate's Life." *The Montgomery Advertiser* (AL). January 16, 1999.

The Birmingham News (AL). "'Prostitute Recruiter' Suspect in Deaths of 10 Women." October 22, 1982.

French, Robert B., Jr. *Beaten, Battered and Damned: The Drano Murder Trial.* Ashland, OR: Blackstone, 1989.

Gordon, Tom, and Frank Sikora. "Husband 'Changed' Accused Murderer." *The Birmingham News* (AL). October 24, 1982.

Gordon, Tom. "Thus Far, No Help from Alvin Neelley on Alabama Cases." *The Birmingham News* (AL). October 27, 1982.

Holden, David and John Peck. "James Saves Neelley from Electric Chair." *The Huntsville Times* (AL). January 16, 1999.

Jaffe, Greg. "Inmate Attempts Suicide." *Montgomery Advertiser* (AL). May 17, 1994.

The Montgomery Advertiser (AL). "Life Sentence Given Neelley in Boy's Death." February 12, 1953.

Krog, Antjie, *Country of My Skull: Guilt, Sorrow, and the Limits of Forgiveness in the New South Africa.* New York: Three Rivers Press, 1998, 2000.

The Montgomery Advertiser (AL). "Murder Trial Slated To Go To Jury Today: Greenville Man Admits Firing .22 Rifle: Denies Aiming At Boy." February 11, 1953.

The Montgomery Advertiser (AL). "State Grants 20 Paroles, Denies 30." April 19, 1959.

Slater, Dashka. "How to Get Out of Prison." *The New York Times Magazine.* January 5, 2020.

Smith, Gita M. "Alabama Governor Commutes Sentence of Georgia Girl's Killer." *The Atlanta Constitution* (GA). January 16, 1999.

Smith, Matt. "Woman Dies in Suicide Pact with Killer, Officials Say." *Montgomery Advertiser.* May 18, 1994.

The Tennessean (TN), "Weekend Traffic Toll." April 1, 1974.

Troup, Randy. "Igou, O'Dell Disgusted with James' [*sic*] Decision." *Times-Journal* (AL). January 16, 1999.

Walker, Lenore E. *The Battered Woman.* New York: Harper Colophon, 1979.

Judy's Personal & Criminal History

July 1953— Alvin Neelley, Jr. is born in Trion, Georgia.

June 1964—Judith (Judy) Ann Adams is born in Murfreesboro, Tennessee.

June 1979— Judy meets Alvin Neelley. She turned fifteen three days earlier. Alvin would soon be twenty-six.

October 1979— Judy runs away with Alvin. Over the next three years, they steal from convenience stores where Alvin works and rob post offices. Judy serves time in youth facilities. Alvin is put in prisons in Georgia.

February 1980— Judy miscarries at about five months.

November 1980— Twins born to Judy while she is in juvenile facility in Georgia.

1981– 1982— After Alvin released from prison, crimes resume.

September 10, 1982— Alvin shoots into the home of Ken Dooley in Georgia.

September 11, 1982— Judy throws Molotov cocktail onto the lawn of the home of Linda Adair in Georgia.

September 25, 1982— Judy gives Cathy Rose Connolly a "ride" from Riverbend Mall in Rome, Georgia. Over the next three days, Alvin rapes her.

September 28, 1982— Alvin and Judy take Cathy Connolly to Little River Canyon in Alabama, where Judy shoots and kills Cathy.

October 3, 1982— Judy abducts Kay MacRae and Steve while they are walking home. Judy shoots Steve. He is injured but survives. Alvin and Judy take Kay to a motel where Alvin rapes her.

October 4, 1982— Judy shoots and kills Kay MacRae.

October 9, 1982— Judy tells her mother to call the police and tell them where to find her.

October 10, 1982— Judy Neelley is arrested at a motel in Murfreesboro, Tennessee. Alvin is arrested a few days later. Judy admits to murdering both MacRae and Connolly and shooting into and firebombing the homes of the Youth Development Center employees.

October 15, 1982— Judy is taken to Alabama and charged in killing Cathy.

January 1983— Judy gives birth to third child.

March 6, 1983— Capital murder trial begins.

March 22, 1983— Judy Neelley is convicted of capital murder, Circuit Court, DeKalb County, Alabama. Jury recommends LWOP.

April 18, 1983— Judge Randall Cole overrides jury and sentences Judy to death. She is transferred to Julia Tutwiler Prison for Women, Wetumpka, Alabama.

December 1983— The state of Georgia extradites Judy for the murder of Kay MacRae. She testifies against Alvin. She receives a life sentence in Georgia.

January 11, 1999— Legal appeals end when U.S. Supreme Court refuses to hear Judy's case.

January 15, 1999— Alabama Governor Fob James grants clemency, sentencing Judy to life.

May 2018— After extensive legal battles, the Parole Board grants Judy a hearing. She is denied.

May 2023— Second parole hearing. Judy is denied.

Endnotes

1   *Krog, Antjie, Country of My Skull: Guilt, Sorrow, and the Limits of Forgiveness in the New South Africa. New York: Three Rivers Press, 1998, 2000,* p. 312.

2   Statistics vary on the incidence of domestic abuse or intimate partner violence. They are hard to get because of differences in definitions and cultural norms from one region to another. The credible threats of further violence against victims make reporting dangerous. The Center for Disease Control and Prevention states that about one in four women and nearly one in ten men experience sexual, physical, or psychological violation. Center for Disease Control and Prevention, "Preventing Intimate Partner Violence," October 9, 2020, https://www.cdc.gov/violenceprevention/intimatepartnerviolence/fastfact.html.

3   Interview with the Rev. Dr. Kathleen J. Greider, Professor of Practical Theology, Spiritual Care and Counseling, at Claremont School of Theology, Claremont, California. March 29, 2001.

4   State of Alabama v. Judith Ann Neelley, Case No. CC-82-276 (Circuit Court of DeKalb Co., AL), Trial Transcript, R–1573. Hereafter Transcript–R (Revised).

5   Transcript R–1373, R–1376, R–1386–87, R–1393, R–1577.

6   Transcript R–1544, 1545.

7   Transcript R–1660–73.

8   Transcript R–460.

9   Transcript R–464.

10   Transcript R–1676, 1677.

11   Julia Tutwiler (1841–1916) was born in Alabama. She saw the deplorable conditions in jails and prisons and campaigned for humane treatment. Tutwiler is the composer of the state song of Alabama. A one-woman play, "My Name is Julia," was written and performed by Kathryn Tucker Windham and published by the Birmingham Public Library Press, 1991. Tucker lived in Selma, Alabama, and is known as a Southern folklorist who wrote stories of haunted places, mostly inhabited by benevolent ghosts.

12   I learned that male officers are governed by the regulations of the Alabama Department of Corrections. They were blocked from advancing in rank in a women's institution. Therefore, their pay and position had a lower ceiling. Within the next year, that regulation was overturned through a lawsuit brought by Robert D. Edwards, an officer at Tutwiler. The court concluded that Edwards had been a victim of sex discrimination. That opened the way for advancement in rank. Edwards was entitled to relief, including back pay.

13   At the time I was chaplain, my surname was not hyphenated Stowe-Johns.

14   *The Tennessean* (TN), "Weekend Traffic Toll," April 1, 1974, 20.

15   Transcript R–1228–30.

16   Transcript R–1231.

17   Transcript R–1231.

18   Transcript R–1233.

19   *The Montgomery Advertiser* (AL), "Murder Trial Slated to Go to Jury Today," February 11, 1953, 1.

20   *The Montgomery Advertiser* (AL), "Life Sentence Given Neelley in Boy's Death," February 12, 1953, 1.

21   *The Montgomery Advertiser* (AL), "State Grants 20 Paroles, Denies 30," April 19, 1959, 56.

22   Transcript R–1455.

23   Transcript R–407.

24   Transcript R–1090.

25   Transcript R–1162.

26   Transcript R–1314.

27   Transcript R–1281–82.

28   Transcript R–1296–97.

29   Transcript R–1528–29.

30   Transcript R–1539–40.

31   Transcript R–1540.

32   Transcript R–1559.

33   Transcript R–1541.

34   Transcript R–1568.

35   Case No. CC-82-276.

36   Transcript R–1097, 1099.

37   Transcript R–1104, 1105, 1106.

38   Transcript R–1193.

39   Transcript R–1108, 1109.

40   Transcript R–1186.

41   Transcript R–1114.

42   Transcript R–1115.

43   Transcript R–1116.

44   Transcript R–1120–21.

45   Transcript R–1122, 1124.

46   Transcript R–1118.

47   Transcript R–1135, 1136.

48   Transcript R–1137.

49   Transcript R–1138.

50   Transcript R–1139, 1140.

51   Transcript R–1141–42.

52   Transcript R–1160–61.

53   Transcript R–1179–81.

54   Transcript R–1182–83.

55   Transcript R–1151.

56   Transcript R–1184.

57   Transcript R–1187.

58   Transcript R–1201.

59   Transcript R–1202.

60   Transcript R–1202–03.

61   Transcript R–1204–05.

62   Transcript R–1205.

63   Transcript R–1207.

64   Transcript R–1207, 1208, 1209.

65   Transcript R–1210–11.

66   Transcript from that Q&A.:

Igou. "Did he ever force you to pick up a 13-year-old girl?"

Laurie. "No."

Igou: "Did he ever force you to shoot a 13-year-old girl?"

Laurie. "No."

Igou. "Mrs. Campbell, you are not with Judith Ann Neelley back on September 28, 1982, were you?"

Laurie. "No."

Igou. "You are not with her when she shot Cathy Rose Connolly, were you?"

Laurie. "No."

Igou. "And you are not with her when she shot Mrs. Campbell, were you?"

"(Witness is crying)" Transcript R–1218–19.

67   Transcript R–1218–19.

68   Transcript R–1221.

69   Transcript R–1221, 1222, 1223.

70   Transcript R–1128.

71   Transcript R–1306–07.

72   Transcript R–1309–10.

73   Transcript R–1291.

74   Transcript R–1400.

75   Transcript R–1402.

76   Transcript R–1405–06.

77   Transcript R–1469, R–1426, R–1436, R–1542.

78   Transcript R–1423, R–1425–26.

79   Transcript R–1437–38.

80   Transcript R–1440. The prison was Georgia Diagnostic and Classification.

81   Transcript R–1442, 1443.

82   Letters read in court and transcribed do not reflect spelling errors. Letters read by the author in the Court House in Fort Payne, Alabama, October 2010 are verbatim. To present an accurate picture of the writer, grammatical errors are not corrected. "*Sic*" is not used, so that the reading is uninterrupted.

83   Transcript R–1497.

84   Evidence #182.

85   Transcript R–1433–34, 1435.

86   Transcript R-1436, 1437.

87   Transcript R–1446, 1447.

88   Transcript R–1455.

89   Transcript R–1449–50, 1451–52.

90   Transcript R–1458–60, 1462.

91   Transcript R–1468.

92   Transcript R–1469.

93   Transcript R–1472–74.

94   Transcript R–1486, 1487–89.

95   Transcript R–1489–91.

96   Judy described some of Alvin's beatings as being "run-of-the-mill regular beatings." Transcript R–1364.

97   Transcript R–1508–11.

98   Transcript R–1511–12.

99   Transcript R–1526.

100   Transcript R–1526, 1539, 1542.

101   Transcript R–1528.

102   Transcript R–1586, 1587–88.

103   Transcript R–1589–90.

104   Transcript R–2033.

105   Bryce Hospital: Hospitalization Summary, February 14, 1983.

106   Transcript R–1941.

107   Transcript R–1925–26, 1927.

108   Transcript R–1931.

109   Transcript R–1932, R–1936–37.

110   Transcript R–1939.

111   Transcript R–1945-46, R–2001.

112   Transcript R–1947, R–1953, R–1954.

113   Transcript R–1975.

114   Transcript R–990, R–2001.

115   Robert B. French Jr., *Beaten, Battered and Damned*, Black Stone Company, 1989, 192. The book is dedicated to "Criminal Defense Lawyers who represent shockingly evil clients."

116   Transcript R–2327.

117   Transcript R–2284–87.

118   Transcript R–2334.

119   Transcript R–2338.

120   Transcript R–2343, R–2344.

121   Transcript R–2345, R–2346-7.

122   Stephen Bussman was French's co-counsel. Judy described him as one who did research. "Very nice guy. Big brother type."

123   Transcript R–2348.

124   Transcript R–2349, 2350.

125   Transcript R–2350, 2351.

126   Transcript R–2352.

127 Interview of Judy by Mike Wilson, July 27, 1998.

128 Associated Press, "Neelley Fears Jailed Wife," *The Montgomery Advertiser* (AL), November 2, 1984, 12B.

129 A sample of the amendments: Amendment #1: Reliance on Judy's testimony re crimes and suppressing the testimonies of some in law enforcement. #2: Misconduct of the forewoman of the jury, Eileen Hargis. #3: Questions as to legality of testimony regarding a shooting and murder that occurred after Cathy's death. #5: Eileen Hargis not replaced with an alternate juror. Transcript R–2408, 2444, 2462.

130 Transcript R–2377, 2386.

131 Lenore E. A. Walker wrote the first edition of *The Battered Woman,* 1979. It is now in its fourth edition. As a licensed psychologist, she leads in the field of battered women through research, teaching, consulting, and being an expert witness in trials.

132 Transcript R–2559.

133 Transcript R–2563, R–2565.

134 Transcript R–2566, R–2567.

135 Transcript R–2569.

136 Transcript R–2579.

137 Transcript R–2588, 2589.

138 Epiphany is a three-day spiritual retreat for juveniles in detention led by volunteers from outside the prison. It is a national ministry.

139 Geraldo Rivera, "Murder: Live from Death Row," 1988, https://www.youtube.com/watch?v=NLYPI-iEq8g.

140 "Murder: Live from Death Row."

141 The author changed the name of the organization.

142 Letter from Barry A. Ragsdale to the president of the organization, March 4, 1998.

143 *The Birmingham News* (AL), "'Prostitute recruiter' Suspect in Deaths,", October 22, 1982.

144 Tom Gordon, "Thus far, no help from Alvin Neelley," *The Birmingham News* (AL), October 27, 1982.

145 Tom Gordon and Frank Sikora, "Husband 'changed' accused murderer," *The Birmingham News* (AL), October 24, 1982.

146 Paulette Beete, "Notable Quotable: August Wilson," National Endowment for the Arts, June 2, 2020, https://www.arts.gov/stories/blog/2020/notable-quotable-august-wilson.

147 *New Revised Standard Version Bible*, copyright © 1989 National Council of the Churches of Christ in the United States of America, unless otherwise noted. Used by permission. All rights reserved worldwide. Scripture quotations are from the *New Revised Standard Version Bible* unless otherwise noted.

148 Lindsay Slater, "Growing up as Judith Ann Neelley's daughter," *Times-Journal*, February 9, 2009, https://times-journal.com/news/article_47fc90e4-3ac8-583f-8d10-945ea3d451e0.html. Other articles: "Forgiveness not easy for killer's child," February 10, 2009; "Daughter felt sentence was unfair," February 11, 2009.

149 When family was at the prison on July 27, 1997, officers allowed the regulation for a two-hour visit to be expanded to nearly four hours.

150 WGNS News Radio, "Man killed after being struck by a vehicle on Highway 70," December 26, 2016, https://www.wgnsradio.com/update-man-killed-after-being-struck-by-a-vehicle-on-highway-70-in-murfreesboro-area-cms-36880.

151 Matt Smith, "Woman Dies in Suicide Pact," *Montgomery Advertiser*, May 18, 1994, 1A, 7A.

152 Greg Jaffe, "Inmate Attempts Suicide," *Montgomery Advertiser*, May 17, 1994, 1A, 4A.

153 Alabama Department of Corrections, Disciplinary, 1.

154 Alabama Department of Corrections, Administrative Regulation #403, 2.

155 Lethal injection with a three-drug cocktail was legalized in 2002 in Alabama. A death-row inmate may choose the electric chair rather than lethal injection.

156 The Prison Project was an advocacy organization founded in

1976 to assist people on death row and their families in humanitarian aid. It also assisted attorneys appointed to represent indigent death-penalty defendants by uncovering mitigating evidence.

157   Carol Gundlach was the CEO of the State Coalition Against Domestic Violence.

158   Michael Curry was the reporter.

159   Judy told her mother on that visit that she was sorry for all she'd put her mother through. She took Judy in her arms and held her. Judy said, "You know how when your mother holds you, you feel safe from everything, that nothing can harm you?" She began crying. "That's the way it felt."

160   Those who bristle at the idea that an inmate, particularly one on death row, should have access to college courses raise valid questions. The more educated inmate is generally less of a threat to prison staff and other inmates and, if released, healthier for communities.

161   David Holden & John Peck, "James Saves Neelley from Electric Chair," *The Huntsville Times*, January 16, 1999.

162   Gita M. Smith, "Alabama Governor Commutes Sentence," *The Atlanta Constitution* (GA). January 16, 1999, 1.

163   Alvin Benn, "James Spares Inmate's Life," *The Montgomery Advertiser*, January 16, 1999, 4a.

164   William H. Stewart, "Forrest 'Fob' James Jr." *Encyclopedia of Alabama*, 2015, http://www.encyclopediaofalabama.org/article/h-1469.

165   Stewart, "Forrest 'Fob' James Jr."

166   Randy Troup, "Igou, O'Dell Disgusted with James' [*sic*] Decision," *Times-Journal*, Fort Payne, Alabama, January 16, 1999.

167   Troup, "Igou, O'Dell disgusted."

168   Priests for Equality, *The Inclusive Bible,* New York: Oxford University Press, 1989. Used by permission.

169   In 2016, as Alabama's longest serving state judge, Randall Cole was named 2015 Trial Judge of the Year. It was the first time the honor was bestowed.

170 In 2018, Alabama passed a law ending practice of judicial override. Capital Clemency Resource Initiative. "Alabama: Capital Clemency," n.d., https://www.capitalclemency.org/state-clemency-information/alabama/.

171 Transcript R–542, R–661.

172 Letter from author to Bussman, French, Cole, and Igou, March 24, 2001.

173 Conversation of author with Robert French Jr., October 19, 2010.

174 Transcript R–2445.

175 French, *Beaten, Battered, and Damned,* 21.

176 Conference of the American Friends Service Committee held the conference in San Antonio, April 1999.

177 "Shipped" is a word commonly used to mean movement of an inmate. It sounds like inanimate cargo, not humans.

178 Neelley v. Walker, 2017 WL 359647.

179 Ibid.

180 The United States Constitution states that a state legislature cannot increase a person's punishment retroactively. Judith A. Neelley v. Alabama Board of Pardons and Paroles, 3:14-cv-269.

181 Ivana Hrynkiw, "Judith Ann Neelley Waives Parole Hearing in Teen's Brutal 1982 Rape, Murder," *AL.com,* May 1, 2018, https://www.al.com/news/birmingham/2018/05/judith_ann_neelley_waives_paro.html.

182 Anna Beahm, "Victim's Advocates Ask for Judith Ann Neeley's [*sic*] Parole," *AL.com,* April 18, 2018, https://www.al.com/news/2018/05/vocal_asks_parole_board_to_go.html.

183 Anna Beahm, "Ivey Says Neelley Should Not be Paroled," *AL.com.,* May 21, 2018, https://www.al.com/news/2018/05/ivey_says_neelley_should_not_b.html.

184 Troy King was in the Republican runoff but was not elected. Michael O'Dell was district attorney for DeKalb County.

185 Mike Cason, "Parole Denied for Judith Ann Neelley," *AL.com,*

May 23, 2018, https://www.al.com/news/2018/05/judith_ann_neelleys_parole_hea.html.

186   Alabama and North Carolina do not allow inmates face-to-face interviews with the parole board. They are the exceptions in state parole boards. Dashka Slater, "How to get out of prison," *The New York Times Magazine*, January 5, 2020, 35.

187   Ibid.

188   *Common English Translation*, 2011, https://www.commonenglishBible.com/.

189   Telephone conversation of author with Ken Dooley, July 17, 1996.

190   Transcript R–1703–09.

191   Rick Halperin, "Death Penalty News," January 26, 1999, http://venus.soci.niu.edu/-archives/ABOLISH/rick-halperin/jan99/0289.html.

192   Miranda Lambert and Heather Little wrote "Gunpowder and Lead." Since the song is about a woman who is beaten by her boyfriend, gets no justice, and then waits for him with a shotgun, it would have resonance in a prison with many women who have been abused.

193 $30,160 is the average cost per inmate according to the report from the Alabama Department of Corrections for fiscal year 2021.

194   Lucille Stewart Beeson, a Birmingham, Alabama philanthropist.